Employment and Work Relations in Context Series

Series Editors
Tony Elger
Centre for Comparative Labour Studies
Department of Sociology
University of Warwick

Peter Fairbrother
Centre for Research on Social and Economic Transformation
Cardiff School of Social Sciences
Cardiff University

The aim of the *Employment and Work Relations in Context Series* is to address questions relating to the evolving patterns and politics of work, employment, management and industrial relations. There is a concern to trace out the ways in which wider policy-making, especially by national governments and transnational corporations, impinges upon specific workplaces, occupations, labour markets, localities and regions. This invites attention to developments at an international level, marking out patterns of globalization, state policy and practice in the context of globalization and the impact of these processes on labour. A particular feature of the series is the consideration of forms of worker and citizen organization and mobilization. Thus the studies address major analytical and policy issues through case study and comparative research.

WORK AND EMPLOYMENT RELATIONS IN THE HIGH PERFORMANCE WORKPLACE

**Edited by Gregor Murray, Jacques Bélanger,
Anthony Giles and Paul-André Lapointe**

continuum
LONDON • NEW YORK

Continuum
The Tower Building, 11 York Road, London SE1 7NX
370 Lexington Avenue, New York, NY 10017–6503

First published 2002

British Library Cataloguing-in-Publication Data
A catalogue record for this book is available from the British Library.

ISBN 0–8264–4705–8 (hardback)
    0–8264–4706–6 (paperback)

Library of Congress Cataloging-in-Publication Data
Work and employment relations in the high performance workplace/edited by Gregor
Murray . . . [et al.].
       p. cm. — (Employment and work relations in context series)
    Includes bibliographical references and index.
    ISBN 0–8264–4705–8 — ISBN 0–8264–4706–6 (pbk.)
     1. Work. 2. Industrial relations. 3. Industrial sociology. 4. Production (Economic
    theory) 5. Labor productivity. I. Murray, Gregor II. Employment and work relations in
    context.

    HD4904. W6433 2002
    331—dc21
                                                                            2001042539

Typeset by YHT Ltd, London
Printed and bound in Great Britain by
TheCromwellPress,Trowbridge,Wiltshire

CONTENTS

Notes on Contributors

Eileen Appelbaum is the Research Director at the Economic Policy Institute and was formerly Professor of Economics at Temple University and Guest Research Fellow at the Wissenschaftszentrum Berlin. She has published numerous articles on employment and labour market developments, and on the employment relationship. She is co-editor of *Labor Market Adjustments to Structural Change and Technological Progress* (1990) and author or co-author of *Back to Work: Determinants of Women's Successful Reentry* (1981); *Job Saving Strategies: Worker Buyouts and QWL* (1988); *The New American Workplace* (1994); and *Manufacturing Advantage: Why High Performance Work Systems Pay Off* (2000).

Jacques Bélanger is a Professor in the Industrial Relations Department at Université Laval in Quebec City. The results of workplace studies he completed in multinational firms such as Alcan and ABB have appeared in various industrial relations and sociological journals. He is co-editor of *Workplace Industrial Relations and the Global Challenge* (1994) and of *Being Local Worldwide: ABB and the Challenge of Global Management* (1999). He is currently co-ordinating an international study of workplace efficiency within two multinationals.

Paul R. Bélanger is a Professor in the Department of Sociology at Université du Québec à Montréal and Associate Director of the Centre de recherche sur les innovations sociales dans l'économie sociale, les entreprises et les syndicats (CRISES), an inter-university research centre concerned with organizational and institutional innovation. His primary research interests are in the area of work organization, social modernization and social theory. He is co-editor of *La modernisation sociale des entreprises* (1994) and *Nouvelles formes d'organisation du travail* (1997), and co-author of *Le Fonds de solidarité FTQ* (2001).

Richard P. Chaykowski is a faculty member in the School of Industrial Relations at Queen's University, Kingston, Ontario, Canada. He is also a co-founder and is currently a co-chair of the Canadian Workplace Research

Network, which facilitates a national network among human resources and industrial relations researchers. Dr Chaykowski's teaching and research interests include public policy in labour markets, labour relations and collective bargaining, workplace innovation, and the impacts of technological change in the workplace. He has edited (with Lisa Powell) *Women and Work* (1999).

Paul Edwards is Professor of Industrial Relations and Director of the Industrial Relations Research Unit, Warwick University. He is a Fellow of the British Academy. His recent work on high performance work systems includes an article (with Martyn Wright) in the *International Journal of Human Resource Management* (June 2001). Recent books include (with John Storey and Keith Sisson) *Managers in the Making* (Sage 1997) and (edited with Tony Elger) *The Global Economy, National States and the Regulation of Labour* (Mansell 1999).

John Geary is at the Graduate School of Business, University College, Dublin, Ireland. Before that he was Research Fellow at the Industrial Relations Research Unit, University of Warwick. He holds a doctorate from the University of Oxford. He is currently on sabbatical leave at the European University Institute, Florence, where he is a Jean Monnet Fellow in the Department of Political and Social Sciences. His research has focused on industrial relations and human resource management in multinational companies and on new forms of work organization. He is currently examining the dynamics of voluntary forms of management-union co-operation.

Anthony Giles is a Professor of Industrial Relations at Laval University in Quebec City, Canada. A specialist in international and comparative industrial relations, his recent research and publications have focused on globalization and its impact on work and employment as well as on the management of work in transnational firms. He has also conducted research and published in the areas of industrial relations theory, collective agreements and work reorganization.

Morley Gunderson holds the Canadian Imperial Bank of Commerce Chair in Youth Employment at the University of Toronto, where he is a Professor at the Centre for Industrial Relations (Director 1985–97) and the Department of Economics. He is also a Research Associate of the Institute of Policy Analysis, the Centre for International Studies, and the Institute for Human

Development, Life Course, and Ageing as well as an Adjunct Scientist at the Institute for Work and Health. His current research interests include: the impact of globalization on the employment relationship and labour policy; youth employment; voluntary activity; gender discrimination; the ageing workforce, pensions and mandatory retirement; public sector wages; the determinants and impact of immigration; childcare arrangements and labour market behaviour; and workers' compensation and reasonable accommodation.

Paul-André Lapointe is a Professor in the Industrial Relations Department at Université Laval in Quebec City and director of research on work, firms and public and private organizations in the Centre de recherche sur les innovations sociales dans l'économie sociale, les entreprises et les syndicats (CRISES). His research focuses on workplace innovation, worker participation in management and the dynamics of union-management partnerships in both public and private sectors and on which he has published a wide range of studies.

Benoît Lévesque is a Professor in the Department of Sociology at Université du Québec à Montréal and Director of the Centre de recherche sur les innovations sociales dans l'économie sociale, les entreprises et les syndicats (CRISES), an inter-university research centre concerned with organizational and institutional innovation. His primary research interests are in the area of organizational modernization and the social economy. He is co-author or co-editor of *La modernisation sociale des entreprises* (1994), *Respenser l'économie pour contrer l'exclusion* (1995), *Nouvelles formes d'organisation du travail* (1997), *Désjardins: Une entreprise et un mouvement?* (1997), *La nouvelle sociologie économique* (2000) and *Le Fonds de solidarité FTQ* (2001).

Gregor Murray is currently a Professor in the Industrial Relations Department at Université Laval in Quebec City and will soon take up an appointment at the School of Industrial Relations at Université de Montréal. His research focuses on different aspects of trade unionism, new forms of work organization, the legal regulation of collective representation and industrial relations theory in the context of globalization. He is also editor of *RI/IR Relations industrielles/Industrial Relations* and director of an interdisciplinary and inter-university research centre (CRIMT) studying the impact of globalization on the regulation of work. Among his recent publications are *La représentation syndicale* (1999) and *L'état des relations professionelles* (1995).

Keith Sisson is Emeritus Professor of Industrial Relations at the University of Warwick Business School's Industrial Relations Research Unit, having previously been its Director for thirteen years. His main interest has been in management policy, recent publications including *Personnel Management: A Comprehensive Guide to Theory and Practice* (2000) and *The Realities of Human Resource Management* (2000). He was also editor of and convenor of the group responsible for *New Forms of Work Organisation. Can Europe Realise its Potential? Results of a Survey of Direct Employee Participation in Europe* (1997). He is currently working with Paul Marginson on the study of the emerging forms of European collective bargaining under the 'One Europe or Several?' programme of the UK's Economic and Social Research Council.

TABLES

PREFACE AND ACKNOWLEDGEMENTS

This volume had its genesis in a colloquium organized by the editors at Université Laval in Québec City, Canada. All of the chapters have permutated rather dramatically since that time, but the colloquium provided a first and vital opportunity for all of the authors to discuss their views on the nature of the new workplace and to develop the arguments that they present in this volume. Interested readers might note that we also edited a special issue of *RI/IR (Relations industrielles/Industrial Relations*, 54:1, 1999), which featured a selection of original empirical research presented at this colloquium.

Special thanks are due to the Continuum Employment and Work Relations in Context Series editors, Tony Elger and Peter Fairbrother, for their continuing support for this project and their insightful comments on the content and structure of the book. We also wish to acknowledge the support of Caroline Wintersgill, Senior Commissioning Editor for the series, and Neil Dowden, also of Continuum Publishers. The manuscript also benefited from key contributions along the way and we would like to thank the individuals concerned: Francine Jacques, for her important role in the organization of the colloquium and in the early development of the project; Maureen Magee and Châu Nguyen for the translation of Chapter 4; Nicolas Roby and Leonor Da Cunha Rego for their detailed bibliographic and stylistic work on all of the chapters; and Judith Paquet for her subsequent work in helping to finalize the manuscript.
We also wish to acknowledge the significant financial support of a number of different agencies that helped to sponsor the original event and without whose support this volume would not have been possible. In particular, financial support was provided by Human Resources Development Canada's Labour-Management Partnerships Program, the Social Sciences and Humanities Research Council of Canada, the Ministère de l'Industrie, du Commerce, de la Science et de la Technologie, the Ministère de l'Emploi et de la Solidarité, the Ministère du Travail, the Fonds de solidarité des travailleurs du Québec of the

Fédération des travailleurs et travailleuses du Québec, the Fonds pour la Formation de Chercheurs et l'Aide à la Recherche (FCAR) and last, but certainly not least, the Département des relations industrielles, Université Laval, and the Canadian Workplace Research Network, which co-sponsored the symposium and the subsequent publications.

Gregor Murray
Jacques Bélanger
Anthony Giles
Paul-André Lapointe

Introduction: Assessing the Prospects for the High Performance Workplace[1]

Anthony Giles, Gregor Murray and Jacques Bélanger

Over the past decade or so a widespread consensus has taken root around the proposition that work systems are being fundamentally transformed, an idea often encapsulated in the expression 'high performance workplace'. This consensus is remarkably broad, stretching as it does from the university classroom to the corporate boardroom, from the seat of government to offices, stores and factory floors, from the pages of magazines and newspapers to the outer reaches of the Internet. Virtually everyone is agreed that deep-seated changes are reshaping the way production and work are organized, the way employees and employers deal with each other, and the way governments seek to shape the workplace and the labour market.

There is, of course, a wide range of explanations of these changes, running from the thesis that we are caught in a maelstrom of technological innovations that are propelling us willy-nilly into new ways of organizing the way society produces, all the way to the conspiracy-tinged thesis that a global elite (central bankers and their ilk) are orchestrating a revival of nineteenth-century methods of squeezing out more work for less. There is also a deep cleavage between those who celebrate the productive potential and 'empowerment' of workers in the emerging high performance work systems, confidently predicting that we are on the threshold of another of capitalism's golden ages, and those who decry the changes, painting an alarming scenario of a world divided into an elite of 'knowledge workers' and an underclass of dispossessed, disenchanted and potentially troublesome unemployed, underemployed and unemployable. To round out the cast of characters, let us not forget the sceptics who, although hopelessly outgunned in the war of words that characterizes the academic and public debates

1

around the changing workplace, perform the invaluable role of reminding us that, when all is said and done, most of us are still either managers or managed, bosses or employees, and that we should not allow the rhetoric of innovation and change to obscure the fundamental continuities with the recent (and not-so-recent) history of employment relations in capitalist societies. To mix cultural referents, the times they are a-changin', but *plus ça change, plus c'est pareil.*

Considerable academic effort has been devoted to describing the patterns of diffusion of workplace change, explaining the decline of previous models of organizing production and seeking to characterize the new high performance models. The gist of all this research might be summarized as follows: there is fairly wide agreement that what are known as 'Fordist' models of production are crumbling, that new models are emerging, but that this process has only just begun, is unfolding slowly and unevenly and is still open-ended. However, just below the surface calm of this general consensus lies a stratum of turbulence: although most observers are agreed that production systems and the work they put in motion are changing in fundamental ways, there is much less agreement about both the extent of change taking place and its consequences for employment relations. Indeed, there are deep cleavages between those who celebrate both the efficiency and the emancipating potential of these new systems and those who bear witness to a workplace increasingly characterized by stress, insecurity and seemingly arbitrary responses to contingency.

A detailed examination of the state of thinking on the new workplace is all the more important because, while a torrent of words has been spoken and written about the new 'high performance' workplace, the research into these changes has not entirely kept pace. The purpose of this book, then, is to advance our understanding of the consequences and challenges of the new high performance production model. To this end, we have brought together a group of leading researchers to take stock of the evidence and implications of the new workplace. Specially commissioned for this project, we asked each group to assess a particular facet of the so-called new workplace, to indicate what they see to be the state of knowledge about their particular question, to highlight what they view as important, and to explore the implications for both research and practice. Drawing on examples from a variety of national contexts, they seek to characterize the nature of current workplace change and assess the implications of these changes for the organization of work, the workers who do the work, employment relations and public policy. The thesis underlying the volume as a whole is that fundamental changes are taking place, sufficient to justify the notion of a new production model, but that they are frequently uneven and profoundly contradictory in character. Hence, the new work systems are typically very fragile, characterized by significant tensions because of their impact on workers and the contradictory exigencies that they imply for employment relations.

The result is a strongly interwoven series of contributions offering a critical look at the transformations observed in many workplaces in the advanced, industrialized economies. In particular, we seek to address three sets of concerns that we believe command the attention of both practitioners and researchers. First, what is the shape of the new production model (or models)? There is certainly a need to develop a fuller understanding of the different permutations of the new production systems that are displacing Fordism and their implications for the nature of work. Second, what are the consequences and implications of new production models for work and work relations? In particular, is teamwork one of the defining characteristics of the new workplace? What is the actual impact of the new ways of organizing production on workers? A third set of concerns relates to the institutional implications of the new workplace. As suggested by Boyer and Hollingsworth, 'for a new social system of production to occur, there must be a new configuration of institutions concerning industrial relations, training systems, state interventions, and financial intermediation, as well as a complementary international regime' (Boyer and Hollingsworth, 1997, p. 193). Here there are two areas where academic research and practical reflection need to be brought into closer contact: the impact of the new models of production on the institutions of labour–management relations and on the role of government. All of these questions are critical to an understanding of the conditions that foster or impede the emergence of new models of production. Indeed, it is only by tracing the consequences within the productive organization, through to the institutional framework and then to the sphere of public policy, that we will be able to develop a full understanding of what new models of production portend.

In tackling these issues, the approaches followed in the various chapters that make up this volume are characterized by three common features worth noting. First, this book seeks to bring the insights of the tradition of industrial relations research to bear on our understanding of the changing workplace. This tradition is one that places a special emphasis on the importance of blending conceptual development with detailed empirical analysis, a characteristic that is reflected in all of the chapters. But, second, the industrial relations tradition is also distinctive in the attention that it pays to bridging the gap between the interests of researchers and the concerns of practitioners and policy makers. Our hope is that the traffic across this bridge will not all flow in one direction, but that the transfer will be two-way, that the practitioners, artisans and students of workplace change can measure the utility of the ideas advanced in this book in terms of their own experiences of change and bring that experience to bear on our broader understanding of the future shape of the workplace. Third, all of the contributions are international in outlook, permitting the authors to go beyond a literature too narrowly focused on the normative requirements of 'high performance' work organizations. Yet all of the chapters are driven by a common agenda designed to understand the nature of changes taking place in a way that it is hopefully accessible for students and a broader audience.

The remainder of this introduction briefly presents the major themes in this book. Our purpose is neither to conduct an exhaustive review of the scientific literature nor to advocate particular models or practices; instead, our intention is to try to highlight the importance of each of these issues, their connection with the broader themes of the book and with each other, and to highlight some questions that run through the chapters.

New Models of Production

Progress needs to be made in identifying the types of new models that are taking shape. This will involve an effort to go beyond the fascination with whatever management fad is currently being touted, whether 'total quality management', 'cellular manufacturing', 'reengineering', or whatever. Technological and organizational innovations may assume a variety of forms and there is considerable debate over their various permutations, both theoretical and observed, as well as their relative merits. To cite but a few of the distinctions, Boyer and Hollingsworth (1997, p. 194) distinguish a number of alternatives to mass standardized production: customized production, which 'assumes a certain reduction in volume'; diversified quality mass production, which purportedly 'combines the benefits derived from product differentiation with significant quantities of production'; adaptive or reactive production, which 'builds upon the constant redefinition of market niches and the fastest possible use of new technologies'. Another alternative, flexible specialization might be described as 'the manufacture of a wide and changing array of customized products using flexible, general-purpose machinery and skilled, adaptable workers' (Hirst and Zeitlin, 1997, p. 221). Each of these, and they represent only a few of the possibilities already identified in the literature, imply certain configurations as regards different dimensions of the production process, be it in terms of production cycles, customer relations or networks of suppliers and subcontractors. The precise choices involved in the organization of production have significant implications for the overall characterization of the new model.

The principal objective of Chapter 1 is to look closely at the different permutations of the core principles that define the new models. In that chapter, Jacques Bélanger, Anthony Giles and Gregor Murray examine the evidence for the emergence of a new production model. After setting out the rationale for looking at production models and the broad characteristics of the Fordist production model, they argue that we can now discern the emergence of a new production model. That model can be summed up by three sets of interrelated principles: productive flexibility and the standardization of processes in the sphere of production management; greater application of skills and knowledge, increased 'multi-skilling' and more self-regulation in the sphere of work organization; and the transfer of risk and insecurity to the workforce and increased social adhesion or employee commitment to organizational goals and the ways of achieving them in the sphere of employment relations. These are the principles that cut across the variegated terrain of most workplace change currently taking place. They can be combined in quite different permutations – greater flexibility at the cost of increased standardization, greater self-regulation to the detriment of standardization, less social adhesion (or employee commitment) in favour of increased insecurity, to name but a few. Not only are these principles difficult to achieve in practice but they often result in important tensions and even significant contradictions, so much so that the new model exhibits a high degree of instability. Yet, however difficult to reconcile, these principles are at the heart of efforts to transcend 'Fordist' production arrangements – be it in the goods sector, in private services or, increasingly, in public services – because the prize of unleashed productive potential in a context of increasing competition appears to be so great.

Bélanger, Giles and Murray go on to explore the sources of this instability in order to assess the future prospects of the new production model. Apart from the natural process of trial and error, they point to two significant sources of variation and instability. The first concerns the internal tensions and contradictions between the core principles of the new model. The second is related to the lack of an appropriate institutional framework, both at the level of the firm and in society more generally, that could improve the internal coherence and stability of the emerging model of production.

This first chapter then gives an overview of the dynamics of this new production model and, in so doing, sets out the major themes for the entire book. It will be of particular interest for readers seeking to build bridges between the different contributions to this book, especially between the first chapters, which focus primarily on different facets of the new model, and the latter chapters concerned with the institutional framework.

Employee Involvement in Work and the Workplace

Given the widespread agreement that a key factor in the crisis of Fordism is the lack of worker autonomy, it is less than surprising that nearly every analyst of workplace change identifies increased employee involvement or participation as a central feature of emerging models. There is, moreover, widespread empirical evidence of an increased incidence of various forms of employee involvement in the workplace, ranging from quality circles to problem-solving groups to autonomous work teams. There is also an enormous normative literature inciting managers to encourage employee involvement in order to harness the gains in flexibility and efficiency required by the new production systems (see, for example, Walton, 1985). This has given rise to a new participative lexicography of team members, associates, facilitators, and the like. However, once we move beyond the general observation of increased participation, there is much less consensus as regards the significance and efficacy of these forms of employee participation.

A first question concerns the nature of these different types of participative mechanisms. Here we might look at the extent of participation, which ranges from little more than the introduction of suggestion boxes or the opportunity to participate in quality circles to, at the other end of the continuum, the devolution of substantial autonomy to workers or work groups, allowing them much greater scope to define and regulate their jobs. Another consideration in distinguishing between the different types is the level of employee involvement. Participation is typically limited to a narrow focus on certain issues of operational concern to one's job at the point of production. However, it is possible, albeit much less frequently observed, to conceive of more substantial employee involvement in questions which concern the actual design and operation of productive organizations.

A second question concerns the permanence of different forms of participation since it is now well established in the literature that many such experiences start with considerable initial enthusiasm but, whether because of flaws in conception or contradictory pressures resulting from the pursuit of other objectives, finish in disappointed expectations and a reversion to traditional patterns of work organization. A related question therefore must be the consideration of the conditions associated with the introduction of various forms of employee involvement. This involves questions about the process through which certain types of participation are introduced but also, to adopt the vernacular, the particular organizational 'fits' or the way that certain practices must be 'bundled' together.

One of the core principles at the heart of recent experiences in work reorganization is greater autonomy and self-regulation and there is growing evidence of its complex and contradictory effects in the context of the reorganization of production designed to achieve maximal results on vectors of both flexibility and efficiency. A frequent example, particularly in assembly-line production such as that of the automobile industry, is greater worker discretion over work process at the cost of a loss of control over the pace of work or in the context of a considerable work intensification sparked by general insecurity. It is clear that almost everywhere the innovation process is rooted in a frantic drive for greater organizational efficiency and flexibility, whether through quality, customer satisfaction or good old-fashioned cost reduction. However, it can be argued that the fundamental dynamics of the relationship between workers and employers are manifestly not being altered in a significant way. Indeed, the inescapable tensions that arise from a relationship that is imbued with hierarchical power relations is the very rationale for innovation in work organization. In other words, there is more than a little justified scepticism as regards the overblown rhetoric on employee 'empowerment' and organizational liberation, a virtual 'new Jerusalem' of the supposed changes in the relationship between workers and managers in an era of work innovations. By the same token, and as has often been observed, there is little likelihood of mass worker mobilization in favour of a return to the Fordist organization of production. Traditional methods of production are the source of considerable employee alienation and there is certainly evidence of a positive worker response to the principles of both wider scope and self-regulation. Thus the new forms of employee involvement merit close scrutiny as regards their complex effects, their interrelations with other aspects of the reorganization of production and employee relations, and their transformative potential.

The second chapter, by Paul Edwards, John Geary and Keith Sisson, focuses on the significance and efficacy of new forms of employee participation that appear to characterize many of the new forms of work organization. Drawing on both the international literature and a major European survey in which they played a leading role, Edwards, Geary and Sisson attempt to distinguish fact from fiction as regards the degree of diffusion of different types of employee participation and the conditions associated with their establishment. The results of this ten-country survey confirm that the employers' interest in 'task participation' has increased in recent years. However, the diffusion and intensity of change are more limited than is often suggested in the international literature. They actually report that the 'team work which has dominated so much of the debate is very much the exception rather than the rule'.

Edwards, Geary and Sisson further assess the possibilities and limits of these new forms of direct participation, with a particular emphasis on what they identify as the predominant form of employee involvement: 'task participation'. They situate this trend in a broader theoretical approach that sees a perpetual, dynamic tension between autonomy and control in the work process. In their view, inasmuch as teamwork is increasingly associated with superior performance in the workplace, it is likely to remain on the agenda for the foreseeable future. However, they are much more circumspect as to whether it will come to define an entire period of development of work organization.

The Impact of New Forms of Work Organization on Workers

Given the important role allotted to the principle of self-regulation in work organization and the principle of social adhesion in employee relations, the impact of new production systems on workers is clearly a critical issue. Yet research focusing principally on the concerns of employees is dismayingly rare. Instead, the focus of much of the research carried out to date on the recent wave of workplace change has been centred squarely on the concerns of management: the practices to implement; the fostering of change; the impact on productivity, quality and profitability. According to this management agenda, workers are viewed either as obstacles to change or as passive recipients of change. In either case, training is the buzzword inasmuch as workers will require, at a minimum, new social skills and, when they are perceived as obstacles to change, an appropriate dosage of motivational techniques. Thus, although there have been tremendous efforts to comprehend the 'performance effects' of innovative work practices on organizations, much less work has been done on workers' concerns (see, for example, Ichniowski *et al.*, 1996).

The research that does focus on workers tends to be considerably more caustic about the possibilities and potential of the reform of work organization. In particular, it draws attention to the many problems encountered in the implementation of these new work systems: deteriorating working conditions in many circumstances; a narrowing of autonomy, especially under lean production; an increase in stress, pace and work effort with the many attendant health and safety consequences; reduced job security in many cases, which obliges workers to accept these changes; a sense of decreased membership support for their unions and a decline in labour's capacity to act as a countervailing force to management. And yet, while there is considerable empirical support for this more insidious characterization, at least in some circumstances, there is also support for a more positive set of outcomes. In particular, certain kinds of work reorganization, such as some forms of teamwork, are more likely to garner the support of workers than others. Just as was argued above in relation to employee involvement, the impact of such practices is all the more important because of the increasing evidence of their complex, contradictory and often varied effects.

These themes are featured in the third chapter, in which Eileen Appelbaum considers the implications of new forms of production for workers themselves. Appelbaum surveys the evidence of the impact of work reorganization on a number of key dimensions of working conditions and the quality of work life, including workload, the intensity of work, job stress, job satisfaction and health and safety in order to identify the tensions underlying some of the new models of work organization as well as the avenues most likely to lead to workers' acceptance of these models. Her broad assessment of actual studies of the effects of workplace changes that characterize the high performance workplace on workers is that they are much more positive than negative.

Workplace Innovation and the Institutional Framework of Labour–Management Relations

Are traditional institutions incompatible with new production models and forms of work organization? And if, as many believe, there is a mismatch, then what should be done? This latter question, it must be stressed, can be posed from two different perspectives: on the one hand, for those who wish to promote innovation, the incompatibility is seen as an obstacle to innovation; on the other hand, for those who defend the traditional institutions, it is seen as a problem of maintaining mechanisms that protect workers from arbitrary managerial power.

The traditional system of industrial relations would appear to be under challenge in terms of the structure, content and the process of collective bargaining (see, for example, Katz and Darbishire, 2000). In terms of the structure of bargaining, there is a continuing trend towards decentralization with, in particular, the redefinition of points of comparison and an unambiguous effort to structure negotiations in line with the notion of business units or profit centres, regardless of its relation to the traditional establishment. Thus there are stresses and strains between pressures to calibrate negotiations solely in terms of local conditions, as opposed to the kinds of comparative considerations of relative equity and union solidarity that have characterized pattern and multi-establishment bargaining. As regards the content of collective agreements, the search for greater flexibility suggests much more fluid forms of contract codification: in essence, definitions which allow maximum scope for flexibility. In terms of process, there has been considerable promotion of new forms of 'jointness' which favour more co-operative, problem-solving arrangements. Betcherman and Chaykowski note that in Canada, there is some limited 'evidence of firms and unions that have developed new approaches to collective bargaining and the conduct of labour relations that reduce traditional "adversarialism" and that facilitate solutions yielding a greater level of mutual gain' (Betcherman and Chaykowski, 1996, p. 27). On this latter point, particularly in the United States, there has been a considerable effort to promote this 'new' labour relations as an alternative both to traditional forms of bargaining but also to what many industrial relations scholars see as the real alternative of non-unionism. This is the basis of a strategic conundrum for unions: risk promoting the decline of the union as an institution if the union does not collaborate in some of the new forms of workplace regulation; yet risk declining support from their members if the abandonment of many of the collective defence mechanisms, associated with the traditional institutional model, translates into increased work intensity and declining employment security. In other words, in this new context, unions risk being 'damned if they do and damned if they don't!'.

The pressures on the traditional framework of labour–management relations and the genuine uncertainty about its possible replacements make it clear that much remains to be clarified as regards the precise character of the institutional framework of labour–management relations in the context of this new production model. The fourth chapter, by Paul R. Bélanger, Paul-André Lapointe and Benoît Lévesque, explores the implications of the new production models for the study of the modernization of social relations at the level of the firm. They seek to draw lessons from the available evidence on organizational innovation and the institutions of work regulation. In particular, they make a broader argument for a kind of systemic paralysis or institutional blockage in the evolution of the new model of work or the high performance workplace. The new model of production is predicated on social partnership between unions and management at the level of the firm. Bélanger, Lapointe and Lévesque argue, however, that the ability to achieve such partnership appears exceedingly fragile and is often temporary. They locate the source of this fragility in the broader social context, notably the absence of institutional support for innovation and partnership. In other words, the reasons for the uneven and partial diffusion of the new production model is to be found as much at the societal level as at the level of the firm. In order to illustrate their case, they draw on research conducted in the Canadian province of Quebec. For many observers, Quebec presents many of the features of a best case scenario for achieving the new kinds of social compromises that must underlie the new production model. These include a high level of unionization, a union movement favourable to workplace innovation, a significant role for public or social capital in the modernization of firms, and a tradition of tripartite consultation between employers, unions and the state. Yet the Quebec experience of labour–management partnerships around workplace innovation remains very uneven. For Bélanger, Lapointe and Lévesque, the spread of this new model consistently founders on the absence of changes in the macro-social institutions that are needed to support local innovation in the organization of work.

The Role of the State in the Diffusion of Workplace Innovation

What role does the state play in the development and diffusion of new models of production and work organization? What role should it play? These two questions, the one empirical the other normative, are of considerable importance to the understanding and practice of workplace innovation. Yet they are questions that have been rarely broached and still more rarely addressed in any substance. This is not to say that government policy has been overlooked in the debate, for the literature is fairly littered with suggestions for specific reforms. But there have been few attempts to consider the question in depth.

This is perhaps not surprising in an era in which the state has fallen out of intellectual fashion. There seems little doubt that governments and state officials across the advanced industrial world, if not in all of its four corners, are exceedingly anxious to see new production models develop more quickly and new forms of work organization take firmer root. After all, it is clear (or so common knowledge says) that the competitiveness of the nation (upon which rests the revenues, domestic acquiescence and international standing which are the lifeblood of the state apparatus) depends on the ability of the national economy to develop and mobilize its human resources. The problem, in short, is not a lack of interest or concern. In fact, the problem is a dual one of new constraints and persistent institutions.

The new constraints are easily summarized. First, under the twin pressures of the new fiscal orthodoxy of deficit reduction and tax regime competition, the resources available to the state have, or have been made to appear as if they have, diminished radically. Second, the ideological ascendancy of neo-liberalism has put deregulation and privatization at the top of the political agenda. Third, globalization of markets and production has instilled a fear of falling out of step with one's competitors and falling behind in the global race for investment and markets, thereby making it dangerous to propose policies that might be seen as too radical. Finally, the weight of existing public institutions and practices is such that they are often difficult to modify, inasmuch as they are, in essence, the continuing manifestation of a certain compromise between social forces within a society.

What then should public policy on workplace innovation be in an age of globalization? Can public policy be used to shape the contours of new forms of work organization? The answers to these questions are the subject of some considerable debate. The neo-liberal response is, of course, to leave workplace innovation in the hands of managers and, should they deem it to be appropriate, in the hands of their workers. The concern of a number of American scholars is that such an approach tends to promote the proverbial 'low road' to workplace change as opposed to the 'high road'. As observed by Locke:

> Value-added-based strategies are expected to lead to the most fundamental transformations in employment relations and have the best chance of producing outcomes of mutual benefit to firms and their employees. Cost-based strategies, on the other hand, are expected to lead to a downward spiral of wages, working conditions, and labor standards and to reinforce adversarial relations at the workplace. (Locke, 1995, p. 23)

Ray Marshall (1992) has been a leading exponent of the activist view of the role of public policy in the promotion and adoption of 'high performance systems'. Such an approach is, of course, predicated on a view that high performance, value-added strategies also lead to a set of desirable macro-economic results and public policy should therefore seek to promote the adoption of such practices. While initially emphasizing the importance of managerial values in the choice of industrial relations strategies, Kochan *et al.*

(1986; 1991) have increasingly pointed to the role of public policies in the dissemination of workplace change, notably because of the way that public policy promotes acceptable sets of behaviour and influences managerial actions. Similarly, Locke suggests that the institutional framework plays an important role in the types of strategies pursued: 'The low-cost response to market pressures and changes appears to be most frequent in countries with weak institutions, low levels of unionization, decentralized bargaining structures, and a limited government role in labor market affairs' (Locke, 1995, p. 24).

Thus, increasing attention is being focused on the possible role of public policies in the diffusion of workplace change, but what kinds of public policies? Here there is much less consensus. Beyond the level of the firm, there are various suggestions to promote different kinds of sectoral and/or national consultation. Indeed, this has been the focus of some experimentation in Canada in terms of both sectoral bodies to deal with training and new consultative mechanisms such as the Canadian Labour and Business Centre, formerly known as the Canadian Labour Market and Productivity Centre. Some also point to the existence of national institutions, in countries such as Japan and Australia, to study and promote workplace innovation (Locke, 1995). There is also the possibility of a legislative obligation to promote workplace consultation on change, a theme which appears to be increasingly important in a number of European Community directives. This latter approach has the additional merit of crossing national boundaries which, in principle at least, decreases the possibility of transnational whipsawing. For others, forms of workplace and company consultation presume that the union or an equivalent representative body is a viable actor in the workplace, a considerable presumption in a number of national contexts, that can safeguard workers from some of the more contradictory effects of the new model. In this respect, the process of workplace innovation is ultimately tied to the collective power of actors in the workplace. It can, therefore, be argued that the reinforcement of employee access to collective representation is a necessary prerequisite for the development of proactive union policies on workplace innovation. Indeed, the whole issue of labour movement strength is critical to an understanding of why institutions are strong in some national contexts and their levels of unionization high.

The fifth chapter, by Richard P. Chaykowski and Morley Gunderson, considers the role of the state and the challenges for public policy in the evolution of the new model of production. Drawing on their analysis of North American public policy, they highlight an increasing paradox between the growing need for labour policy initiatives to support innovation and adjustment in the organization of work and the increasing difficulty of sustaining a national consensus on such public policy initiatives. Chaykowski and Gunderson undertake a broad review of the current state of research on this question in order to set out the principal choices facing public policy as regards the new production model. In particular, they make an argument for a more strategic and proactive public policy role in the construction of the new workplace.

By now it will be clear that this book does not seek to add yet another tome to the how-to section of business books in your local library. Indeed, if our ambition had been to join the seemingly endless stream of prescriptive prattle about 'empowerment' or 'post-capitalism', we would surely have come up with a catchier title and used more bullet points. Instead, we and the other contributors have sought to bring the traditions of scepticism and critical thinking to bear on recent workplace change. In so doing, we have sought to steer clear of the two extremes that so often characterize treatments of this issue: on the one hand, the tendency of many critics to dismiss the ongoing changes as nothing more than a clever smokescreen intended to disguise intensified exploitation; and, on the other, the naive celebration of the new workplace served up by all too many enthusiasts of the high performance workplace.

But this stance does not mean that we offer a neutral assessment, one that is shorn of any concern for those who are struggling to contend with the changing reality of production, work and employment. Although the contributors to this volume range across the ideological spectrum, all are fundamentally persuaded that the construction of healthier, more democratic and more rewarding jobs must, as a matter of both principle and pragmatism, involve full, genuine and independent participation on the part of the employees who are being asked to embark upon this journey and on the part of the employee organizations and unions that represent them.

Note

1. This Introduction draws on Giles *et al.* (1999).

1 TOWARDS A NEW PRODUCTION MODEL: POTENTIALITIES, TENSIONS AND CONTRADICTIONS

Jacques Bélanger, Anthony Giles and Gregor Murray

Judging by the dizzying pace of terminological invention over the past two decades, the modern workplace has become a phantasmagoria of swiftly evolving new practices, innovations, models and paradigms. Who has not heard of the 'high-performance workplace' or its recent offspring, the 'high-commitment' and 'high-involvement' workplaces? Who has not been subject to the siren calls of achieving greater competitiveness through lean production, diversified quality production, flexible specialization or world-class manufacturing? What self-respecting production manager has not considered the merits of 'pulling' instead of 'pushing' production along the value chain, of promoting a 'customer focus', of reconfiguring supply management chains by means of just-in-time and sub-contracting, of harnessing employee potential in teams to generate corporate productivity gains through knowledge-driven work systems, or of achieving 'six sigma' targets for value enhancement and customer satisfaction? Are there any corporations that have not been 'reengineered', 'refocused on their core competencies,' 'downsized', 'delayered', or otherwise discombobulated? What worker has not been invited, or instructed, to join a quality circle or problem-solving group, to work in an off-line, on-line, autonomous, semi-autonomous or other type of team or to engage in *kaizen* or systematic problem-solving and incremental improvement in all aspects of the work process? And what local or national union leader has not been urged to be a partner for progress, to rethink the social contract at work and to rewrite collective agreements to reflect the new realities of the marketplace in a global context?

The incessant invitations to partake of this new productive cornucopia certainly provide fodder for the sceptical-minded. After all, many of the currently popular ideas are not so new; others seem to have an exceedingly brief shelf-life; and still others fall far short of their promise to 'radically transform' work, the workplace or labour–management relations. Nevertheless, it is difficult to dismiss the wave of recent changes as entirely a case of old wine in new bottles or as a mere smokescreen laid down to disguise deepening exploitation.

The aim of this chapter is to offer a critical understanding of the changing workplace. We will argue that it is indeed possible to identify the contours of a new model of production, one that is likely to yield significant gains in productivity, quality and flexibility. The key operative principles of this model, however, are so fluid and contradictory that the entire amalgam remains fragile, uneven and often unstable. The daunting yet compelling task for observers of the contemporary workplace – students, researchers, practitioners and policy-makers alike – is to understand whether and how these tensions might develop into a more stable and enduring productive model.

To simplify the task and to sharpen our analytical focus, we start with two sets of distinctions: the different spheres of workplace change; and the analytical levels at which we can analyse workplace change. These distinctions are important for a clear understanding of the objectives of this chapter.

Our analysis of the changing workplace starts from a distinction between production management, work organization and employment relations.

Production management concerns the overall organization of the processes through which goods and services are produced and delivered. The way production is managed is, of course, intimately related to the type of product or service being provided as well as to the nature of the technologies used to manufacture or deliver them. However, production management's key focus is the systems and processes that govern the organization of service delivery or product manufacture. For instance, the production process can be organized on the basis of continuous assembly or process, in batches or by unit production. It also concerns the ways in which the production process is laid out (e.g. in assembly lines or modular groupings), as well as the ways in which supplies are delivered (e.g. the size and management of buffer stocks). Also of concern is the degree to which particular parts of the process are internal to or external to the production process (i.e. whether subcontracting or outsourcing is used). A key focus of production management is control over productivity and quality.

Work organization relates to the ways in which one of the factors of production, labour, is utilized in the production process. More concretely, work organization concerns the ways jobs are defined or configured within the overall organization of production of goods or services. For example, do jobs entail a relatively narrow range of pre-defined tasks or do employees enjoy a degree of discretion in the way that they do their jobs? Do employees work individually or in teams? And are employees subject to tight supervision or do they enjoy a degree of autonomy in meeting performance objectives?

Employment relations are the policies and practices governing the employment relationships of individuals and groups involved in production. These include the broad range of human resource management practices, such as recruitment, remuneration, training or promotion, that are designed to direct the abilities of employees towards the achievement of the objectives of their employer. Employment relations also include the negotiation and application of rules, taking the form of either collective agreements or customs and practices arising from successive dealings with informal work groups.

It is crucial to consider all three spheres of the workplace if we are to make sense of the dizzying array of workplace change. All too often analysis is focused on just one or two of these spheres to the detriment of a more global understanding of the changes taking place. Industrial relations and human resource management specialists, for example, often neglect the nature of change taking place in the management of production and the organization of work. Similarly, some production management specialists are blissfully ignorant of the implications of their work for employment relations. In our view, one of the key challenges for the analysis and practice of workplace change is to better understand the relations between these different spheres. Indeed, we will argue that the often observed fragility of new work systems is partly related to the tensions between the sometimes conflicting objectives pursued in each sphere.

The second distinction which informs this chapter is the level of analysis. Our objective is to offer a general understanding of changes taking place in the contemporary workplace. Such generality, however, can only be achieved by not delving into the full complexity of particular practices or patterns of changes. It is perhaps helpful here to think of three possible levels of analysis of workplace change and practice.

At a first, perhaps microscopic, level, specific practices can be isolated for detailed scrutiny, as in the case of the considerable literature on teamwork or total quality management. This research into individual practices plays an indispensable role in developing our understanding of the changing workplace. However informative the analysis of particular practices might be, most observers would probably agree that the study of individual practices cannot fully capture the extent of change in the contemporary workplace. Instead, it is necessary to go a step further and examine the relationships among the various practices and their contexts.

Thus, at a second level of analysis, one might focus on changing patterns, sets or 'bundles', of firm- or establishment-level practices. These are often conceived as systems that, depending on the point of view of the analyst in question, can embrace the areas of production management, work organization and employment relations policies and practices. Among the most common are 'flexible production systems', 'lean production systems', 'high performance work practices or systems' and the 'high involvement' workplace. All of these aspire to bring together a range of different practices into more general systems or models. This is at the heart of much of the recent US literature on workplace change (see, for example, Becker and Huselid, 1998b; Appelbaum *et al.*, 2000; Pil and MacDuffie, 2000). The key notion at this level of analysis is the difficulty of implementing one practice in the absence of another or, alternatively, the incompatibility of certain practices. Research frequently focuses on the linkages between the different practices, on the question of whether particular sets of practices constitute coherent models or systems, or on the synergies to be achieved through the 'fit' of different types of practices. Also of considerable interest is the degree to which other organizational characteristics, such as corporate structure or product market types, facilitate or inhibit the adoption of particular models or systems. Related to this is a sometimes almost existential literature concerned with the role of strategic human resource management within the larger objectives of the firm (see, for example, Guérin and Wils, 1992; Lawler, 1995; or, for a more critical view, Guest, 1990). Much of the current literature on workplace innovation and high performance work systems focuses on this level of analysis in a search for the Holy Grail of new production systems.

This brings us to a third, more abstract level of analysis – that of the 'production model'. A model is a simplified theoretical representation of the relations that exist between different concepts or parts of a whole. Irrespective of variations that might be observed in practice or in particular contexts, the key notion at this level of analysis is that it is possible to generalize about certain sets of relations between different components of the model. Although we shall develop this idea in much greater detail through the course of this chapter, it needs to be emphasized here that this level of analysis allows generalizations about the underlying principles at work. Observers of the world of work, for example, often refer to 'Taylorism' or 'Fordism'. Such representations of the complexities of the world of work are not meant to depict specific workplaces but rather a set of principles that underlie the organization of work in many different workplaces. Wrongly used, such representations can easily distort our understanding of particular situations. However, their analytical value lies in their ability to distil complex sets of relations into a broader whole. This chapter is pitched precisely at this more abstract level.

Our core argument is that we can now identify the major principles underlying an emerging model of production, one that is different in significant ways from what preceded it. However, it is important to stress that the mere identification of distinctive principles does not confer internal cohesion on the model. On the contrary, we will argue that while the emerging model is characterized by a number of key principles which do offer some plausible consistency in the way that they operate, the model is also traversed by significant tensions and contradictions. In other words, and in contrast to much of the normative literature offering magic recipes for more productive workplaces, we do not believe that the emergence of this model abolishes the age-old difficulties inherent in the realization of value within the production process. Many of these difficulties remain intractable and are indeed exacerbated in the changing workplace, hence the real and often remarked fragility of these new production systems.

The objective of this chapter, then, is to analyse the underlying relations between new practices in the spheres of production management, work organization and employment relations, the linkages between these three spheres, and the relationship between firm-level practices and their wider organizational and institutional setting. Since many of the issues concerning new production models and the high performance workplace are defined, sometimes implicitly, in terms of a transformation or transition away from a previously dominant production model, the first part of the chapter examines that traditional model, commonly labelled Fordism. This term is here used as a shorthand to refer to a particular set of relations between the management of production, the organization of work and employee relations. The second part of the chapter sketches out the broad contours of the model now taking shape. The final part assesses the prospects for the consolidation of the new model. We argue that the slow, variable and tension-laden diffusion of this new model of production is partly a natural feature of social change, but is also due to significant tensions and contradictions within the new model. These are twofold in nature: first, the internal tensions between the most salient characteristics of the new model; second, its uncertain insertion into a wider set of social institutions.

Jacques Bélanger, Anthony Giles and Gregor Murray

The Rise and Fall of Fordism

A basic premise shared by virtually all analysts of workplace change is that recent innovations in production management, work organization and employment relations constitute a response to growing problems with the social system of production that dominated advanced capitalist economies during the long boom of the post-war years. However, beyond this premise, there are a number of questions and issues that have generated considerable debate. First, there is the basic issue of definition. As a quick glance through the literature soon reveals, the notion of Fordism has been used in a wide variety of ways, and so our first task is to clarify its meaning. Second, there is a plethora of explanations why Fordism is faltering, explanations that are intimately connected to attempts to characterize recent innovations. Accordingly, we briefly review some of these explanations as a prelude to our discussion, in the second part of the chapter, of the emergence of a new model that departs from Fordism.

The Fordist Production Model

The term 'Fordism' has come to be applied widely, and not a little casually, as shorthand for a number of distinct phenomena. It is common, for example, for Fordism to be equated simply with 'mass production' or with assembly-line production. Fordism is also often treated as the extension or mechanization of the 'Taylorist' model of work organization, i.e. the narrow definition of highly specialized tasks separated from conception and subject to the tight control of engineers and supervisors. Finally, Fordism is sometimes used to describe the pattern of labour–management relations in which employers accept the existence of unions, collective bargaining and relatively high wages in return for union and worker acquiescence to the retention of management control over work and production.

These different uses of the notion of Fordism are not surprising since the term has also been applied in a much broader sense that encompasses all of these specific meanings. Indeed, the Italian communist leader Antonio Gramsci (1971, pp. 277–320) is usually credited with having coined the term in the late 1920s as a way of encapsulating not simply a particular method of production or pattern of work and employment relations, but as both a whole system of production marking a rupture with previous modes of industrial organization and as a 'way of life'. More recently, this broad use of the term has been taken up by French political economists belonging to the 'regulation' school. Thus, for Lipietz, Fordism refers to the 'model of economic development *actually* established in advanced capitalist countries after World War II' (Lipietz, 1994, p. 230; see also Aglietta, 1979). On this view, although Fordism rested on the productivity gains made possible by the application of Taylorist principles of work organization to mass production, it was not until the post-Second World War era that what the regulation school labels a 'regime of accumulation', combining mass consumption with mass production, was finally put in place. This regime was held together by what is labelled a Fordist 'mode of regulation' that entailed a specific wage relation, monetary and credit regime, pattern of competition, role of the state and insertion in the international political economy. It is argued that this particular formula underlay what 'regulationists' refer to as the *trente glorieuses* or 'Golden Age', namely the approximately thirty post-war years of unrivalled economic expansion in most of the major capitalist industrialized economies.

For present purposes, neither the complex theoretical architecture of the regulation school nor its oftentimes arcane vocabulary need be adopted in their entirety (for a full-blown self account, see Boyer and Saillard, 1995; for a more critical view, see Clarke, 1992). Instead, we focus on three elements of the more general Fordist model that, taken together, cover the range of innovations and experiments that are commonly treated under the rubric of the 'new workplace': production management; work organization; and employment relations. That said, as is often stressed by the regulation school and by other analysts, it is important not to lose sight of the connections between models of production at the level of the firm and the wider (usually national) set of institutions. These connections reflect the social relations between actors – employers, unions and the state, for example – and the institutional arrangements to which they give rise. Indeed, as will be argued later in this chapter, the arduous birth of the new production model can be attributed, in part at least, to a lack of coherence between changes at the level of the firm and their institutional setting – an incoherence that expresses the still evolving state of social relations in the new model. Let us now look at each of the three spheres of the Fordist model of production at the level of the workplace.

Production Management
In the area of production management, Fordism rested squarely on the principles of standardized mass production, i.e. the production of 'highly standardized goods on a large scale with highly specialized equipment, operated by semiskilled workers' (Hollingsworth and Boyer, 1997, p. 20). The

characteristics of this type of production management are, of course, already well rehearsed in the literature. Suffice it to depict the broad argument as it applies to basic manufacturing. National product markets were characterized by a fairly constant demand for standardized and relatively undifferentiated goods produced by a small number of dominant or oligopolistic producers. This was the result of the ability of certain firms to achieve competitive advantage through the economies of scale that accrued from mass production, thereby eliminating smaller firms in the process (for example, see Chandler, 1977). These dominant manufacturers were typically able to use highly specialized single-purpose equipment to produce their goods. While there were differences in the quality of the goods produced, overall quality concerns appear to have been less important than the simple ability to get products to market. Thus, this type of production was generally a resource-driven or 'push' system, inasmuch as the amount produced was dominated by supply and output considerations rather than specific demand. Indeed, general economic conditions permitting (hence the importance of overall Keynesian demand management), it was assumed that there would be a demand for the product, not least because of the significant resources invested in mass marketing to create that demand. Production management was therefore characterized by infrequent model changes, long production runs, a limited number of set-ups, and long time lags in set-up changes. Competitive advantage accrued to those producers that could achieve higher levels of productivity through the scale of their production of standardized products and, consequently, could ensure continuous production in order to achieve the efficiency gains associated with the highly specialized equipment being used.

Since the elimination of uncertainty was very important in the production process, firms tended to maintain large buffer stocks and to pursue a strategy of vertical integration in which dominant firms often sought to control the key resources and parts suppliers as well as the specific skills on which their production process depended. Indeed, the economies obtained in mass production were so significant that firms were willing to internalize costs associated with excess capacity in order to reduce levels of uncertainty about the ability to respond to demand when national economies were running at full tilt. The resulting organizational structure of the firm was both complex, in terms of the multiple functions to be performed, and hierarchical, in terms of the many levels associated with the planning and operation of production process. Mintzberg's (1979) typological depiction of a mechanical bureaucracy is entirely apposite to the kind of organizational structure associated with this model and the way that production management was calibrated to operate within it.

This portrait is obviously not applicable in either the same degree or in the same way to all firms. Moreover, the model was not immune from internal tensions or contradictions. In particular, there were limits to which firms could pursue vertical integration strategies, carry costs associated with decreased uncertainty in the supply chain, abandon quality concerns in favour of unbridled output, or even aspire to market dominance without significant research, technological innovation and product differentiation. In fact, as we shall see below, the ability to achieve many of the necessary efficiencies was crucially dependent on the realization of objectives in the other two spheres of the production model, objectives that were character-ized by their own inherent difficulties. In other words, it should scarcely astonish to discover that the management of production was continuously subject to many kinds of uncertainty and trade-offs between competing objectives. Moreover, by the very nature of the competitive process at work, although many firms aspired to such advantage, few actually achieved it. Yet, as was so characteristic of much of twentieth-century industrial production, and what so differentiated it from production management prior to the emergence of the Fordist paradigm from the 1920s onwards, was that the prize of productive dominance was there to be obtained for those firms best able to reconcile the sometimes competing objectives in the application of this new set of techniques. It was on the basis of their production management that such firms became household names in virtually every post-war consumer economy.

Work organization

In the sphere of work organization, Fordism entailed the application of the core features of Taylorism. Indeed, it was Frederick Taylor's (1911) pioneering work in the area of industrial engineering that later led the way to the possibility of mechanized assembly line production from which the real productivity gains were secured. These core features included the separation of conception from execution, the division of labour into a series of highly fragmented and simplified tasks, and the 'scientific' analysis of each task in order to prescribe the best method of accomplishing it. Scientific management implied, in turn, the development of a hierarchy of supervision and control methods in order to ensure that the production process was planned and co-ordinated. Taylorism implied little in the way of training or involvement on the part of these 'low-' or 'semi-skilled' workers, who were perceived, as in Charlie Chaplin's brilliant cinemagraphic depiction of the production worker in *Modern Times*, as mere cogs in the productive wheel.

The net result was typically a complex job structure detailing fragmented sets of interdependent tasks.

Here too the power and coherence of Taylorism has often been exaggerated. In particular, the idea of almost disembodied workers mechanically performing alienating tasks does violence to the reflexivity and subjectivity inherent in human labour. More prosaically, the central problem for the management of labour remains how to elicit employee co-operation in the transformation of their productive abilities into real work performed (see Edwards, 1986). For those familiar with the complexities of managing production, the idea that it is possible to achieve such a high degree of perfection in the conception of work organization that worker intelligence and tacit knowledge are no longer required is quite ludicrous. It is for precisely that reason that workplace researchers have invariably discovered complex forms of worker influence over the production process, be they expressed in terms of overt or tacit forms of influence over the work process and its results in terms of productivity and control over the 'effort bargain', i.e. over how hard or fast employees are actually willing to work (see, for example, Brown, 1973; Burawoy, 1979; Bélanger, 1989). Similarly, while tasks might be fragmented, the problems of managing uncertainty in the production process no doubt erected an invisible frontier beyond which it was no longer feasible to divide up jobs or to even want to destroy the synergies that might accrue from informal work groups. Yet, despite these tensions in the operation of Fordist production, it must be acknowledged that the mass production characteristic of much of the twentieth century was characterized by an elaborate and complex division of labour designed to achieve the objectives associated with this new type of production.

Employment relations

The management of employment relations was a crucial dimension of the Fordist paradigm. Indeed, it was so central that it gave rise to new areas of functional specialization such as industrial relations and human resource management. The pattern of employment relations typical of the Fordist era entailed what is often termed a broad 'compromise' between labour, management and the state. The central issue for the realization of the tremendous productivity gains to be achieved in this new productive model was how to secure employee co-operation in what was manifestly a more alienating division of labour (see, for example, Lazonick, 1983). This led to the emergence of a panoply of techniques designed to ensure worker co-operation in assembly-line production, including new forms of recruitment and selection, the development of elaborate internal labour markets and job ladders that rewarded long service or continuous effort, new forms of compensation, and corporate cultures designed to elicit employee loyalty and commitment.

These techniques were supplemented by the spread of mass trade unionism and the negotiation of collective rules that, to some extent at least, legitimized the dominant forms of employment relations (Brody, 1980). At the heart of this compromise was a trade-off between security and control. As Standing (1997) has argued, workers and their unions in the advanced capitalist world won a greater degree of security along a number of dimensions: representational security through the acceptance of unions and collective bargaining; enhanced employment security thanks both to continual economic growth and to the development of a range of mechanisms to protect individual workers against arbitrary dismissal and groups of workers from mass layoffs; income security through a combination of collective bargaining and welfare-state initiatives; and job security, ensured through the construction of internal labour markets in large firms.[1] In return, irrespective of continuing worker influence over the actual work process, workers and unions generally acquiesced to a certain consolidation of formal management control over the organization of production and work and over the strategic direction of the firm. Thus, at least in the realm of production, unions were seen to be interested in a limited range of economic issues and workers themselves were not expected to take on any responsibility for the way in which their work was organized or the firm was operated.

This pattern of collective employment relations was not wholly isolated from the production process. As was argued above, by its very nature, human labour is subject to a complex variety of trade-offs that cannot be disembodied from the very workers whose labour is to be realized. Nor can the trade-off between security and control ever be absolute. Nevertheless, through successive struggles and conflicts over the control of labour and the production process, over the right to collective representation in this process and over the appropriate division of labour between what workers and their organizations might negotiate with their employers and what they might negotiate with the state, Fordism entailed a certain regularization and, indeed, institutionalization of social relations at work. Although Fordist institutions were variable, both geographically and over time, they generally reinforced this new set of productive arrangements by ensuring a degree of cohesion between the key characteristics of production management, work organization and the major dimensions of employment relations.

The consolidation of national trade unions took place within this context and it is worth pursuing this point about unions since the typical structures and strategies of modern trade unions are so entwined with the rise of the Fordist production model. The evolution of national union structures in many ways mirrored the emergence of a few dominant firms in particular industries. Whether in terms of national craft and general unions spread across multiple industries, as in the UK, or single-industry national and international unions, as in the USA and Canada, there arose large-scale union organizations to counter the giant firms that came to dominate the industrial landscape. Depending on the national context, this union representation could be consolidated in a winner-take-all monopoly representation system, as in the USA and Canada where one union represented most employees within a firm. Or it could be found in forms of multi-unionism predicated on pockets of workplace presence, as in the UK where worker allegiance was divided among competing craft and general unions that, in the absence of a positive right to organize, had to impose their presence on the employer. Or, union representation was channelled in regimes of universal worker representation where multiple union centres, as with Catholic and Communist unions in France and Belgium, struggled to exert their influence over the course of wages and conditions within the structures provided by the state for worker representation.

Apart from securing representation rights, the typical union focus in the Fordist production model was fourfold: first, to maintain a degree of job security through national and local bargaining; second, to ensure a degree of procedural justice within the operation of internal labour markets and in opposition to the broad expression of management rights accruing to employers in the organization of production and work; third, to improve wages and working conditions in keeping with productivity gains; fourth, to exert pressure on the state through political party and direct government lobbying activity in order to achieve these other objectives in the industrial sphere (see, for example, Murray *et al.*, 1999). These objectives were typically pursued in the context of either multi-employer bargaining at national and/or regional levels or of pattern bargaining within and between national firms. The central focus of union organizational activity, at least in North America and the UK, was therefore on contract negotiation and servicing, but there was also scope for complementary political activity in order to influence the general framework under which such bargaining took place. While there was considerable local bargaining, there was at least a presumption that local bargaining strength should be co-ordinated within these larger, articulated bargaining strategies designed to achieve broad gains for workers across industries. Union organizing or recruitment outside the core industries was limited and, outside of industries characterized by a high degree of labour and capital mobility, most recruitment simply sought to mitigate the effects of a weakening core structure; in other words, to maintain a threshold of union organization sufficient to maintain patterns through successive bargaining rounds.

While employers did not necessarily seek to redistribute their productivity gains to their unionized employees, it was possible to share out these gains, inasmuch as their unionized workforce presented sufficient strength and other employers were doing likewise. Indeed, collective worker organization played a critical role in the consolidation of the Fordist model, simultaneously both a source of instability because the exact terms of the compromise were always to be renegotiated, but also of stability inasmuch as the model epitomized a generic understanding about respective zones of influence, the promise of shared gains and a certain institutional continuity in order to provide a framework to negotiate these trade-offs.

The Fordist paradigm

In sum, then, Fordism can be portrayed as a production model that entailed a set of principles governing production management, work organization and employment relations. In practice, of course, Fordism did not emerge fully formed when Henry Ford introduced the first automobile assembly line in 1913. Instead, it was built over a considerable length of time and only truly became consolidated as the dominant social system of production in the post-World War II era. This process also entailed much trial and error and a significant degree of conflict. Indeed, in an important sense Fordism was only possible because the conflicts to which it gave rise, for example around the emergence of mass unionism and the right to collective representation, or the pursuit of procedural justice and equitable working conditions at the level of the workplace, were contained to a degree by a wider social compromise. Although the terms of this compromise certainly varied in important ways from one national context to another, it can be argued that this compromise rested on the consolidation of a set of labour-relations institutions at the level of the firm, on a wider set of institutions at the level of the society and on certain guarantees provided or underwritten by the state. Indeed, it can be argued that collective worker organization was one of the key factors driving a kind of dynamic stability within this production model.

Fordism was neither a homogeneous nor a singular system. There were a variety of variants of Fordism shaped by the features of individual countries, sectors and firms. Although automobile production in the USA still serves as the theoretical archetype of Fordist production, this particular model was not imposed everywhere without modification. Nor did Fordism wash away all other ways of organizing production, but instead co-existed with these (Piore and Sabel, 1984; Sabel and Zeitlin, 1985). In other words, a general model of production is not a logically coherent, conscious design imposed unilaterally but, is characterized instead by overlaps, discontinuities and reversals.

The Decline of Fordism

Explanations of the growing difficulties, if not actual decline, of Fordism are varied. The simplest and most common explanation is that the generalized pressure of 'increased competition', commonly linked to 'globalization', 'deregulation' and 'privatization' has driven managers to search for more efficient and less costly ways of producing goods and services. On this view, Fordism is no longer able to offer additional productivity gains, and so alternatives are being sought.

A more sophisticated version of this thesis holds that competition has not merely increased, but that its nature has changed in fundamental ways (Piore and Sabel, 1984). More particularly, driven essentially by consumer preferences, the nature of product demand has changed, becoming more exacting in terms of quality, uniqueness, variety and other factors. Fordist production is ill-suited to these new product markets because its organizational dynamics are predicated on the concept of standardized mass production. In particular, the compromise between workers and management at the heart of Fordist production neither facilitates the kinds of flexibility required by the competitive environment nor does it favour the acquisition of new skills and the horizontal transfer of knowledge between workers that enlightened management now seeks to promote.

A third explanation of the travails of Fordism is rooted in technology and organizational innovation. Here the focus is not so much on how markets shape production, but rather on how technological and managerial advances, particularly those pioneered in Japan, have opened up a wide range of new ways of producing goods and services, including flexible automation, just-in-time inventory management systems, robotization, cellular manufacturing and computerization. As one of the best-known exponents of this view puts it in his analysis of 'post-Fordism': 'The re-engineering of work is eliminating jobs of all kinds and in greater numbers than at any time in recent memory. All of these problems are likely to accelerate dramatically in the years ahead as companies, faced with more intense global competition, use increasingly sophisticated technologies to raise productivity and reduce labor force requirements' (Rifkin, 1996, p. 106). The seemingly huge recent productivity gains to be secured from the application of new information technologies to the production process clearly reinforce the thrust of this argument.

A fourth explanation concerns the producers themselves, i.e. employees who, it is said, are no longer content to be treated as part of the assembly line (on the social failures of Taylorism, see Durand, 1978, pp. 69–80). In effect, the assumptions that underlay the post-war 'compromise' in the advanced capitalist nations consolidated managerial prerogatives on the choice of technology and the management of production. Coupled with Taylorist principles of work organization, this compromise, while bringing material advantages to workers and institutional rights to their unions, had the effect of inhibiting workers' actual involvement in their work. Although traditional forms of worker autonomy persisted, the post-war system of joint regulation clearly was not designed to produce the forms of employee involvement most organizations are now purported to be seeking. Quite the contrary: over time, the traditional model of production generated disillusionment among the workforce towards technological and industrial progress and withdrawal of part of their creative potential, because it was not solicited in a way acceptable to them. Hence, besides creating social tensions, this mode of labour regulation adversely affected productivity. To borrow Lipietz's formulation (1989, p. 29), these arrangements end up exhausting the very source of the previous productivity gains so characteristic of the model.

A final and complementary explanation concerns the erosion of the material and institutional basis of the social compromises that underlay the Fordist model. It can be argued that forces associated with globalization, notably the internationalization of product markets and the ability to organize production across borders, fundamentally alter the parameters of the hitherto national social compromises associated with the emergence and endurance of the Fordist model of production. In the absence of some form of international or global Keynesiasm (see Petrella, 1994), national models of social compromise can no longer sustain the social arrangements that underwrite a productive bargain between security and control in the production process on a local or national level. In particular, the weakening of these national compromises would appear to be bound up with diminished union influence. This can alternatively be linked to the reduced coverage and erosion of collective worker strength as expressed in relative trade union density in a context of rapidly restructuring industries and the movement of employment to poorly unionized services (ILO, 1997); or to the rise of employer-led alternatives to collective union strength, such as human resource strategies designed to avoid unions (Kochan et al., 1986); or to the decline of alternative production models, as characterized the conflict between capitalist and socialist models during the 'Cold War'; or simply to the apparent insufficiency of national social compromises in an increasingly internationalized environment.

While some analysts might stress one or another of the factors listed above, they are closely interrelated. So much so indeed, that they can be situated in a more sweeping analysis of the interconnected elements of the Fordist regime that was pioneered by the regulation school (see, for example, Boyer and Saillard, 1995). It is thus argued that we are witnessing not an accumulation of separate pressures but a systemic failure that is shaking the political and social foundations of the post-war era. In this analysis, a central element of Fordism was the apparent solution to the Keynesian problem of how to counter cyclical economic crises through the linking of production and consumption in national economies. By assuring workers annual wage increases in return for their basic co-operation in the production process, Fordism also assured its own renewal through the ready markets for mass production. In brief, mass production required mass consumption and this basic relationship was assured by the emergence of a complex set of national institutions. This institutional consolidation ensured a degree of stability for capital accumulation, a fundamental requirement for the stable reproduction and expansion of the capitalist economic system. The larger crisis of the Fordist regime, which first became apparent in the two economic recessions of the 1970s, is not only about increased competition, technological changes and worker alienation, it is also fundamentally about the unhinging of this stable relationship between production and consumption and the reconstruction of institutional arrangements in order to ensure a new period of stable economic expansion.

Again, the particular diagnosis put forward by the regulation school is less important than the underlying principle of explanation: the various pressures on Fordism cannot usefully be seen as isolated trends, but should instead be seen as part of a wider pattern of change in the political economy of advanced capitalism. Changes in the way production is managed, work is organized and employee relations are structured need to be related to the wider pattern of social relations that underlie the structures and institutions shaping the relations between actors in the workplace. Thus the instability and multiple tensions associated with the previous model have given rise to a tremendous wave of experimentation and innovation in the way that production and work are organized as well as in the ways that social relations are organized to underpin those methods of production management and work organization. This change in the workplace is the necessary precondition for the possible emergence of a new productive model and it is to the characteristics of this model that we now turn.

The Contours of a New Model

How then might we characterize the contours of the emerging production system? In this part of the chapter, we look at the three spheres of the production process: production management, work organization and employee relations. We argue that it is possible to identify key characteristics within each that differ in important ways from the previous Fordist model. A central theme in our argument is that the interaction of these operative principles, both within each sphere and between the spheres, is characterized by tensions and contradictions which make the emergent model highly fragile and unstable.

However, before outlining the major features of the emerging model, two caveats are in order. First, it should not be surprising at this stage of its development that the emerging model is made up of somewhat disparate elements, often melded together in a rather precarious and not always internally coherent balance. In short, the new model is a 'work in progress'. Second, it is worth re-emphasizing the abstract character of the model. Our intention is not to describe a particular workplace or a particular pattern of workplace change but rather to distil from the complex processes of change currently taking place a number of basic principles that characterize the emerging model of production. This is, of course, a perilous exercise but one that has the analytical merit of identifying what we perceive as the core features of these new ways of organizing work and also some of the key tensions which account for the considerable variety of productive arrangements to be observed in workplaces experimenting with change across the industrialized world and their relative volatility in terms of employment relations. To paraphrase the famed British historian E. P. Thompson (1968, p. 11), in the way that he once depicted his understanding of social class: if we stop history at a given point, then there are no *production models* (*social classes* in the original) but simply a multitude of experiences. But if we watch these social relations of production over an adequate period of social change, we observe patterns in their relationships, their ideas, and their institutions. . . In other words, the argument is not that this new production model can be seen on a particular day at a particular time but, rather, there emerge distinct patterns in the way that firms have sought to restructure their production, their organization of work and their employment relations, and it is to the contours of this new model that we now turn our attention.

JACQUES BÉLANGER, ANTHONY GILES AND GREGOR MURRAY

Production Management

Greater product variety, the uncertainty associated with increased competition in the context of globalization, and the rapid evolution of technologies are all part of the universe of new pressures driving transformations in the organization of production. In many sectors of the economy, demand has gradually evolved towards less standardized products and services. The need for flexibility and speed in production adjustments is imperative in the race to produce less standardized and more varied products. But placing all the emphasis on flexibility would make systems of production highly vulnerable. To make production efficient, some form of standardization has to be achieved somewhere in the production chain, and so standardization is being gradually transferred from product to processes. In short, developments in production management can best be understood as a continuous effort on the part of management to reconcile two principles: productive flexibility and process standardization.

The transformation of the principles of production management was noted in the mid-1980s by Katz and Sabel in their discussion of the car industry:

> There are signs of a slow movement towards a model of production which turns the principles of mass production upside down. Instead of producing a standard car by means of highly specialised resources . . . the tendency is to produce specialised goods by means of general-purpose resources. (Katz and Sabel, 1985, p. 298)

Katz and Sabel emphasized, as did Piore and Sabel (1984), the trend towards more flexible production systems. In essence, this was predicated on the spread of computer-controlled technologies to respond to structural changes in the economy.

Since then, the automobile industry has shifted steadily towards a form of flexible mass production. It is also in this industry, in which product diversification is compatible with 'standard' models sold in large volume throughout the year, that the key concepts of lean production (such as just-in-time inventory and the pull system) seem to apply in their most pure form. Nevertheless, the notion of flexibility in production systems applies to most sectors of the economy, albeit in different forms and to various degrees. As described by Coriat, product variety and business speed have become key elements in firms' struggles to experiment with new forms of corporate strategy and organization: 'competitive position increasingly rests on a firm's ability to differentiate and adapt its products, to do so rapidly in response to demand changes, and to anticipate such changes so as to identify and occupy lucrative market niches' (Coriat, 1997, p. 243). In particular, shortened product life cycles mean a much closer relationship between marketing and operational functions within the organization as firms attempt to be closer to their clients. This represents an important departure from many of the assumptions that governed the archetypal mechanical bureaucracies that dominated the workplaces of the golden years of Fordist mass production. New forms of horizontal co-ordination of production activities are replacing previous forms of vertical control; organizational hierarchy is thereby flattened out.

Although there is a need for flexibility and speed of adjustment in production, in most industries placing all the emphasis on flexibility might mean that the system of production generates neither the efficiencies nor the quality required by ever more competitive and demanding product markets. Some form of standardization, therefore, has to be achieved.

There are essentially two ways to standardize production processes, namely technology and production management. In contrast to the robust, single-purpose equipment typical of the previous generation, information technology is relatively flexible. Its versatility was seen as a positive influence in the conception of post-Fordist production models such as 'flexible specialisation' (Piore and Sabel, 1984, pp. 258–63) or 'diversified quality production' (Streeck, 1992, pp. 4–10), a view confirmed by more recent investigations of the impact of information technology in the sphere of production (Castells, 1996).

As distinct from hardware equipment, production management is made up of programmes, procedures and rules for regulating the transformation of resources. The development of procedures and measures by which the successive stages in the production chain can be assessed and performance monitored is therefore very much on the agenda. Indeed, the tendency seems to be more pronounced in organizations in which process controls are not already integrated in the technology *per se*. Like Taylorism and other advances in industrial management in the early twentieth century, current developments are being instigated mostly by industrial engineers; but at the beginning of a new century, the tools of the trade are much more sophisticated. So far, the importance of these developments in the sphere of production management has been underestimated by social scientists. Such developments represent a further phase of rationalization, in the Weberian sense, by which engineers and production managers seek to reduce as much as they can the variability and uncertainty associated with the production of non-standard goods and services.

The main goal is to develop production systems that are leaner and more fluid. In the search for a more continuous flow of production, two main concepts underlie the various programmes of production management: 'process management', in which production is conceived as a global process and not as a succession of different activities organized in separate departments; and 'customer focus', which holds that operations should be driven, or 'pulled', by customer specifications. The 'theory' holds that once these concepts are well established, and shared as widely as possible among all participants, significant progress can be achieved in the reduction of 'non-value-added activities'.

This phase of standardization was first observed in the sphere of quality management, where it remains quite important. It is worth noting here that, contrary to what is often suggested, total quality management (TQM) is not necessarily designed to promote worker participation or employee involvement. As conceived by William Deming and others, the idea was to use statistical tools to analyse variance from tolerance margins at each stage in the process and to monitor production activities in order to bring about more consistency and less variability. A good example is the 'Six Sigma' programme, a sophisticated tool of statistical quality control first implemented in large corporations such as Motorola, ABB and General Electric (Björkman, 1999, pp. 51–2). In the view of the industrial engineers who conceive these systems, the objective is to standardize operations and procedures, a goal that seeks not to expand but to reduce the autonomy of workers in the execution of their tasks. According to this rationale, quality is clearly management's responsibility.

Much of the confusion about the place of employee involvement in such programmes derives from the fact that, to be effective, they have to be accepted by workers. This is the case in particular for procedures of standardization such as ISO, at least at the implementation stage. The degree of employee involvement depends on the extent to which TQM programmes really have a strong statistical or technical dimension, as opposed to more watered-down versions. Hackman and Wageman, for example, bemoan the fact that there are many cases where 'rhetoric is winning out over substance' (1995, p. 338), where TQM has more to do with a search for employee involvement than with quality control *per se*. It follows that the real impact of such programmes on workers' autonomy and influence is a complex issue, one that remains to be clarified by empirical research.

As evidenced by an international study of ABB (Bélanger *et al.*, 1999), such developments in process management are by no means limited to quality control. At ABB, programmes have also been developed to monitor supply management and, even more importantly, to introduce time-based management. ABB corporate management does much more than set objectives. It has developed benchmarking measures through which similar plants are systematically compared over time. Although social and institutional forces still create considerable differences between similar production units in different countries, real forces for diffusion of 'best practices' and process standardization can thus be driven by central corporate managers.

In a sense, these methods and programmes could be interpreted as a further phase of rationalization, an idea that dates back to the development of industrial capitalism. But recent developments also mark a rupture with the orientation that prevailed in previous decades, when the emphasis was more on 'soft management', i.e. on the human side of the industrial organization. While the objective of stimulating employee participation and involvement usually remains on the agenda, the necessity of controlling performance and 'being more productive in a more competitive environment' is being expressed more explicitly in management's dealings with workers and their representatives. This context has given rise to a veritable industry of consultants and academic business writers on 're-engineering', process management, organizational learning, and a host of other managerial neologisms that have yet to be invented (for a critical analysis, see Micklethwait and Wooldridge, 1996). But to be critical of such fads is not to suggest that there is no substance in current developments. Behind the rapidly changing flavours of the month, there is continuity in the attempt to rationalize the production of non-standard goods and services.

However, contrary to some well-known arguments (e.g. Womack *et al.*, 1990), there is no 'one best way' in industrial management. None of the programmes mentioned here has the potential for wholly solving the social tensions and technical constraints that occur at the point of production. As noted by Knights and McCabe (1998a) in reference to TQM, there is an unfortunate tendency on the part of both management gurus and social critics to exaggerate the rationality and effectiveness of such programmes. Part of the difficulty lies in a confusion between intent, implementation and outcomes. As pointed out by Smith and Thompson, there is a tendency to confuse 'the formal characteristics of systems such as JIT, TQM or team working, and the intent of some managements, with the real outcomes, which remain influenced by uneven and incompetent management implementation, plus continued resistance and informal workforce controls' (Smith and Thompson, 1998, p. 559). In the current phase of rationalization, besides the fundamental conflict associated with the conversion of labour power, the difficulty of achieving flexible production through standardized processes remains considerable.

To summarize, two key operative principles characterize the emerging model of production in the sphere of production management. These are productive flexibility and standardization of processes. Tremendous competitive advantage is likely to accrue to firms able to achieve these twin principles. Rapid adjustments in the provision of goods and services ensure that firms can achieve economies of scope in the range of products and services offered and tailored to respond to consumer demand. Standardized processes seek to ensure that the organization of production and services is done with maximum quality and efficiency.

Such a dream scenario is, of course, more easily espoused than achieved. The implementation of these principles is complex and problematical. First, to draw on the core insights of critical labour process theory, this is because of the inherent difficulties of managing human labour power 'through shifting patterns of coercion, accommodation and compliance, into forms of profitable production' (see Elger and Smith, 1994, p. 12). Second, there are institutional obstacles in the structuring of collective agreements and labour–management relations, not least as concerns the kinds of contentious issues such as sub-contracting, workplace flexibility and minimum levels of employment on which union co-operation needs to be secured in order to achieve these twin objectives. Third, since other firms are pursuing similar objectives, so the possible reconciliation of these principles is still not a guarantee of success in larger competitive markets. The tensions at the heart of this new model in the sphere of production management do not, however, eliminate its innovative character. On the contrary, they represent a tremendous productive potential that has profound ramifications in the spheres of work organization and employment relations.

Work Organization

Work organization can be analysed along three dimensions, namely the application of knowledge, the degree of task specialization (or polyvalence) and the form of supervision. These different facets of work organization are related, and the ways they are combined produce various patterns or configurations of labour utilization. But there are also natural tensions between them. In particular, efforts to enhance the skills and cognitive abilities of employees and, at the same time, to require more polyvalence on their part, often create problems. This has always been a key problem among groups of skilled craftsmen supporting manufacturing, and it is now a recurrent difficulty among technicians and professionals more generally.

Although the number of configurations has always been considerable, with hindsight we can identify a contrast between the Fordist era and the organizational models now emerging. As we saw earlier, work organization under Fordism was governed by the key principles of Taylorism: a sharp distinction between conception and execution; a high degree of task specialization; and systematic and direct supervision to ensure co-ordination and discipline. This was very much the model Henry Ford also had in mind when he introduced the moving assembly line.[2]

While these principles of Taylorism remain influential, two major developments in production systems have occurred in recent decades that have undermined the Taylorist model. The first is the development of the more flexible production systems discussed above. The second is the more intensive application of information technology in most production systems. Innovations related to computer-based technology and their diffusion throughout the economy are reducing the importance of manual work and making output and quality more dependent upon the application of skills and knowledge at the point of production (Zuboff, 1988; Castells, 1996; Bell, 1999). Moreover, contrary to what is suggested in many popular accounts, this development is not limited to 'high-tech' sectors such as telecommunications equipment, but is pervading much of manufacturing, either as a support to production or as a driving force.

These changes have two major implications for work organization: first, as regards the nature of work; second, on the assessment of labour productivity. The development of production activities based on knowledge, cognition and abstract labour renders individual worker output more intangible. Emphasis on the discretionary nature of effort, deriving from the original distinction between labour power and actual labour, was a key intuition behind the critical labour process literature. This notion remains decisive. In spite of the drive for rationalization discussed above, production planning and productivity measures are often based on 'soft' foundations. Even in manufacturing, sophisticated calculations are often made on the basis of production norms that have more to do with shopfloor relations over time than with strictly technical considerations. In fact, unless work is routinized by a technical device such as a moving conveyor belt or assembly line, the conversion of labour power remains quite variable.

It follows that the traditional notion of labour productivity – or, more specifically, the way it should be measured – now needs to be reconsidered (Drucker, 1999; Veltz, 2000). In the Taylorist conception of manual work, the emphasis was on the intensity of effort and on the resulting volume of output per unit of time. Students of Taylor will recall that his system 'worked best' when output was dependent upon individual effort and could be measured on a short-term basis. Labour was seen as a more or less homogeneous resource and the standard unit of measure was time (Veltz, 2000). In many contemporary work situations, however, productivity now depends more on the application of skills and less on work pace. Productive activity often involves monitoring a flow of production or processes designed to provide customers with what is perceived as professional, high-quality service. Appraisal of performance is now as important an issue for management as the more traditional measurement of unit output.

Students of the automobile industry, a sector on which much of the research and analysis on patterns of work is still concentrated, may take exception to this line of analysis. But the point is that the technological configuration in operation for the core employees of this sector is exceptional, even within the manufacturing sector. On the basis of a major national survey covering all sectors of employment in Britain, Duncan Gallie and his colleagues stress 'how exceptional it is for individuals to be controlled by a machine-paced or assembly-line system. *Only 6 per cent of employees said a machine or assembly line was important for their work effort, and only 4 per cent for their work quality*' (Gallie *et al.*, 1998, p. 65; emphasis in original). Similarly, in their analysis of the growing service sector in the USA, Herzenberg *et al.* estimate that only 4 per cent of jobs fall into the category of what they describe as tightly constrained work systems, i.e. where operations 'are broken down into simplified tasks performed by workers who are closely monitored, often today by computers as well as supervisors' (Herzenberg *et al.*, 1998, p. 47). The point is that the more work is based on knowledge, the more the objective of 'measuring output' becomes elusive and, often, inappropriate.

This growing importance of the mobilization of tacit knowledge and worker discretion underlies much of the burgeoning literature on knowledge creation and diffusion, and on the 'learning organization'. As Cutcher-Gershenfeld *et al.* note: 'the knowledge-creation process must be understood as the engine driving modern organizations' (Cutcher-Gershenfeld *et al.*, 1998, p. 158). Although empirical research indicates that actual practice is more demanding and uneven than the prescriptive literature suggests, workplace practices such as teamwork or 'off-line' activities within problem-solving groups or quality circles represent a range of ways of going beyond the limitations of the Taylorist approach. This trend also accounts for the greater importance of various kinds of 'soft' training associated with new forms of work organization (Whitfield, 2000). Indeed, it is this link between knowledge and specialization that leads us to identify a second dimension of work organization in the new production model, namely the degree of task specialization.

Cutcher-Gershenfeld and his colleagues see teamwork as a way to reconsider the link between knowledge and specialization in new production systems: 'virtual knowledge[,] . . . created as individually held tacit knowledge[,] is shared among a group of people who will develop it into explicit knowledge as they work toward solving a problem' (Cutcher-Gershenfeld *et al.*, 1998, p. 4). In other words, the set of interactions fostered within teams or problem-solving groups helps disseminate tacit skills and knowledge from individuals to groups of workers and then between groups of workers. This practice of sharing skills across traditional demarcations defined in job classifications, and also across the occupational specializations acquired as a result of a long (and individual) investment in formal qualification and human capital, is thus a fundamental feature of the emerging model. This is true not only of team-based work systems and the many other forms of direct participation at the point of production, but also of the various forms of management by project and networking through which organizations are now seeking to improve their efficiently. Even professional employees, who once felt that their formal qualifications meant they were free of interference within their field of expertise, now feel much greater pressure on their so-called professional autonomy. The emphasis is now on cross-functional and multidisciplinary teams and horizontal co-ordination; and this represents a distinct movement away from the narrow specialization and direct supervision that characterized the previous model of production.

This growing importance of team or group work highlights the third dimension of work organization in the new model: the form of supervision. Some degree of self-regulation is reported in many workplaces, but the possibility of reducing direct supervision appears to depend to a considerable extent on the system of production. In the automobile industry, for example, where the rigour of the assembly line remains a major constraint, it seems more difficult to move away from direct control. Such assembly-line production, be it modular or otherwise, is much more conducive to the maintenance of prevailing forms of Taylorism in work organization (see, for example, Wells, 1996; Rinehart *et al.*, 1997). This is also the case in other kinds of routine assembly work, such as electronic equipment manufacturing, where performance depends directly on the volume and quality of output of each individual on a daily basis. In such contexts, some research suggests that teamwork may lead to 'peer pressure' and excessive forms of social control (Barker, 1993; Sewell, 1998). In contrast, under continuous process technology (e.g. in aluminium, steel and other metal smelters, as well as in oil refineries), production workers have to monitor technical systems. They have large areas to monitor, and performance does not depend directly on individual effort on a day-to-day basis. Rather it requires good co-ordination within and between teams, as well as with other employees (e.g. maintenance craftsmen, engineers and technicians) whose task is to assist production. Such a system of production creates favourable conditions for self-regulation and limited direct supervision. In such cases, the movement away from Taylorism is often well under way, on each of the three facets of work organization analysed here.

Similarly, in the service sector, Herzenberg *et al.* (1998, pp. 76–7) identify a rapid growth in high-skill autonomous work systems as opposed to a declining number of jobs in tightly constrained work systems. As they argue, most work is resistant to the spread of Taylorist work practices and employers are likely to rely on some combination of other forms of work organization to achieve objectives of increased cost efficiency and greater flexibility.

To summarize, the operative principles of work organization in the emerging model of production represent a clear move away from the previous model. While the diffusion of the new model will no doubt vary from one industry to the next, both the pursuit of productive flexibility by firms and the characteristics of the new technologies used in production are leading to a greater emphasis on the mobilization of tacit knowledge and worker discretion in the control of the production process and the achievement of production objectives. Similarly, the new model places much more emphasis on polyvalence than did the previous model, which accounts for the emergence of so many forms of job rotation, cross-training and teamwork. Finally, both greater mobilization of knowledge and task discretion imply less emphasis on direct supervision in favour of greater worker autonomy in the achievement of individual jobs, albeit generally not in favour of greater employee influence on overall organizational objectives.[3] These characteristics do not eliminate the problems inherent in the conversion of labour power into actual labour in the production process. This challenge remains unchanged. Rather, these characteristics are intimately related to the greater flexibility sought in the organization of production and the need to elicit and, where possible, harmonize worker inputs in the standardization of processes as opposed to products.

However, the achievement of these objectives is daunting. First, the encroachment of traditional demarcation lines and professional 'territories' is bound to create some resistance, especially among more highly skilled employees. Not only does it represent a drastic change from the traditional conception of the technical division of labour, but the objectives of increasing formal qualifications and cognitive abilities on the one hand, and increasing polyvalence on the other hand, will always be fraught with difficulties.

Second, the move to new forms of work organization can be especially problematical in a context of organizational downsizing and it is precisely such a context that has characterized so many workplaces engaged in work restructuring. Whereas 'multi-skilling' might well be beneficial to employees, 'multi-tasking' can often simply entail working more, i.e. 'doing the jobs of others as well as your own'. It is an open question whether this type of change is experienced as an improvement or a deterioration of working conditions by individual employees, hence the possibility of employee disenchantment with new forms of work organization characterizing the emerging model of production.

Third, although process standardization can conceivably mitigate the need for direct supervision, it is more difficult to give full scope to workers' tacit skills while pursuing hyper-efficiency in the standardization of processes. Not to put too fine a point on it, there is a significant tension between relative autonomy and discretion in the application of skills and knowledge and the relentless pursuit of standardization, notably through the incorporation of these skills and knowledge into processes. In an ideal world, perhaps this is eminently achievable. In the real world of production, traversed as it is by power relations and the formal capacity of supervisors to dictate behaviour, it is much more difficult.

Fourth, these desired changes in work organization can significantly alter the terrain of union–management relations in the workplace. Insistence on tight job definitions and clear demarcations between different trades and job categories has been at the heart of traditional union strategies to protect employment and safeguard workers from undue demands in the work process in the Fordist model. Moreover, the language of collective agreements was often predicated on certain assumptions about the nature of managerial supervision. All of these changes raise a thorny dilemma for local and national union organizations seeking to articulate their strategies within this new production model (see, for example, Kumar, 1995; Ackers *et al.*, 1996; Nissen, 1997). In particular, the challenge for unions appears to be how to give greater scope to some of the positive aspects of the new model, which workers themselves naturally espouse (expression of tacit skills, teamwork and decreased supervision), while protecting against the typical problems experienced by workers and their unions through institutional safeguards to ensure employment security, relieve stress and, more generally, to ensure that the new model delivers on its promises.

These problems do not obviate the need to pursue these three managerial objectives in the organization of work – the prizes to be gained are too great – but they do mean that many of the solutions to these problems in the realm of production management and work organization are seen to rely on achieving employee consent and commitment in the sphere of employment relations.

Employment Relations

The changes outlined above in production management and the organization of work have important implications for conditions of employment and their modes of regulation. Changes in the sphere of employment relations, in terms of both industrial relations and human resource management practices, reflect the imperatives of this emerging model of production in the other two spheres. The new production model has both material and social objectives as regards employment relations: relax existing rules to maximize flexibility in the terms and conditions of employment (and the range of tasks to be performed) but promote social adhesion to ensure forms of commitment consistent with the greater autonomy being devolved to workers in different production systems. Social adhesion here refers to employees' belief in, identification with, or commitment to, the possibilities and potential of the new ways of organizing production and their consequences for firm performance. Once again, it is not always apparent that these twin objectives – increased individual insecurity and social adhesion – are compatible, hence the variety of configurations and the overwhelming complexity in their implantation. Moreover, they might be pursued in the absence or the presence of a union, with a greater or a lesser focus on the collectivity as opposed to the individual.

The principle of increased individual risk in employment relations is a seemingly necessary corollary to the achievement of greater flexibility in the organization of production and in work organization. The need for flexibility and speed of adjustment in the organization of production requires much greater flexibility in the operation and regulation of internal labour markets, and this has consequences for the individuals within those labour markets. It is thus that a first wave of scholars used the concept of flexibility to examine the different ways in which the rules of the old production model were being refashioned in response to the environmental changes of the late 1970s and 1980s (see, for example, Atkinson, 1985; Boyer, 1988; Osterman, 1988). A basic feature of employment relations in the emergent model is the importance of such a high degree of flexibility that the frontiers between internal and external labour markets become blurred, as does the distinction between employment contracts for the provision of labour and commercial contracts for the provision of services (Supiot, 2000).

Employment flexibility can be achieved in a variety of ways, both individual and collective. For individuals, there is an increasing tendency to diversify contract status in terms of working time, in terms of degree of permanency, and often even in terms of who employs whom. A telling example is the growth of temporary employment (see Rogers, 2000). Similarly, whereas some highly skilled jobs in the manufacturing sector used to be performed by regular employees, such work is increasingly being transformed into maintenance contracts stemming from guarantees associated with the purchase of equipment. Most of these contractual changes, in individual terms at least, reduce employment security for workers. There is also a trend towards more variable forms of compensation, particularly where pay increases are tied to performance or skills acquisition. Flexibility can also mean, of course, attempts to weaken other mechanisms for regulating the mobility of labour: in the North American context, the key target has been seniority; but in other contexts it can also affect similarly cherished principles, such as life-time employment in Japan.

In a unionized setting, most such changes are, of course, subject to joint regulation and so they have been at the heart of much collective bargaining over the past decade. There has been an almost universal move to decentralize the level of collective bargaining so as to tie its outcome more closely to the results of particular business units (Katz, 1993). This objective has assumed a variety of organizational forms depending on the particular institutional context. In the United States and Canada, there has been a move to secure increased flexibility by extending the length of collective agreements. This is designed to provide an envelope of security within which it is possible to negotiate a multitude of new, more flexible arrangements. In the UK, employers first sought to reduce the constraints of multi-unionism within the workplace by securing single-union agreements focused on partnership. With the election of a Labour government, there evolved a full-blown discourse to promote workplace partnerships (TUC, 1999; Brown, 2000). In industrial relations systems with more centralized traditions, such as Australia and France, the advent of workplace agreements is meant to remove the perceived constraints of national collective agreements or awards. In most countries, union movements have experienced often divisive internal debates over the degree to which they should be engaged in negotiating increased employment insecurity and productive flexibility.

The second core principle of the new model is the pursuit of social adhesion or commitment to the new production systems and to organizational goals. The goal of social adhesion involves efforts to fashion employment conditions, and the modes of regulation of those conditions, in such a way as to elicit the tacit skills of workers and to tie them more closely to the goals of their firms. What marks a change from the traditional Fordist configuration is the apparent centrality of social adhesion in fashioning the employment relationship. This social dimension is arguably one of the most striking characteristics of the emerging models of employee relations. The recourse to self-regulation as a core principle of work organization, the effort to unleash tacit skills, the importance of ever greater flexibility and efficiency entail, at least in principle, a significant internalization of managerial norms about production objectives. Laurie Graham, for example, highlights the distinct and important character of social adhesion in the case of the Japanese transplants in North America: 'the Japanese model is clearly post-Fordist in its approach to control over the workforce because it incorporates social elements as well as traditional Fordist methods of control' (Graham, 1995, p. 3). Similarly, Tixier (1992, pp. 113–36) highlights what he labels the post-rational character of modern management strategies and the importance of the mobilization of 'subjectivities', by both management and union, within this new productive universe. Indeed, some of the more expansive proponents in the post-modernist organizational literature tend to depict this trend as a veritable social transformation of the firm: organizations are henceforth to be constructed on employee reflexivity, on the creativity of the persons that inhabit them. It is but a small step then for the organizations 'themselves' to become reflexive – so-called 'learning organizations'.

It is important here to be wary of some of the more overblown rhetoric about the objective of social adhesion. Firms' attempts to heighten employee identification with organizational objectives is certainly not to be confused with a veritable fusion of interests into a single unitarist paradigm, even though the emphasis on social adhesion has given new life to a previous generation of managerial philosophies seeking to tie employees more closely to the objectives of firm performance (on this trend in the managerial literature, see Giles and Murray, 1996). Indeed, there is a growing body of research that suggests that worker commitment is neither easily, nor unproblematically, engineered. In a context of threats to job security and declining high-wage employment opportunities for blue-collar workers, there is considerable evidence of worker submission as opposed to worker adhesion (Wells, 1996, pp. 192–3). But there has also been much discussion of the possibilities for employees to internalize managerial norms (see, for example, Scott, 1994). In a context of expanding employment opportunities and greater career mobility, particularly in the United States, there is also an emerging literature on the problems of engendering loyalty in a 'market-driven workforce', which is now accustomed to the lack of employment security (Cappelli, 1999) and is probably more circumspect about any enduring attachment to the objectives of particular firms. Certainly some of the key insights that emerge from the various empirical studies of workers in the context of new production models is, first, their openness to changes in the way that work is organized but, second, and contrary to its promises, the new model is often associated with a reduced sense of employment security and a continuing lack of influence over organizational goals. Therein lies the conundrum of engineering an enduring individual commitment to the new model. However, the multiple efforts to develop human resource management practices designed to enhance individual identification with organizational objectives and forms of remuneration that tie individual workers and groups of workers to the achievement of these objectives bear witness to the imperative of pursuing enhanced social adhesion on the part of individual employees.

As opposed to managerial strategies seeking to mobilize individual adhesion to organizational goals, another method, and one that might well enjoy greater worker legitimacy, is through the joint negotiation of new sets of rules, most frequently with a representative body such as a union. Indeed, as we saw above, this was a key aspect of Fordist employment relations that gave some degree of continuity, if not stability, to that production regime. Once again, the potential for joint governance in the new production model has given rise to considerable hyperbole, but it is also clear that various forms of joint regulation can be used to secure greater employee co-operation in the introduction of new forms of work organization. If perceptions of relative equity are grounded in due process and the observance of negotiated rules, then the re-negotiation of rules might well lead to new forms of social adhesion, albeit forms that are more equivocal than the apologists of employee adhesion would have us believe. This is the essence of the somewhat hopeful theoretical proposal advanced by a number of US authors for the renewal of pluralist labour relations through a 'mutual gains' approach to corporate modernization (see, in particular, Kochan and Osterman, 1994; but also Kochan, 2000). For others, this trend brings some representative arrangements dangerously close to the kind of enterprise unionism, which many see as characteristic of the organization of employee relations in Japanese firms. Moreover, some US observers are also beginning to moot the idea of intermediary, non-union forms of representation on issues of more limited scope as a method of securing greater employee voice and involvement (see Ichniowski *et al.*, 1996, p. 329).

To summarize, the central focus of employment relations in the emerging model of production is twofold. First, there is a transfer of risk and the costs of flexibility to the workforce. This can be achieved in a variety of ways, ranging from new contractual arrangements, which entail an erosion of the core labour force, to a rewriting of formal and informal workplace rules to ensure that firms enjoy greater flexibility in the use of their labour force, to variable forms of pay where employees are rewarded on the basis of output or even firm performance. In essence, workers rather than firms are asked to assume the risk and uncertainty of product markets and the realization of their labour in those product markets through the sale of the goods and services of the firms for which they work. Second, firms are seeking increased employee commitment, which is seen as a necessary pre-condition for the realization of the gains to be achieved in the new production systems, and these gains depend on employees' use of their knowledge and skills in the resolution of problems.

The dilemma of how to promote employee adhesion in a context of uncertainty and increased insecurity is undoubtedly one of the most complex and fundamentally intractable problems for the emerging model of production, several aspects of which need to be pointed out.

In the first place, social adhesion must be secured in the context of an employment relationship that remains fundamentally unequal. This is not to suggest that social adhesion is impossible in such a context; some degree of adhesion certainly is possible inasmuch as employees find both intrinsic and extrinsic rewards in that relationship, not to mention a degree of security in a volatile and uncertain labour market. However, the emergent model of production is still grounded in the structural constraints of that relationship, and social adhesion is neither automatically nor easily secured in the context of a relationship structured on quite asymmetrical sources of power.

Second, the need to reconcile social adhesion and increased risk is likely to run up against the scarcity of certain types of skills and knowledge. In a labour market that is increasingly likely to be favourable to more specialized employees, firms have to contend with increased worker mobility, which is difficult to reconcile with increased social adhesion. In other words, faced with the problem of retaining scarce employees and assuring the continuity of production, firms might have to forego contractual arrangements intended to maximize their degree of flexibility and the transfer of risk to individual employees through new forms of employment arrangements. Firms would then have to assume the infrastructural costs associated with carrying these scarce employees even in times of reduced demand and/or despite precepts about the new flexible workforce.

Third, in this changing labour market context, the search for greater social adhesion is likely to encounter several other obstacles. Increased employee bargaining power is likely to demonstrate that employee commitment is not so easily engineered. Moreover, the hyperbole too often associated with the discourse about the emergence of the high involvement work systems means that the promise of participation often runs up against the realities and constraints of workplace relations, not least in terms of the lack of employee influence over often rapidly changing organizational objectives that have more to do with the complexities of corporate financing than with the performance of particular establishments or work units. Faced with the stark realities of the need to get the product to market and the command structure that underlies the basic contract of employment, there is a strong potential for disappointed expectations as regards the scope for employee input in the production process. Freeman and Rogers (1999, p. 47), for example, identify a high degree of correlation between what they term the 'discontented third' in American workplaces (i.e. the roughly one-third of employees who wish they did not have to go to work or who feel indifferent about their work), and the high degree of employee dissatisfaction with their influence over workplace decisions.

Fourth, the movement from older sets of rules underlying the Fordist model, which enjoyed considerable legitimacy, to new sets of rules is frequently problematical. The overall configuration of the latter is still unclear and they have often emerged in the context of either extreme contingency or the threat of sanction. Minimally, this movement involves considerable experimentation, a period of experimentation that is currently under way and one in which the way forward is not entirely apparent. This is certainly the focus of much experiential and intellectual effort. The new literature on trust, stakeholding, partnership and loyalty is a renewal of many of the older themes of the social sciences in ages of uncertainty when there were many interrogations about the possibilities for social cohesion in industrial societies (see, for example, Bendix, 1956; Dahrendorf, 1959). And the frustration about the absence of shared gains in return for greater flexibility, workload and insecurity is one of the paramount themes emerging from the disappointed expectations literature on the experience of change in the new workplace (see, in particular, Osterman, 2000).

Fifth, the continuing erosion of the homogeneity or universality of the employment conditions that characterized the Fordist model has in many ways undermined the social role of the union in the new model of production. In particular, the multiplication of employment status within the firm, the fragmentation of units of employment along more complex and differentiated chains of production, the greater emphasis on individual initiatives, achievements and rewards are but some of the factors that make it more difficult for a union to achieve the kind of unity of purpose and, indeed, collective consciousness that was often associated with the previous model.

Finally, particular workplace and company arrangements are also grounded in a broader set of societal and institutional arrangements, including those resulting from public policy. For example, do public policies facilitate or hinder the adaptation of collective representation on the part of employees to new forms of corporate organization? Do public policies foster increased individual mobility through training, portable pensions and the like to take account of heightened levels of employee insecurity and more discontinuous periods of employment? As we shall see below, it is still far from evident what kind of institutional arrangements might consolidate new forms of workplace regulation and, in particular, facilitate this rather complex arbitrage between the objective of rapid, micro-level adjustments and the broader problems of endemic insecurity in the labour market. We shall return to this theme in the final part of the chapter, but suffice it to say that there is currently considerable evidence of a gap between the blending of the key precepts of the emerging model of production and the evolution of public policy.

Summary

We have argued that the new production model is characterized by a set of interrelated principles (see Table 1.1) that differ in significant ways from the previous Fordist model: productive flexibility and process standardization at the level of the management of production; the application of knowledge, polyvalence and less direct supervision in the sphere of work organization; and flexibility (or insecurity) and social adhesion as regards employment relations. These are the principles that cut across the variegated terrain of the contemporary workplace.

However, as should be apparent from the discussion above, not only are these core principles rather difficult to achieve, they are often in contradiction. Indeed, they can be combined in quite different permutations – greater productive flexibility at the cost of efficiency, greater polyvalence to the detriment of knowledge, less social adhesion in favour of greater insecurity, and so on. Yet, however difficult to reconcile, these principles are

Table 1.1 *Operative principles of the new production model*

	Fordism	New Model
Production management		
Source of competitive advantage	Economies of scale through continuous production; internalization of costs related to a constant flow of supplies	Productive flexibility in the pursuit of niche markets; externalization of costs related to supplies where possible
Source of efficiency	Standardization of product	Standardization of processes in order to achieve high levels of product quality but rapid adjustments in the type of production
Work organization		
Application of knowledge	Lesser mobilization of worker knowledge in favour of separation of conception and execution	Higher mobilization of worker knowledge in order to resolve problems in the production process and to achieve productive flexibility
Degree of specialization	Greater specialization and extensive division of labour	Increased polyvalence in order to overcome jurisdictional and functional problems in the separation of tasks
Degree of supervision	High degree of direct supervision	More self-regulation or process-driven regulation
Employment relations		
Degree of security offered	Higher: less flexibility for employers	Lower: more flexibility for employers
Social adhesion required	Lower: technical division of labour reduces the need for social commitment	Higher: integral to the achievement of production objectives

at the heart of most efforts to transcend Fordist production arrangements, whether in the goods sector, in private services or, increasingly, in public services. The result is a production model of immense potential in terms of the transformation of existing processes of work and employment, but one that is still highly variable and often unstable.

JACQUES BÉLANGER, ANTHONY GILES AND GREGOR MURRAY

Prospects for the Consolidation of the New Model

Although it is possible to discern the rough outlines of a new model of production, it is also clear that this model is experiencing quite a few growing pains. Indeed, the literature on workplace change is characterized by a striking amount of handwringing and despair about the inchoate, variegated and halting nature of change. In stark contrast to the vast normative literature extolling the virtues of the high commitment/high performance workplace, survey and case-study evidence from many countries suggests that the putative new model is an elusive and temperamental creature. In this final part of the chapter, we seek to interpret this considerable body of evidence in order to assess the prospects for the consolidation of the new model. We begin with a brief overview of the key problems identified in the research literature, focusing on weaknesses in the diffusion of the new model, problems rooted in the process of change, and the pronounced variability of the new model. We then argue that, although a number of these differences are to be expected, there are more fundamental problems at work: first, those that derive from the tensions and contradictions that we have previously identified; second, those that arise from one of the fundamental lacuna in the new model – its lack of accommodation at the societal level and the resulting lack of institutions that might mediate these tensions.

Diffusion, Change and Variability

There is now fairly widespread agreement that the sum of changes taking place in the workplace amounts to more than a rejigging of traditional forms of the organization of production. However, it is worth considering the rate of diffusion of these changes, the nature of the change process, and the apparent variability of the forms of change.

Rate of Diffusion

Although there is considerable evidence of workplace innovations, research suggests that the rate of diffusion is uneven and not particularly systematic.

Although caution must be exercised in comparing national surveys using different methodologies and different definitions, and where similar terminology does not necessarily cover the same sets of practices, there is mounting evidence that the various innovations identified with the new production model are being implemented in workplaces in a variety of countries and that these practices are, by and large, on the increase. In the United States, Osterman (2000, p. 182) points to survey evidence that by the early 1990s 'a significant minority of establishments' had implemented a range of practices associated with high performance work organization. He notes that 24.6 per cent of establishments in his 1992 survey had implemented at least two of these practices (i.e. quality circles, job rotation, teams and TQM) for at least 50 per cent of their core non-supervisory employees. Using the same definition, this degree of diffusion rose to 38.3 per cent of establishments in a similar 1997 survey. Drawing on a much larger 1993 US Bureau of Labor Statistics training survey, Gittleman *et al.* (1998) found that although only a minority (42 per cent) of establishments engaged in any so-called innovative work organization practices, this figure rose to nearly 70 per cent among establishments with 50 or more employees.[4] Although Edwards, Geary and Sisson (see Chapter 2) are circumspect about fulsome portrayals of the diffusion in Europe of one of the key dimensions of the high performance work system, self-managing teams, they do point to an apparent growth of a number of variants of this type of innovation. Canadian survey evidence reviewed by Kumar (2000) similarly points to an increase in many of the practices associated with the new model (also see Statistics Canada, 1998). And the comprehensive 1995 Australian Workplace Survey indicates that a substantial proportion of employees in Australia work in workplaces with practices such as TQM, quality circles, autonomous work groups, team-building and the use of task forces and *ad hoc* committees (Morehead *et al.*, 1997, p. 507). Comparing the 1990 and 1995 Australia Workplace Surveys, Harley (1999) notes little increase in the incidence of quality circles but substantial increases in the use of task forces or *ad hoc* committees and joint consultative committees. This international survey evidence, then, suggests that at least some of the kinds of changes associated with the new model of production are taking place and that their incidence does appear to be increasing.

Second, the diffusion of these new practices appears to be fairly uneven, with changes being concentrated in particular firms and sectors. North American research suggests, for example, that the incidence of new forms of work is concentrated in larger firms, in the manufacturing sector, and in firms and sectors exposed to international competition (Smith, 1993; Betcherman *et al.*, 1994; Osterman, 1994; Kumar, 1995; Meltz and Verma, 1995; Murray *et al.*, 1999). Moreover, as reported by Storey and Harrison (1999) in their case study of work reorganization in a British manufacturing firm, the adoption of these practices can also vary markedly within individual firms and even in the same workplaces.

Finally, while recent studies in the United States and Canada clearly indicate that many, and perhaps most, firms have adopted at least some of the elements of the new production model, change frequently falls well short of a wholesale transformation of production, work organization and employment relations practices. For example, drawing on a survey of American workers and their workplaces, Freeman and Rogers (1999, p. 95) note that the distribution of practices follows a fairly normal bell-shaped curve with only a very small proportion of firms having many practices. Similarly, reviewing US research, Godard and Delaney stress that 'while a majority of employers have experimented with innovations, only a small percentage have adopted a full system of these practices' (Godard and Delaney, 2000, p. 484). On the basis of their 1993 training survey, Gittleman *et al.* (1998, p. 106) were unable to find any distinct patterns in the adoption of innovative practices: the clusters of practices that they could identify 'tended to be quite heterogeneous and thus difficult to characterize'. Osterman (1994) was also unable to identify distinct clusters of change. In analysing the same data set, Wood (1999) arrives at much the same conclusion. In other words, the changes tend not to be systematic.

This latter finding represents an especially intriguing paradox given that it is often argued that the positive impact of such practices on organizational performance depends on the adoption of whole 'systems' or 'bundles' of mutually reinforcing practices. Certainly the consensus in the literature on the new forms of work organization is that a partial adoption of these principles is insufficient to achieve the promised organizational outcomes. Ichniowski *et al.*, for example, conclude that innovative human resource management practices 'can improve business productivity, primarily through the use of systems of related work practices designed to enhance worker participation and flexibility in the design of work and decentralization of managerial tasks and responsibilities' (Ichniowski *et al.*, 1996, p. 322). They emphasize, however, that particular work practices alone, such as work teams or quality circles, 'are not enough. Rather, whole systems need to be changed' (*ibid.*, p. 322). Appelbaum *et al.*'s analysis of the steel industry in the USA suggests that 'bundles of high-performance work practices increase uptime substantially compared with a traditional work system, with implementation of an HPWS [high performance work system] having the largest effect of all' (Appelbaum *et al.*, 2000, p. 142). For them, the conclusion is compelling since such systems set in motion 'positive productivity dynamics' entailing more participatory work systems supported by a range of human resource and organizational practices, which translate into enhanced levels of trust and commitment, increased levels of discretionary effort and skill investment on the part of employees and more rapid productivity growth (*ibid.*, pp. 234–5). In other words, there is a high degree of interdependence between the different facets of the new model and, when implemented, this new model delivers overwhelmingly positive results.

Faced with such unequivocal conclusions, the mystery in many ways deepens as regards the diffusion and implementation of the new model. There can be little doubt that widespread changes are taking place. However, its diffusion appears to be slow and uneven, often consisting of small steps rather than wholesale change. For example, Wood (1999) highlights the need for due diligence in the more exaggerated portrayals of the emergence of coherent sets of interrelated practices in workplace change. Drawing on a separate analysis of Osterman's US data, he stresses the apparent non-linear, experimental and unco-ordinated nature of workplace change. However, he does suggest, as we have also argued throughout this chapter, that new personnel and HRM (human resource management) practices are more likely to be driven by innovations in the organization of production. Change in the realm of production management thus appears to engender related changes at the level of work organization and so too for changes in the organization of production and work organization for the sphere of employment relations. Thus, change cuts through multiple levels of productive organizations. As has been argued throughout this chapter, change in one of the spheres of production clearly has ramifications in the other spheres. Yet these changes do not appear to cohere into clear patterns of change, or into neat prescriptions as to what should emerge; hence the interest in looking more closely at the process of change and the variability of the configurations observed.

Process of Diffusion
Much of the literature on the new workplace also points to a range of difficulties experienced by firms seeking to adopt the new model or elements of it, which suggests that the problems run deeper than the pace of change. In this respect, it is interesting to note that stories of failed experiments, setbacks, and full or partial retreats from change are common. For example, Osterman (2000) reports that slightly less than half of the establishments that had implemented teamwork for 50 per cent of their core employees in 1992 continued this practice at the same level of coverage in 1997. However, the degree of continuity for quality circles (85.8 per cent) and TQM (76.0 per cent) was much higher than for job rotation (60.2 per cent) and teamwork (48.4 per cent). In addition, case-study evidence reveals that the implementation of the new model has generated conflict and resistance, from workers

as well as middle-managers, sometimes leading to the abandonment of some elements and the modification of others. Although this dynamic does not show up well in the survey research, especially cross-sectional surveys, it does emerge as a consistent theme in the case-study literature and is also highlighted in the second chapter of this book by Edwards, Geary and Sisson. There is considerable evidence that new work practices are often introduced in a context of constraint and downsizing, that they lead to an intensification of work, and that the results vary considerably both in terms of the types of changes and other contingencies (Geary, 1995).

These results make it particularly difficult for the strategic positioning of local and national unions. Simple opposition to these workplace changes is a risky option, particularly in a context where members wish to safeguard their jobs and when some of these changes in the realm of work organization represent an improvement over the Fordist model. Yet simple acceptance of many of the features of the new model risk allying the union with some of the negative consequences of these changes. These dilemmas are well documented in the literature and accentuate what has already been identified as the volatility of the new model.

Variability

The two previous points help account for another finding in the literature – the high variability of the new model. Indeed, the plethora of descriptions of change – running from lean production to the high performance workplace – is indicative of more than analytical confusion. As was argued in the second part of this chapter, it suggests a high degree of variability in the implementation of the core principles of the new model. Instead of a single recipe, change is messy, experimental and uncertain.

The overwhelming temptation is to fix on just a few aspects of these production arrangements. Two caricatures come readily to mind. So-called 'high performance' or 'high commitment' work organizations emphasize a high-skills/high-wages/high-commitment approach, commonly allied with union participation and aimed at achieving competitiveness through quality, the ability to respond quickly to changes in market demand, and customer service. In contrast, 'lean and mean' organizations search for competitiveness through lower labour costs, enhanced numerical flexibility, and an aggressive move away from the traditional security of the employment relationship. These approaches merit closer scrutiny, not just because there is empirical support for each, but because they can even represent different faces of the same production model.

The so-called 'high performance' workplace literature is said to rest on productive flexibility in the realm of the organization of production, increased worker autonomy in the area of work organization, and increased social adhesion or organizational commitment in the area of employment relations. While it is difficult to find hard evidence of this apparent 'fairy tale' model, the search continues unabated. Moreover, many elements of this model can be found within a wide variety of workplaces. Managers clearly feel obliged to experiment with at least some elements of what is purported to be the future. Indeed, there is a burgeoning literature inciting human resource managers to assemble the requisite bundles of practices that will support such a virtuous circle of innovation: advanced training practices, sophisticated communication strategies, variable but collective forms of remuneration, and so on. More substantially, there is also much evidence of positive worker response to some of the key elements of this model, notably greater worker autonomy (see, in particular, the chapter by Appelbaum in this book). The key problem in the pursuit of this kind of model is the apparent abolition of the contradictory tendencies within the model itself, namely the simultaneous need for increased standardization of processes, the overwhelming pressures towards work intensification, and, hitherto at least, the attendant negative effects on employment security.

In opposition to the high performance model is 'lean production', typically characterized by accentuated standardization of processes, a greater intensity in the way that worker knowledge is utilized, and increased insecurity. While there is no doubt considerable evidence that these principles can easily coalesce into a seeming vicious circle of heightened productivity through multiple constraints, there is much less evidence that such a model is either sustainable or new. Many of the more innovative aspects of the new production arrangements are thus absent and, more likely than not, particularly in the absence of external labour market constraints, managers will be compelled to move away from many aspects of such a model because of the difficulty of sustaining it.

Problems and Obstacles

Given the differential, uneven and sometimes halting diffusion of the core principles of what we have identified as the new production model, is it not in the end a myth? We believe not. First, none of the evidence about the slow diffusion, variability and instability of the post-Fordist model of production is particularly surprising when seen in the light of both how Fordism actually developed and the level of analysis at which we believe a model of production makes any sense at all. Second, as we have argued throughout this chapter, the emergence of a number of distinct principles characterizing these new forms of production does not suspend the tensions and contradictions inherent in the production process. On the contrary, and this is the third prong of the argument, these lines of tension are likely to be even more manifest in the absence of some way of regularizing them and providing for their institutionalization. This is undoubtedly one of the most telling of the unresolved problems of the new production model. We shall briefly explore each of these propositions below.

On Production Models, Emergent and Consolidated

As was argued at the outset of this chapter, variety was always a feature of the Fordist era. It is far from surprising, then, that the current era is marked by a multiplicity of versions of the new production model. Indeed, it is only in comparison to the idealized and abstract version of the Fordist model that the hesitant and awkward birth of post-Fordism can be seen as problematical. The currently dominant national models are, to a certain extent, the products of the Fordist era. Locke and Thelen (1995), for example, have argued that the different patterns of change across countries are at least partly explicable in terms of such pre-existing differences: in countries such as the USA, Canada and the UK, the entrenched tradition of job control unionism and the strong hold of Taylorist work organization have made the transition to post-Fordist production a more radical and wrenching change than in countries such as Japan and Germany, where a tradition of greater workplace flexibility and communication developed within the broader parameters of the Fordist model.

Furthermore, even within individual countries there has always been significant variation between sectors and firms. While it may be plausible to argue that diversity is increasing, there does not seem to be any way of actually measuring this. But does all this suggest that post-Fordism is merely experiencing normal growing pains and that it is therefore only a matter of time before it is more fully and completely diffused, albeit in a range of different variants? In our view, not all of the problems of post-Fordism can be explained away on these grounds.

Tensions, Contradictions and Internal Coherence

Despite its promise, the new production model is characterized by considerable internal tensions and contradictions that constitute a perm-anent source of instability and give rise to a highly variable, indeed often volatile set of production arrangements. This is one of the basic features of many of the changes taking place and underscores why such a variety of patterns have been observed. The core principles of the new model can be combined into a wide variety of specific configurations of varying degrees of stability. It is precisely this variability that allows researchers to arrive at such different conclusions about the search for new methods of organizing production and the delivery of services. It would appear that the operative mode for much workplace change is typically one of organizational tinkering, of successive sediments of organizational innovation, which vary greatly from one workplace to another. Hence our analysis of an emergent model in terms of the sets of principles enumerated above points to the multiple and often contradictory faces of what is often called the 'high performance workplace'. The tensions are essentially threefold: between the core principles within each of the spheres of production, between the changes sought in the different spheres of production, and in terms of the internal consistency of the emerging model as a whole.

In the second part of the chapter, we set out the core principles within each of the three spheres of the new production model and identified the tensions between the objectives within each sphere. As regards the management of production, it was argued that productivity gains can be achieved by firms able to pursue both productive flexibility and process standardization. However, not only is the pursuit of these operative principles subject to the problems inherent in the management of the labour process, there would also appear to be logical limits to the simultaneous achievement of productive flexibility and process standardization. While it is certainly possible to imagine the co-existence of these two principles, it is equally plausible that in a context of market constraint and human contingencies associated with the labour process, that the emphasis on productive flexibility can run up against the core precepts of process standardization.

Similarly, in the sphere of work organization, the principles of knowledge, 'multi-skilling' and worker self-regulation mark a distinct movement away from prevailing Fordist principles of work organization. There is considerable evidence of synergies to be achieved between them. But, as we have previously emphasized, the combination of these principles must contend with the real problems of organizing co-operation and productivity in the labour process in what remains, in the end, a legally ensconced, hierarchical command structure. Moreover, while it is entirely possible to place greater emphasis on the use of worker knowledge and, thereby, to decrease direct supervision, the additional requirement of greater job flexibility or polyvalence can be the source of considerable tensions, not to mention stress. In this respect, it is scarcely surprising that one of the most frequently reported sources of resistance to these new forms of work organization comes from the most skilled workers, who by the very nature of the objectives pursued in the management of production must play a key role in achieving productive flexibility through rapid adjustments of machinery. Again, and this observation is also true of less skilled workers who must meet rigorous production and service delivery standards, there appears to be a logical limit in terms of the degree to which they can both upgrade their specialist knowledge and exercise a wider range of skills or tasks. This problem is further compounded in a context of downsizing. These elements are certainly a recipe for the often observed stress associated with the so-called high performance workplace. And, as was argued above, these problems manifested in work organization are further exacerbated by the possibility of disappointed expectations, in particular the gap between some greater manifestation of skill and self-regulation in the job and the continuing lack of influence as regards overall, and often changing, organizational objectives.

The key objectives pursued in the sphere of employment relations are undoubtedly the most difficult to achieve. We identified twin objectives: first, the transfer of risk and the costs of productive flexibility onto the workforce; second, increased employee commitment, which is seen as a pre-condition for the realization of the gains to be achieved in the new productive systems. The management of these often contradictory objectives is surely a 'high-wire' act. Quite apart from the inherent variability of social relations between workers and management from one workplace to another, not to mention from one firm, industry or country to another, it should hardly be surprising that it is in the sphere of employment relations that we are likely to observe the widest variability. This is because of the manifest tensions between these core principles. As has often been observed, employee commitment is notoriously difficult to engineer in the context of the structural constraints of the employment relationship. This is further compounded in a context where employers seek to transfer the risks and the cost of greater flexibility onto employees or other workers, irrespective of their legal status as employees or contractors. The contradiction between these objectives is a source of real instability, particularly in the absence of an accepted model of collective employment relations and a role for employee representation therein.

There is obviously a high degree of interdependence between the core principles pursued in each of the spheres of the new production model. The objectives of process standardization and flexibility in the sphere of production management require a different type of work organization, notably as regards the mobilization of knowledge, increased polyvalence and greater worker autonomy to resolve problems as and when they occur. Similarly, it is difficult to imagine that the changes in the sphere of work organization, such as the upgrading of skills specific to a workplace or work in teams, can take place without a sufficient degree of employee commitment to their jobs. And productive flexibility seems to entail a transfer of risk from firm to employee or worker contractor. The considerable potential of the new model lies precisely in the synergies to be realized in the pursuit of these different objectives.

Yet tensions are also to be observed between these core principles. First, in practice there is a tension between the relative autonomy and discretion in the application of skills and knowledge offered to workers, as espoused in the realm of work organization, and the relentless pursuit of process standardization in production management. Second, many of the solutions to the tensions observed both between the core principles within production management and work organization and between these two spheres are seen to lie in the sphere of employment relations. Several examples spring to mind. Firms that seek to mobilize the specialized skills and knowledge of workers, to encourage them to develop a wider range of skills and execute more tasks, and to exercise a greater degree of autonomy certainly will encounter difficulties in transferring the costs of productive flexibility onto their workforce. Similarly, not only is enduring commitment difficult to secure at the best of times, but it is all the more problematical in the face of increasing demands to implement standardization in the sphere of production management and the apparent increase in workload and stress associated with such changes in work organization in many firms. Third, whereas the workplace union came to play an important role in regularizing employment relations in the previous Fordist model, the role for a union, where it is even present, is not entirely apparent in the new production model. In particular, it appears more difficult, though certainly not impossible, to organize its social basis within the workplace. Moreover, given the ambiguities and tensions associated with the emergence of the new model, local and national unions are typically caught between a 'rock' and 'a hard place' in terms of whether they should be strategically allied with, in opposition to or somewhere in between as regards the implantation of the new production model in particular workplaces.

Such is the paradox of the emerging production model. It offers huge potential in terms of the gains to be made in the realm of production management and work organization; and many of the changes in work organization, notably the greater use of worker skills and increased autonomy, do offer the promise of a more interesting working life for many workers. Overall, however, the new model is characterized by so many internal tensions that its implementation is difficult, uneven and highly variable. This brings us to our third line of argument as regards the consolidation of the new model. The tensions observed, particularly as regards employment relations, require a degree of institutional innovation and support. It is to the absence of this institutional support that we now turn.

Institutional Embeddedness

As we have seen, Fordism was never a seamless, harmonious system. It is normal for conflicts and tensions to exist within a model and between it and other ways of organizing production. However, there was an extended period of relative stability under Fordism, due in large part to the institutions fashioned by trade unions, employers and the state in the workplace, the firm, the labour market and society. The tensions of Fordism were thus contained and muted through these micro- and macro-level political and social institutions founded on a broad compromise in the post-war era.

In the case of the newly emerging production model, it is apparent that such institutions have yet to be constructed. Indeed, the dominant neo-liberal discourse predominates, and its faith in open markets and deregulation particularly is a key obstacle to the consolidation of the new production model. While the new principles of production and work organization are – irrespective of their internal tensions – fairly well settled, employee relations remain highly unstable, particularly in the absence of a wider social compromise and the recasting of the relevant institutions that regulate employment relations in the workplace. This problem is attracting increasing attention in the research literature and might be divided into several streams of analysis: first, the general challenge of recasting the role of public policy; second, how to rethink and rebuild the institutions of collective representation; third, how to devise and support a new social contract at work; fourth, the search for a 'new deal' for the new labour market; and, fifth, how to transform power relations in the labour market and society.

In traditional policy terms, there is considerable angst about the shift to an appropriate set of public policies for the new economy. From the onset of stagflation in the 1970s, international institutions such as the Organization for Economic Co-operation and Development (OECD) played a key advocacy role in recasting state policies. In particular, the OECD (1989) promoted labour market deregulation, privatization, workplace flexibility and the like. Faced with continuing high levels of unemployment, particularly in Europe, the OECD also begin to promote training and social transfer policies designed to encourage labour market mobility. Individual states have, of course, sought to adapt these policy prescriptions to their own set of circumstances. Apart from traditional industrial and fiscal policies designed to promote new investments in equipment and material and reduce other types of social expenditure, many states steered clear of workplace innovation. Others, notably in Canada, have launched a variety of programmes designed to promote the diffusion of new workplace practices (see Chaykowski and Gunderson in this volume). There has also been some experimentation in Canada with a number of novel sectoral initiatives designed to encourage the diffusion of workplace innovation (see Gunderson and Sharpe, 1998). The UK Government is now also promoting workplace partnership programmes (TUC, 1999; Brown, 2000). Suffice it to say, however, that state policies designed to facilitate the transition and to achieve the stability of these new methods of organizing production remain fairly tentative, where and when they even exist.

A second area of concern is the future of collective representation. The dramatic decline in the level of unionization in the USA has naturally raised questions about the role of collective worker organizations in the changing organization of production. Thus a line of analysis prevalent in that country has focused on the renewal of labour law. It is argued that the original objectives of labour legislation have been derailed through a successive narrowing of the scope of application of collective labour legislation and the addition of ever more onerous legal hurdles standing in the way of workers' access to union representation. Access to collective representation must therefore be facilitated if collective actors, i.e. unions, are to play the role that they must play in the transition to the new production model (see, for example, Weiler, 1983). Similarly, in the UK, it has been argued that there is a need to address the so-called 'representation gap' by facilitating access to a framework of collective representation (Towers, 1997). While the jury is still out on the fairly modest recent reforms to the law of collective labour representation in the UK (see Brown, 2000), the basic direction of this reform is fairly similar to what had been advocated in the USA, namely small changes designed to facilitate access to collective representation. In the meantime, in the USA, attempts to facilitate access to collective union representation have encountered the twin obstacles of employer opposition and institutional stasis. This has led a number of authors to recommend a more radical rethinking of the assumptions underlying union representation. In particular, there is an increasing advocacy of a basic floor of participative rights for all employees, independent of union status, through a combined system of works council and statutory minima (e.g. Freeman and Rogers, 1993; Weiler, 1993). However, given the continuing forces of inertia in the US legislative process and opposition by the US labour movement, the prospects of such a reform are not bright. Other scholars have argued for a revamping of the existing labour law framework so that it might better take account of the tremendous changes in the economy and their effect on traditional assumptions about who is an employee and how employees can be represented in the firm and the labour market. Murray and Verge (1999), for example, argue that the existing Canadian legal framework of collective representation is out of step with the changing forms of employment and the locus of corporate decision-making, as well as with changing patterns of employee knowledge and skills.

A third line of argument may be labelled the 'stalled workplace innovation' literature. The evolution of this literature in the USA is of particular interest. Much of the voluntarism that characterized the early work of Kochan *et al.* (1986) as regards the innovative practices that actors might adopt in order to pursue new workplace practices, ran aground on the difficulty of implementing these practices in a non-adversarial way. In particular, there was much evidence of employer opposition and a dawning realization that employers most likely had to be coaxed into generalizing innovations through public policy initiatives (see Kochan *et al.*, 1991). Thus has emerged an increased emphasis on the obstacles to achieving a generalization of the model on the basis of changes in individual workplaces and a consequent shift towards a more substantive engagement with public policy as an integral part of the promotion of the high performance workplace. This, of course, paralleled the early optimism of the first term of the Clinton presidency when Robert Reich was Secretary of Labor, but it quickly hit a kind of institutional stasis in the face of the lack of legislative interest and/or will in securing significant changes. Even some exponents of the new model recognize this. In the USA, in particular, while the Massachusetts Institute of Technology (MIT) school continues to emphasize the importance of convincing individual employers of the merits of adopting a progressive version of workplace practice, they increasingly discuss the need for a new 'social contract' (e.g. Kochan and Osterman, 1994; Kochan, 2000). Although oftentimes vague and idealistic in its pluralist formulation, it is of no little significance that this now entails not just labour law reform, but the call for a wider reconstruction of institutions that would better match the needs of workplace actors (see also Chaykowski and Gunderson in this volume). The problem is that such a project, although it probably needs intellectual framing, is not likely to be accepted by employers or the state in the absence of sustained popular pressure. More recently, this analysis has tended to go further and this is some ways represents a qualitative shift in discourse. Osterman (2000), in particular, has continued to grapple with the problem of the limited diffusion of the high performance workplace model. He highlights what he sees as an institutional blockage at the heart of the new workplace practices, namely the fact that workers are not sharing the productivity gains reaped by employers. From this perspective, a more adequate sharing of gains would contribute to the internal institutional coherence of the new model at the workplace level. The problem remains, however, as to why there is such an unequal distribution of productivity gains.[5]

This leads directly to a fourth stream of analysis, which might be termed 'societal' or 'systemic dis-synchronization'. This thesis is at the heart of the chapter later in this volume by Paul R. Bélanger, Paul-André Lapointe and Benoît Lévesque. They argue that, despite the evidence of many so-called models of co-operative workplaces based on a social contract in the Canadian province of Quebec, and what they see as the presence of a number of factors that should facilitate a wider diffusion of new workplace practices (a high level of union density, new institutional mechanisms such as worker investment funds, a strong 'statist' tradition, a history of tripartite and multipartite consultation on labour and social policy issues and a union movement that espouses the virtues of the new co-operative workplace policies and practices), there remains a fundamental discontinuity between innovation at the level of the workplace and innovation more generally in society. In essence, workplace change is unlikely to be consolidated until there are more systematic changes at the societal level.

In his recent work, *Securing Prosperity*, Osterman (1999) also pursues this line of analysis. He too adopts the Gordian knot approach, i.e. that the full potential of the new production model cannot be realized until the disequilibrium of power is redressed, and that this paradox needs to be resolved before the new high performance workplace prevails. Osterman (1999, pp. 146–78) sets out two basic avenues to effect change in the balance of power: rethinking corporate governance in order to go beyond the narrow view of maximizing the wealth of shareholders; and building up counter-vailing power, notably in the community, in the workplace and through the expansion of employee representation. Such an approach has strong parallels with Piore's (1991 and 1995) earlier advocacy of the need to look for new kinds of institutions that better fit the emerging labour market. Herzenberg *et al.*'s (1998, pp. 149–73) call for 'a New Deal for a New Economy' offers one of the more imaginative visions of the broad range of changes in public policies and practices required for the new service economy. These include facilitating multiple establishment career paths, the promotion of multi-employer structures, of sectoral and occupation pay, and of regional training alliances, stimulating performance improvements in the service sector, and improving the access and the efficacy of collective representation for workers in the service sector.

The Australian Centre for Industrial Relations Research and Training (ACIRRT, 1999) provides a similar kind of analysis in its advocacy for a movement from the 'wage earner' to the 'working life' model. From this perspective, the twin exigencies of productive flexibility and the transfer of risk onto employees is likely to be a permanent feature of work. Thus, public policy should focus on picking up the slack to ensure that this kind of framework can work. This includes standard rights to entitlements regardless of the legal status of employment, increased portability of benefits, socially responsible recruitment, training and pooling arrangements, a better articulation of income support for periods in and out of work, long-service leave to promote retraining and a range of policy measures to support part-time work and transitional labour markets (ACIRRT, 1999, pp. 156–76).

These and other analyses leave many questions unanswered as to the appropriate institutions of collective labour relations and, indeed, their link with national and transnational forms of macro-economic regulation. However, they do represent a significant improvement in terms of the kinds of institutions that might respond to both the potential and the contra-dictions of the emerging model of production.

This brings us to the fifth and final line of analysis: how do we get from 'here' to 'there'? This approach seeks to locate institutional transformation in the context of broader relations of power. It is hardly novel to suggest that institutions reflect prevailing relations of power, just as the operation of these institutions reflects social forces (for an elaboration of this argument, see Murray et al., 2000; Murray, 2001). Several of the previous lines of argument have much to commend them, but they are unlikely to transpire in the absence of longer-term pressures leading to institutional transformation and renewal. It is extremely difficult, at this point at least, to predict exactly how these pressures might emerge, yet alone to envisage the new institutional forms to which they will give rise. What is clear, however, is the essential role of social forces and actors in bringing about such new stabilizing institutions. What are some of the possible sources of this renewal?

As we have argued at different points above, one source of pressure is likely to be tightening labour markets over the longer term. Another possible source of change could stem from the differential impact on employers of the potential of the new methods of organizing production. Faced with labour market pressures or with problems of internal coherence in their employment policy practices between business units or establishments, firms might well seek a greater degree of stability in their employment practices in order to better generalize the key operative principles informing the 'high performance' model. In other words, it is not inconceivable that employer policy could, in some firms at least, lead to a degree of stability in terms of institutionalizing certain types of trade-offs with this more differentiated work force in return for its collaboration in the pursuit of the new model. One obvious area of compromise for firms able to withstand the associated market pressures would be to reduce individual risk about employment security and enhance rewards, presumably in return for increased employee purchase of the new model. Although this could certainly also lead to an emulation effect (see Di Maggio and Powell, 1983), such employer-driven pressures are unlikely to be generalized in the absence of a more sustained impulsion for change at the societal level.

Another possible source of pressure might emerge as a result of increasing social inequalities. While one part of the population is likely to be tied into and benefit from the superior productive gains on offer in the new production model, another part of the population is likely to be excluded from these benefits. This increasing polarization of fortunes, intimately bound up with the articulation of different firms, industries and/or regions to the global economy (see, for example, Castaingts-Teillery, 2001; Rodrik, 1997, 70–1), could well be the subject of increasing social discontent. Inasmuch as social actors such as community and social groups, be they formal or informal, national or transnational, are able to give voice to this trend as a policy and institutional problem, then the state might well be compelled to intervene in order to broker suitable compromises in employment relations that give firms the kind of productive flexibility they are seeking while socializing or reducing the costs of the transfer of risk and insecurity to employees. In this case, the state, as opposed to individual employers, would assume the cost of this transfer of risk. Again, however, such a result supposes the mobilization of sufficient social pressure so that the failure of the state to play such a brokering role would be perceived as a policy problem.

These two previous avenues of institutional change probably depend on the renewal of the modes and forms of collective representation. We argued in the first part of this chapter that the emergence of a particular regime of collective representation – in essence, national and often industry-based trade unions – was the result of the transformation of production characteristic of Fordism, but that this regime also greatly contributed to the stabilization and regularization of employment relations in the Fordist model. Not only does the new 'high performance' model of production challenge traditional modes of employment regulation but it has, in many ways, eroded the social base of previous forms of union representation. The challenge for organized labour under this new model is therefore to reinvent and consolidate its role in the context of the new production model.

At the level of the workplace, a key question is the role that the union can and should play in the new model. A rich seam in the literature suggests that multiple changes in the way that work and employment are organized have shaken the traditional foundations of union action. While this diagnosis is widely shared within the research community (ILO, 1997), the prognosis is open to debate. One thesis points to an inevitable decline in the strength and influence of unions. The intensification of competition, the emergence of new organizational models of production and service delivery and the proliferation of new, atypical forms of employment are but some of the factors buffeting workers faced with incantations of the need to change. Thus the leverage of the union as an institution in the regulation of work seems to be ever more weakened. While certainly applicable to the new production model, this unidirectional reading of the dynamics of change in the contemporary workplace finds only mixed support in empirical research. A more imposing body of research, in fact, suggests that the effects of the multiple changes in the workplace depend on the power of the actors at play, on their capacity to mobilize their own power resources, and on the particular nature of the contexts in which these actors mobilize their resources. Recent empirical work points in precisely this direction (Lapointe, 1998 and 2000; Lévesque and Murray, 1998; Frost, 2000; Murray *et al.*, 2000; Kumar and Murray, 2001 and 2002). This reading suggests that a renewal of the union role at the local level is a key component to ensure a greater stability in the multiple contradictions of the new 'high performance' model, but that a union is unlikely to be able to play this role in the absence of a renewal of its power resources (see Lévesque and Murray, 2002).

Several examples must suffice to illustrate this thesis. The move from a centralized to a decentralized model, as in both public and private sectors, raises multiple challenges for union organizations compelled to revisit their internal modes of organization in this new context (Fairbrother, 1996) and to enlarge the foundation of union identity in a much more heterogeneous universe of identities at work and beyond (Piore, 1995). Similarly, in the face of increasing competition, the improvement of quality and productivity is imperative and it is thus that we see the emergence of new forms of workplace partnership (Bourque, 1999; Brown, 2000). The resulting social pacts and social contracts represent an attempt to reconcile the interests at play towards greater workplace competitiveness and, inasmuch as it is possible in these new globalized but altogether more volatile local contexts, a degree of employment security. The real paradox of these new forms of partnership, however, is that enduring forms of partnership very much appear to depend on the reinforcement of union power. The challenge for local unions then is how to reinforce their power so that they might be 'partners' in a context where the overwhelming tendency, on the contrary, appears to lead to a weakening of their position. A key question, therefore, concerns the insertion of the local union in the larger union structure, including transnational co-ordinating structures in an increasingly global economy. It can be argued that local unions able to construct and mobilize horizontal and vertical solidarity networks, articulate proactive positions in the face of employer incantations for change and reinforce their internal solidarity and social cohesion through participative and representative mechanisms for democracy are more likely assume an enduring role in the reorganization of production and exert influence on behalf of their members (see Frost, 2000; Lévesque and Murray, 2002; Kumar and Murray, 2002). Simply put, the stabilization of the 'high performance' model depends on the emergence of a degree of autonomous employee power, this latter being predicated on a renewal of existing union power resources.

At the level of the society, there remains the question of the overall strength of labour as a social force. Again, pessimistic readings, at least from the point of view of union renewal, suggest a decline in the saliency of the labour movement as a social force. However, a number of labour movements are putting new emphasis on organizing in order to better match their structures and strategies to the emerging contours of the new economy and thereby reinforce their overall strength. Indeed, there has also been a revival of and renewed emphasis on social unionism in a number of countries, particularly in the USA and Canada, in order to engage in a more forthright advocacy of social change in the context of broader strategies for union renewal (Moody, 1997; Bronfenbrenner et al., 1998). Such strategies, both national and transnational in character, seek to construct broader coalitions of workers and identity-based and community groups interested in social change in order to exert greater pressure on the evolution of public policy.

Existing research certainly points to the need to examine the interface between these transformations of work and community in the new economy and the modes of operation of traditional union organizations. The increasing decentralization of collective bargaining and the role that unions are called on to play in the implementation of new production models entails the development of new services, negotiating skills and forms of co-ordination. But the unionization of traditional services and secondary labour market jobs seems to be predicated on the movement from a servicing model to an organizing model of unionism (Bronfenbrenner *et al.*, 1998; Nissen, 1999). And the increasing fragmentation and dispersion of employment and identities at work appear to entail both the transformation of the union into a new type of intermediary structure in the labour market (Piore, 1991) and a search for new forms of collective solidarity (Lévesque *et al.*, 1997). Yet most current studies highlight the continuing difficulty of effecting these types of transformation and underscore the complexity of the trade-offs involved in the organizational transformation of local unions, for example between external recruitment and the political and practical exigencies of internal representation, hence the need for new forms of membership participation (Fletcher and Hurd, 1999; Voss and Sherman, 1999; Schenk, 2002; and, more generally, Fairbrother and Yates, 2002). Union actors thus remain structurally and strategically challenged and their renewal would seem to be one of the necessary preconditions in order for them to exert more sustained pressure at both the level of the workplace and of the society as a whole.

The outcome of these efforts at renewal is, as yet, far from evident. However, we are arguing, perhaps somewhat paradoxically, that it is from such efforts that the sources of stabilization of the new production model are likely to emerge. In essence, it is such pressure that is likely to engender more systematic trade-offs concerning the operation of the new production model and, thereby, secure a greater degree of overall stability in what will otherwise remain a volatile, emergent model of production. This identification of potential sources of pressures is not to suggest that we are about to witness some miraculous convergence into an entirely stable, homogeneous and harmonious model of production. Rather, it is a possible scenario for a greater stabilization of the new production model, tensions and contra-dictions intact, just as was the case with the previous Fordist model of production.

Conclusion

In this chapter we have sought to advance a way of understanding the basic contours of the emerging model of production. In order to do so, we first set out a number of conceptual distinctions, notably the idea of a 'model' of production and its three main spheres. We then sought to apply these concepts to the Fordist model and its declining influence. Of particular importance here was the notion that a model of production does not solve all problems related to the organization of co-operation in the labour process and the realization of value in production. Rather, it represents a dominant set of operative principles that offer a significant advantage over previous modes of organizing production and that congeal into a more or less stable model over time. In this sense, the model offers a set of principles or precepts designed to resolve on an ongoing basis some of the problems inherent in the organization of production and the delivery of services.

In the second part of the chapter, we set out the core principles of the emerging new model. These principles are to be found in a variety of workplaces and have taken on increasing significance in much of the literature about the 'high commitment' or 'high performance' workplace. These principles include productive flexibility and the standardization of processes in the sphere of production management, greater application of skills and knowledge, more self-regulation as well as increased 'multi-skilling' and 'multi-tasking' in the sphere of work organization, and the transfer of risk and insecurity onto the workforce and increased employee commitment in the sphere of employment relations. It was also emphasized that these principles are characterized by important tensions and, in some cases, significant contradictions. So much so, that, despite its considerable promise, the model currently displays a high degree of instability. This will not prevent management, however, from continuing the drive to organize production and the delivery of services in new ways, since so many of the new operating principles respond to market forces and technological developments that are unlikely to be reversed.

The final part of the chapter focused on the sources of this instability. One of the reasons for the slow diffusion of the model is the natural process of trial and error, as well as market outcomes associated with the development of new methods of organizing production. Another concerns variations that we would expect to observe around what is, after all, an abstraction – an attempt to read larger trends into complex and varied empirical patterns of social behaviour. Two other explanations were, however, deemed to be even more compelling. First, it was argued that the new production model is subject to significant internal tensions that naturally contribute to a high degree of variability. Second, the model still lacks an appropriate institutional framework that could improve its internal coherence and ensure a greater degree of diffusion. The central conclusion here is that many of the new operative principles in the new production model have yet to find adequate institutional support within the new economy. We believe that the model is likely to remain highly unstable in the absence of such institutions.

It was further argued that such institutionalization is unlikely to take place in the absence of social forces likely to prompt some movement on the part of the state and other social actors. Stabilizing institutions cannot be decreed; they emerge from conflict between actors, established and emerging, and their attempts to resolve those conflicts in a more or less enduring way. These institutions might take the form of particular patterns of social relations or they might lead to the genesis of new public policies and formal institutions, or both. We also stressed that the emergence of such institutions presumes a genuine renewal of the labour movement. It should be emphasized that such institutions do not abolish problems inherent to the management of labour at work. Rather, they offer plausible and more or less coherent solutions to these problems over time. In the absence of the development of institutions calibrated to the new production model, the enduring conundrum will remain its hybrid character: superior productive potential frustrated by the real tensions and contradictions that cut through its different spheres. Over the coming years, we are likely to witness a vibrant, open-ended process where, in part at least, this conundrum might well result in a more stable set of social relations, at least until the onset of new sources of change.

Notes

1. Standing adds several other forms of security, including labour market security secured through the state's commitment to full employment, work security gained through the expansion of employment standards and legislation on health and safety at work, and skill reproduction security.
2. Before analysing how the situation has changed, it is important to point out that addressing the 'problem of labour' and solving it are quite different matters. The well known indeterminacy of the employment contract (i.e. how to convert labour power into actual work) is a long-standing question for students of economics, sociology and management. The transformation of employees' abilities into actual production remains so complex that it can never be reduced to a mere technical matter. In contrast to a strong tendency in managerial textbooks to conflate Taylor's programmatic intentions with workplace realities in the post-war Fordist period, a rich tradition of industrial sociology shows how work arrangements regarding patterns of effort rest primarily on social

customs or conventions founded in the workplace. For an analysis of the technical and social limitations of Taylorism in the sociological tradition, see Durand (1978).

3. As suggested by Sennett (1998, p. 56): 'Control can be exercised by setting production or profit targets for a wide variety of groups in the organization, which each unit is free to meet in any way that seems fit.' He emphasizes, however, that such freedom is specious inasmuch as the targets are typically difficult to reach and management maintains a high and constant degree of control over actual results (see also Harrison, 1994).

4. Using a similar definition to that of Osterman (1994), Gittleman *et al.* (1998) note that only 11.1 per cent of all establishments, and 20.2 per cent of establishments with 50 or more employees, had adopted at least two of these practices (more broadly defined to also include peer review of employee performance and worker involvement in purchase decisions).

5. This conundrum has led many to put increased emphasis on variable payment systems at the heart of the implementation of new production systems (see, for example, Freeman and Dube, 2000). However, there remain at least two significant problems with this kind of approach: first, they are not widely diffused; second, they do not offer any possibility of transfer from micro-level solutions to meso and macro levels.

2 NEW FORMS OF WORK ORGANIZATION IN THE WORKPLACE: TRANSFORMATIVE, EXPLOITATIVE, OR LIMITED AND CONTROLLED?

Paul Edwards, John Geary and Keith Sisson

The line in Bob Dylan's song 'Ballad of a Thin Man', 'something is happening here, but you don't know what it is',* summarizes much of the debate on new forms of work organization (NFWO) and their implications for the involvement of employees in work tasks. There are widespread claims that such new forms, notably team work, are growing more common, and the popular management literature contains numerous books on how to manage teams. Yet most serious accounts enter doubts as to the true significance of teams. Having summarized United States surveys on new work organization, Cappelli *et al.* (1997, p. 99) set claims for a transformation alongside evidence that most workers 'work without these innovations'. The British Workplace Employee Relations Survey of 1998 found formally designated teams to be the most common of a list of new management practices that managers claimed to have introduced (65 per cent among a representative sample of workplaces); yet a more stringent definition of team work reduced the proportion to 5 per cent (Cully *et al.*, 1998, p. 11). As well as the extent of work re-organization, when we consider its impact on employee involvement we also have to address the scope of involvement (over how many aspects of work do workers have an influence?) and its depth (how extensive is employee influence?). Assessments of these questions were initially polarized between pundits identifying empowerment and sceptics stressing work intensification. The situation has changed more recently, as researchers examine the costs and benefits of re-organization (Wilkinson *et al.*, 1998). Yet there remains uncertainty as to whether there has or has not been much change in employee involvement and, in relation to situations where change can be clearly identified, what it signifies. The reasons for this uncertainty, we argue, are two. Weak conceptualization of new work organization means that scholars may be discussing different things. Inadequate theory leaves writers saying only that re-organization falls between the extremes of transformation and work intensification, with little means of grasping the nature of re-organization. The lack of theory has also tended to leave the debate at the level of universals, that is, arguing about re-organization as though it has the same effects everywhere.

The first task of this chapter is to improve conceptualization and theory. We can be relatively brief on the theory, since the essentials have been developed at length elsewhere (Geary, 1995; Collinson *et al.*, 1997). In the light of our analytical perspective, we then review survey and case study evidence, drawing in particular on European materials, for it is here that the key issues of the scope and depth of new forms of work organization, and of the conditions promoting different outcomes, have been addressed most fully. As against a transformation thesis, we argue that re-organization has been of limited extent, depth and scope. But, in contrast to an exploitation view, we show that there are conditions, notably where there is high job security, an appropriate system of employee representation and sustained managerial commitment to employee involvement, under which employees genuinely welcome re-structuring. The outcome is not a simple trading of costs and benefits but a fundamental shift in the organization of work: the new organization has a distinct blend of autonomy and responsibility. It is a limited and controlled process but none the less a significant one.

Nature and Theory of 'New' Forms of Work Organization

The present concern with NFWO focuses on those initiatives in which employees have some active participation in defining the nature of work tasks and the way in which they are to be carried out. We concentrate on the more 'advanced' forms of work organization such as team work, problem-solving groups (including quality circles) and total quality management (TQM). These are accepted indices of innovation in work organization and are frequently cited as one of the key dimensions of the new production model (see, for example, Appelbaum and Batt, 1994; Geary and Sisson, 1994; Osterman, 1994; 1998; Ichniowski *et al.*, 1996; Geary, 1999). The significance of these practices is they – potentially, at least – alter the structure of work and supervision in a very fundamental way, primarily through granting employees more discretion to organize, plan and execute work tasks.[1] In addition, their introduction, and particularly team working, have the potential to overcome rigidities often associated with Taylorist traditions of job specialization and work boundaries. The significance of such innovations is naturally going to vary depending on the 'starting points' of a country's tradition of work organization and industrial relations. To this extent, the implications of change are likely to vary greatly between 'Anglo-American' countries (e.g. the USA, UK, Ireland) and 'Rhineland' and other countries (e.g. Germany and Sweden, but also Japan).

An important part of the definition of NFWO is the managerial role in initiating the practice. The contrast here would be with activities which either (a) emerge spontaneously among work groups or (b) are part of an organized campaign by workers to wrest control from management. Obvious examples of (a) are the group rules for the allocation of tasks developed by workers who are organized into gangs or crews, for example dockers or garbage truck crews; in many parts of the world such rules developed into powerful customs governing the whole of a worker's life in the workplace and indeed outside it (Sayles, 1958; Mars, 1982). As for (b), we are in the world of workers' control of production, as discussed in studies such as Goodrich's classic work (1920/75) and Friedman's (1977) and Batstone *et al.*'s (1977) analyses of shop stewards and gang systems in the British car industry (see Edwards, 1988, for discussion).

We cite such evidence to make several points:

- First, working in groups or teams is not necessarily new. As we will see, this fact is important in understanding current evidence on the extent of team work. Much of the debate has taken the auto industry as its illustration and has contrasted Fordist task fragmentation with team autonomy. But in other sectors, there never was this sharp contrast, with 'teams' being taken for granted and with the possibility that, where team work is reported, it is far from being a novel activity or one which is linked to transformative managerial policies. A corollary of this point is that 'new' forms of work organization often build on long-established ideas (Geary, 1993). For example, work groups often have their own norms governing worker effort, and the idea of 'self-discipline' or 'semi-autonomous teams' may well rest on such norms rather than being a sharp break with 'Fordism'.

- Second, workers often pursue team principles. They are not necessarily passive recipients of new ideas. It should not be surprising that there is a welcome of the principles of team work, and it is often managers rather than workers who are wedded to 'old' models of work organization.

- Third, workers' workplace behaviour is fundamentally about control, in that it entails efforts, sometimes against managerial opposition, sometimes without there being a conscious managerial policy, to establish some predictability and order in, and influence over, the important aspects of work experience. Experience with Fordist and other traditional forms of discipline teaches workers that they and managers have interests which are often opposed. So too with NFWO; new initiatives are part of a relationship of control, and not a negation of control.

Let us pursue the second and third points. We need to consider why new NFWO schemes are introduced and what is new about them (and thus how far they have control as a motive) and what their effects are (that is, how far they shift pre-existing relationships).

On all these points, debate has often been polarized. Proponents of NFWO tend to present them as a reflection of managers' escape from old forms of thinking based on controlling workers, and thus as something distinctly new; the effects are felt to be improved trust and commitment by workers. Walton's (1985) celebrated argument that there was a shift from control to commitment illustrates the approach. Or consider Fröhlich and Pekruhl's (1996, p. 188) conclusion from the evidence in Japan that NFWO are well advanced and that 'in the large companies, almost all employees work in groups'.

Much of the critical literature on NFWO takes the more extreme proponents of change at their word and criticizes extant programmes for failing to live up to the rhetoric. To take one example of many, Tuckman (1995) presents Total Quality Management (TQM) as a device which in fact aims to regulate workers more closely. Here the motive is management control, what is new is merely the means used to attain it, and the effect is a tying of workers to managerial demands. Very similar views have been expressed about Business Process Re-engineering (e.g. Grint, 1995). On the Japanese example, there is of course now a substantial literature arguing that Japanese workplaces are not models of employee autonomy but are tightly managed and highly pressurized environments (e.g. Kamata, 1983; Berggren, 1993a). The implication would be that there may be team work but that it does not entail 'real' autonomy and is instead managerially driven.

The critical studies draw on earlier work on the labour process. Thus Ramsay (1977) lays out a 'cycles of control' model wherein managers seek control of the workplace and cede it when their legitimacy is under threat 'from below', but otherwise revert to more autocratic measures. There are close parallels with Friedman's (1977; 1997) theory that managerial control strategies fluctuate between granting workers 'responsible autonomy' when forced by worker pressure to do so and otherwise seeking 'direct control'.

There are some evident weaknesses with such theories. How do they explain the fact that NFWO initiatives developed during the 1980s at the very time that organized labour in many countries was becoming weaker rather than stronger? They also explain NFWO in terms of the control of labour within the workplace, rather than as a response to external forces. Thus Kelly's (1982) careful study of job redesign in the USA and the UK shows that redesign experiments often occurred in situations where unions were weak and were a response to product market pressures rather than problems within the workplace itself. There was also often an implication that any form of employee involvement was simply a device to better control workers, with workers' interests being opposed to such manipulation.

Yet there are features of control models which can be useful. First, there is evidence that workplace problems are sometimes the stimulus to NFWO. Kelly's review mainly covers Anglo-American cases. Yet in a country such as Sweden, NFWO were linked with strong unions and a national political context that favoured industrial democracy, as illustrated by the 1976 Co-determination Act. Yet even here there were links with control. As Pontusson (1992, p. 299) shows in his study of Volvo's experiments with NFWO, a key reason for their introduction was a concern with high levels of turnover and absenteeism; it was hoped that a more humane workplace would remove these symptoms of discontent. NFWO were thus introduced not because of a principled managerial commitment to the idea of employee participation but as a response to specific shopfloor problems. The absence of similar experiments in Volvo plants in other countries, where the problems were less acute, strengthens this interpretation. Thus, rather than assert that NFWO occur either because of product market or because of workplace issues, it seems that, depending on the economic and political context, either can be the key initiator.

Second, we may place the theories in a context broader than their initial focus, which looked at management-worker relations largely in their own terms. Management can be brought under pressure because of changing competitive conditions, and it is now a commonplace that NFWO reflect efforts to respond to intensified competition. This argument is consistent with the logic of Friedman's analysis, which explains fluctuations between direct control and responsible autonomy in terms of competitive conditions.

As he puts it, firms in the British car industry could afford responsible autonomy up to the 1960s, and were forced to concede it by shop stewards, but tighter conditions in the 1970s led them back to a direct control strategy. But how could this explain the 1980s and 1990s? A second part of the answer is that product market conditions exert important but not determinant forces. What is now dignified as strategic choice theory restates this evident proposition. Pressure can lead firms to re-assert control but it can also induce an approach more based on participation, as studies of US airlines showed (Cappelli, 1985). A third proposition links these two by asserting that management adopts NFWO when it is under pressure and when it has overcome shopfloor resistance. The history of the British car industry illustrates this, with the involvement schemes of the late 1980s and the 1990s arguably being built on defeats of the unions in earlier periods (see Scarborough and Terry, 1997).

A third and crucial point sees 'control' in less stark terms than is often implied. Again, the logic of Friedman's analysis (which is shared by an important strand of British writing, notably the important contribution by Cressey and MacInnes (1980)) is that control is not a one-dimensional issue. Managers have interests in releasing workers' creativity as well as regulating them tightly, because workers who are engaged by their tasks are more likely to think constructively about difficulties than are those who are treated as mere cogs in the machine. This simple but critical perception (which, arguably, American labour process work such as that of Edwards (1979) never really grasped) indicates that NFWO are always potentially on the agenda because one way of running a workplace is to encourage workers' active participation. But we are still talking about control because there are limits to the extent to which employers can cede full autonomy to the workforce.

We enter here some complex matters. What is real autonomy and how might we know what it is? Is it not possible to rescue any control theory by denying that NFWO offer any genuine autonomy? A theory of control does not necessarily carry such implications. Consider a theory adumbrated long before the current interest in empowerment:

> [We need to make] an important distinction between what may be called detailed control and general control. The former refers to who controls all the decisions about how immediate work tasks are to be carried out, and is conveniently analysed using the metaphor of a frontier [i.e. this form of control is zero-sum, with the frontier marking whether managers or workers control an issue]. The latter covers the broader issues of securing workers' commitment to the aims of the enterprise. . . . Consider, for example, the

many schemes that have been introduced to increase workers' participation in the enterprise. . . . [W]orkers are not to be de-skilled operatives doing fragmented tasks but competent people thinking about how to produce goods effectively. The aim is to improve general control while reducing the employer's detailed control.

. . . In so far as such efforts help to secure the existence of the firms, they are 'in the interests' of workers. . . . [But] improving general control may not be consistent with the interests of all workers or all the interests of each worker. (Edwards, 1986, pp. 79–80)

What is being argued here is that control is not a zero-sum phenomenon and that managerial and worker motivations contain several elements. Friedman himself tended, and arguably still tends (see Friedman, 1997), to see direct control and responsible autonomy strategies as opposites. Yet the pressures towards exerting tight control and releasing creativity are tendencies which may co-exist. Indeed, they often do, as in the common problem of 'mixed messages': the use of a language of trust and participation along with tighter discipline and the threat of dismissal. Now, putting the matter this way implies that these two forces are always opposed: sending mixed messages is presented as harmful, and as one key reason why NFWO strategies fail. But they may also exist in creative tension. Employees may recognize a need for performance standards and clear objectives while also wanting the autonomy to take decisions. This is what we have called in our studies of TQM (Collinson *et al.*, 1997) the disciplined worker thesis: the argument that in some circumstances (just which circumstances we discuss below) workers accept managerially defined disciplines as boundaries to the exercise of discretion within NFWO schemes. Workers may thus have quite specific expectations of what NFWO will deliver for them, and the schemes should not be measured against a benchmark of total employee freedom.

Thus when we place NFWO in the context of existing theories of workplace relations, we can make the following observations. First, there is its extent (how many firms practise it). Common competitive pressures are likely to push firms towards it. A second influence is 'mimetic isomorphism' (Di Maggio and Powell, 1983): the tendency of firms to become alike because, precisely on account of the uncertainties of the capitalist market, there are pressures to copy each other, particularly models of 'excellence'. To the extent that firms are increasingly subject to the pundits of excellence, this tendency is likely to be greater than it was. However, circumstances differ as do firms' eagerness for novelty. We should thus expect a patchy take-up of NFWO. We should also expect variations according to national context.

Second, there is the depth of NFWO: how many forms of it are practised, and how many firms use the more advanced forms of teams which have extensive autonomy on such indicators as the selection of team leaders and the ability of the team to decide on task allocation? One would naturally expect depth to be less marked than extent.

Third, what conditions encourage the use of NFWO? Evidently, large firms are more likely than are small ones to be able to invest in such activity. It may also be that certain sectors are more appropriate than others. For example, where work is naturally organized on a group basis, for example the continuous process industries, team working may have more value than is the case in more fragmented operations.

Fourth, what conditions are associated with the success of NFWO? Studies of early initiatives such as quality circles have often found that they tend to decay (Hill, 1991). What circumstances sustain other forms of NFWO? It is, for example, commonly argued that job security is a condition for workers' acquiescence in change programmes: German unions, for example, have been seen as favourable to change because of the employment protections in the German system.

Finally, what is the balance of costs and benefits in NFWO? The point of introducing the concept of general control was to escape from the idea that a control-based theory entails an assumption of totally opposed interests between managers and workers. As the above extract stresses, workers may have an interest in change if it helps to secure their jobs. Naturally, this is not the only interest involved. They may also, for example, find that work is more rewarding if they are given more discretion. On the other hand, there may be more work pressure if targets are tightened. Lean production, in particular, is often associated with tight staffing levels and the absence of buffers, the result being more pressure to produce. As the worker famously quoted by Nichols and Beynon (1977), in their study of a 1970s job enrichment programme, put it, 'I don't feel enriched, I just feel knackered'.

The underlying point is that NFWO are unlikely to have neat aims or results. Managers will introduce them for all kinds of reasons, and what goes under the label may differ widely. Workers will respond in varying ways according to the effects on different sets of interests. NFWO are part of a continuing relationship between management and worker, and involve a re-regulation of work: a re-organization of the conduct of work, which will have variable effects, and not a self-contained activity.

Paul Edwards, John Geary and Keith Sisson

Survey Evidence of NFWO

We begin our consideration of the survey evidence by first addressing a number of points in relation to method. We then discuss the findings from a number of national surveys and from the recently completed Employee Participation in Organisational Change (EPOC) cross-national survey of ten EU member countries. Finally, we consider a number of conditions from the research evidence which might explain the observed variation in the adoption of NFWO.

A Note on Methodological Issues

Much of the debate about NFWO has taken place in a vacuum. Many commentators either ignore the survey evidence or take it into account, but go on to argue as if it did not exist. A major problem has been the weakness of the survey evidence. We consider a number of the fundamental limitations in turn. First, NFWO are notoriously difficult to define and measure. It is not unusual in some surveys to see respondents being asked simply, do you have team working or quality circles?, without seeking to add a more precise definition or description as to what might be meant by such concepts. Understanding of what constitutes such popular labels, however, varies enormously.

The second point follows from the first. If NFWO are difficult to define, it becomes virtually impossible to measure their diffusion. For it is not just a question of the simple incidence of NFWO that is at issue. Knowing that a workplace has team work, for example, tells us nothing about the nature of the practice: whether, for example, the team is a loose grouping who work together from time to time or a formally designated and relatively permanent unit; whether the team is semi-autonomous in its working or under close management supervision; and so on.[2]

Third, there are the issues of response rates and response bias. Expectations have tended to be set by the UK and Australian workplaces industrial relations surveys (hereafter UKWIRS[3] and AWIRS respectively), which are models in terms of representativity and comprehensiveness. In both cases, a national representative sample, stratified by workplace size, has been used and a total of over 2,000 workplaces surveyed in face-to-face interviews. The response rate for these surveys has been very high, 87 per cent for the first AWIRS (Callus et al., 1991) and 83 per cent and 80 per cent for the third and fourth UKWIRS respectively (Millward et al., 1992; Cully et *al.*, 1998). The problem is that it is very difficult to get close to these levels of response rates in specialist surveys of NFWO. It is not just that the pressure of resources has usually meant relying on postal or telephone surveys, which are much less effective than the face-to-face surveys, especially if they have 'official' imprimatur. An additional problem, which is developed in more detail below, is that respondents may be reluctant to go beyond the relatively general information required in the WIRS.

An associated issue relates to the 'quality of response'. This depends on the identity of the respondent and the unit of analysis. It would seem reasonable to argue that what is critical in a survey is that the chosen respondent is familiar with the policy, and close to the practice, of NFWO. In most of the surveys cited here, as with the UKWIRS and the AWIRS, the respondent was the senior workplace manager with responsibility for industrial relations and human resource management matters. The unit of analysis has been the workplace. In contrast, and in spite of having the same unit of analysis, the Lawler *et al.* (1992) study relied on a respondent at the level of corporate HQ. In this instance, the quality of responses is suspect as the respondent is likely to be more familiar with company policy than with workplace practice and, in answering in respect of the former and not the latter, is more likely to overstate the diffusion or depth of NFWO; that which is enunciated from the top as company policy may not be replicated as practice at workplace level.

This points to a fourth issue. Where the subject of study is the extent of workplace innovations, it is certainly likely that, where such changes have been introduced, their champions may be anxious and eager to have their efforts recorded. Organizations not associated with such innovations, however, may be less likely to agree to participate in a survey. There is therefore the possibility of over-estimating the diffusion of workplace change. Of course, there is also the additional problem that the reality of NFWO may bear little countenance to its protagonists' proclamation. To act as a check for such exaggeration the UKWIRS and AWIRS have not relied solely on the views of a member of management; an employee representative is also interviewed and, more critically, the most recent surveys have included an employee survey. Other studies (e.g. Oliver, 1997) have sought to minimize such risks by combining surveys of management respondents with site visits for the purpose of 'intensive data collection and verification'. We return to this issue again when we consider some of the benefits associated with case study research.

Fifth, there is the importance of a study's sampling frame. A number of studies often rely on drawing their sample from a list of top performing companies or the largest 1,000 firms. Consider, for example, Lawler *et al.*'s study, which drew its sample from the *Fortune* 1,000 companies in the USA and Oliver and Wilkinson's (1989) study of the extent of Japanese practices in the UK which used *The Times 1000* index for its sample. One would obviously need to exercise extreme caution in making statements as to the diffusion of NFWO when using such sampling frames. After all, such firms are most likely to support, and have present, the conditions necessary for NFWO's introduction. In such circumstances, the diffusion of NFWO is again likely to be considerably overstated.

A number of the more detailed studies also focus on a specific sector, which is usually metalworking, or a sub-sector. The result is that the service sector and, in particular, public services very often get ignored, despite its significance in overall employment terms.

Sixth, there is the durability of NFWO. Unfortunately, there are few surveys with a longitudinal or panel design which can help us provide an answer to such a question. The exceptions are the UKWIRS and AWIRS, which both contain a panel sample. This not only allows us to examine the survival rates of NFWO, but it also carries the additional advantage of allowing us to discriminate between two major sources of change, whether that is 'within-unit' change or compositional change (Millward, 1994). Most of the other surveys looked at here are one-offs and, therefore, only permit a measure of the diffusion or incidence of NFWO at one point in time.

Finally, and perhaps most importantly, there is the problem of comparison and in particular cross-national comparison. The great majority of the studies have been country-specific. Inevitably, as well as suffering from a number of the general weaknesses identified above, they tend to reflect the national concerns and issues not only of researchers but also of policy makers. Thus issues such as the 'quality of working life' have been very much to the fore in European studies, while 'transformation' has tended to be uppermost in their US equivalents. This makes it extremely difficult to compare the extent of NFWO in different countries.

In brief, then, it is not only difficult to define and measure NFWO accurately, but the quality of the survey data available varies tremendously. Data of the quality and authority of the UKWIRS and AWIRS are hard to come by.

National Survey Evidence

In this section, we provide a brief account of the extent of NFWO in a number of countries, concentrating on Japan, the USA and Europe, before going on to consider the results of the EPOC cross-national survey.

Japan

Japan stands out, at least in the popular mind, as being in the forefront in the development of NFWO. In a review, Nakamura and Nitta (1995) draw on a number of studies to show that job rotation, task flexibility, quality circles and team working are extensively practised in Japanese manufacturing. Similarly, Fröhlich and Pekruhl's (1996) review cites a 1994 study by Okubayashi and colleagues which shows NFWO to be widely diffused. More than 90 per cent of companies with over 1,000 employees said that employees were involved in team work in manufacturing and more than 80 per cent in services. The proportions of companies with quality circles (92 per cent and 70 per cent respectively) were also substantial. These results underscore the problem of definition: the case study evidence suggests that the room permitted to employees to act autonomously is tightly regulated in Japan within a demanding and intense workplace regime (Kamata, 1983; Cusumano, 1985; Dohse *et al.*, 1985; Williams *et al.*, 1992; Berggren, 1993a). Further, while large workplaces may be able to introduce new work organization practices, this may be facilitated by the subcontracting of repetitive work to other smaller companies where more traditional work practices prevail. Taylorism is, therefore, 'exported' to subcontracting companies through an intra-industry division of labour (see, for example, Berggren and Nomura's (1997) discussion of the machine tool industry in Japan).

The USA

In the USA in recent years a considerable amount of evidence has become available detailing the diffusion of NFWO initiatives. Perhaps the most noteworthy is the work of Osterman (1994; 1999). Osterman's surveys of innovative work practices (TQM, job rotation, teams and problem-solving groups or quality circles) recorded a wider diffusion of these practices than had many previous surveys. The questions were asked in respect of the largest, non-managerial section of the workforce. Among the main findings were: over half of the establishments reported having team working, 33.5 per cent employed TQM, 40.8 per cent used QCs and 43.4 per cent had job rotation. These figures fall by about 15 percentage points when it was asked if the practices affected 50 per cent or more of the core group. The factors most associated with the introduction of these practices were: the existence of a set of managerial values which accepted responsibility for employees' welfare, competing in international markets, the adoption of a high-skill, high value added competitive posture, being part of a large enterprise and finally being a small workplace. NFWO was also found to be associated with certain HRM practices, most noticeably high levels of pay and contingent pay systems, but surprisingly security of employment was not found to be important.

The main controversy relates to Osterman's use of his findings to discuss the issue of 'transformation'. The difficulty as most commentators see it, is that his suggestion that a third of American workplaces has been 'transformed' is overly reliant on 'surface measurements' of innovation; that is, to have team working or problem-solving groups says nothing about the level of autonomy or discretion enjoyed by employees. As indicated, the meaning of such practices is notoriously varied and 'elastic' and their significance is likely to vary a great deal from one organization to another (see Geary, 1999). Moreover, no attempt is made to examine the persistence or co-existence of traditional work structures with new work practices: without which we have no firm basis to claim that innovation in work systems has replaced or transformed traditional work patterns. In the circumstances, it would seem sensible to accept Weinstein and Kochan's more modest conclusion that the US data paints

> a picture of an economy where substantial workplace innovation has been introduced, but one where these practices are only partially diffused within and across firms and where their staying power is still being tested. . . only a relatively small number of firms can be unambiguously categorised as transformed. (1995, pp. 7, 23)[4]

Nonetheless, Osterman (1998) remains remarkably up-beat in his analysis of innovation in the American workplace. A repeat of his original survey in 1997 showed – apart from team working – that the use of new work practices (QCs, TQM and job rotation) had, in the author's words, 'surged'. The latter initiatives were being used in just over half of the workplaces examined and teams were in place in more than a third. The study also found that these new practices also seem to be more firmly embedded in the labour process than previously assumed and that they are remarkably durable even in the face of job losses; although the case of team working would seem to be more equivocal. To this extent, at least, NFWO would seem to have become a more common feature of the American workplace in recent years.

Against this, however, note must be given to Freeman and Roger's (1999) recent employee survey, *What Workers Want*. At first glance, the picture is not too unlike that of Osterman's: many managers had moved to empower their employees with more than half of those workers surveyed being employed by firms which have introduced some form of employee involvement scheme. However, the so-called 'representation/participation gap' (that is, the difference between the say workers desire in their work and that which they actually have) remains, in the authors' view, ubiquitous. Existing programmes are, it would seem, strikingly unambituous in their scope. At bottom, workers believe management are unwilling to share power or influence, a view with which management respondents are at one.

Europe

Taking the UK first, the country with which we are most familiar, findings from the UKWIRS series up until the late 1980s and early 1990s suggested that NFWO were not widely diffused and had not penetrated the UK workplace to any great extent. The 1990 survey, for instance, found that 'semi-autonomous work groups' (SAWGs) existed in only 2 per cent of establishments (Millward et al., 1992). The most recent workplace survey, however, would suggest that use of NFWO has increased to a significant degree. Although the term SAWGs has been dropped in favour of 'formally designated teams', the proportion of workplaces reporting that such an initiative was practised – 65 per cent – would point towards a significant move by British employers to promote employee involvement. In addition, the proportion of workplaces using problem-solving groups (e.g. quality circles) has grown significantly over the last fifteen years, or so, from a very low base in the early 1980s to 35 per cent in 1990 and now to 42 per cent of workplaces (Cully et al., 1998). Further, there would seem to be a considerable 'bundling' of practices with training, team working, quality circles and supervisors trained in employee relations matters associated with one another. A caveat would need to be entered here, however. Of those workplaces which had team working, only 5 per cent of respondents said that team members had to work together, were given responsibility for specific products or services, jointly decided how work was to be done, and appointed their own team leaders. Thus once a stricter definition is adopted, the incidence of what might be termed an advanced form of team working is very modest indeed.

A further word of caution should also be entered here in regard to the durability of new initiatives in the UK. In respect of QCs, for instance, there is evidence to suggest that their life span has often been short and that the depth of their penetration within organizations has usually been modest (Collard and Dale, 1989; Hill, 1991).

Another finding from the WIRS series that deserves special mention is that organizations recognizing trade unions in the private sector were more likely to employ employee involvement initiatives than non-union companies. A similar finding was reported by Marginson *et al.* (1993) in their second company level industrial relations survey. To this extent, the increase in the take-up of these new initiatives in the UK, modest though it might be, cannot simply be accounted for by the rise of union-free companies.

Duncan Gallie and Michael White's study of the employment relationship in Britain provides a valuable addition to the WIRS series (Gallie and White, 1993; Gallie *et al.*, 1998). The data, derived from a national representative survey of 3,458 employees, of between 20 and 60 years of age, provide a rare insight into the effects of workplace innovations in a way that cannot be derived solely from management or employee representative respondents. Another merit of this study is that in addition to measuring the incidence of given practices, it also gets behind the labels associated with such innovations and examines in a detailed way the nature of the labour process. Some interesting findings are revealed. For instance, in respect of the incidence of new practices, it was found that 20 per cent of employees participated in QCs or similar groups with some significant variations across occupational categories. But notwithstanding the limited reach of QCs, the study revealed that their effects were quite profound: employees felt they had a significant say over the way in which their work was organized; members were more willing to use their discretion and initiative; and enjoyed their work more than non-members. To this extent, the study's findings indicate that QCs can be highly effective in promoting employees' sense of involvement.

A less positive and more mixed picture emerges from the survey as a whole, though. First, in looking at the wider issue of changes in skill levels, the authors found evidence for a striking upskilling of UK employees together with a significant devolution of responsibilities in relation to decisions about work tasks in a manner which would suggest that the 'most prevalent employer policy with regard to work organisation has been a move towards "responsible autonomy"' (Gallie, 1996 p. 156). The consequences of these changes in work organization were not always unambiguous, however: on the plus side, employees enjoyed more autonomy, made greater use of their skills and had more opportunities for self-development, but on the negative side there was an extensive and expanding use of control systems as well as considerable intensification of effort levels. But perhaps the most striking finding from this study was the rarity with which UK employees were permitted to take part in decisions that involved changes in work organization. Only about a third felt they could exercise some significant influence and nearly half were dissatisfied with their level of influence. And when it came to those employees who reported (46 per cent) that they were a member of a work group, only 15 per cent worked in a group which had 'a lot of responsibility'. There was also evidence to suggest that the level of employee participation had not increased from the mid-1980s, but may have declined.

There is another valuable element to the findings of Gallie and White's research, for not only do they show how employees' task discretion and management controls had increased in tandem, but also that there was no simple polarization as between employers who might have adopted high control and low discretion strategies and others who might have preferred low control and high discretion. It should also be emphasized that all categories of employees had experienced high or growing control. There was not therefore, a

> simple trade-off between discretion and control. . . . Employers' practices about task discretion do not appear to map in any straightforward way onto their policies of control. Depending on the type of control used, higher control might be associated with lower discretion, higher discretion or something in the middle. (Gallie *et al.*, 1998, p. 71–2)

The evidence therefore would suggest that even where employer strategies do permit enhanced employee discretion it is not that anything like full autonomy is being ceded: modes of production might have changed and new models of work organization might have been introduced, but the requirement for employers to control their employees remains.

Finally, the introduction of performance management is interesting. It was most evident, not surprisingly, among those employees who enjoyed high task discretion, but it would be wrong to see its introduction simply as an assertion of management control over erstwhile autonomous employees. It was more complex than that: it was also part of a wider strategy of decentralizing work task decision-making within organizations. It was thus a highly ambivalent process with employers relaxing or replacing immediate controls with more remote controls. Managerial control, therefore, was not being revoked but was being recast – sometimes in a more sophisticated way – and, in some important respects, intensified.

In Ireland (Republic of Ireland), the 'starting point', like the UK, is a Taylorist tradition of job specialization, overlaid in unionized companies by a tradition of control linked to employment and skill protection with a climate of industrial relations which has historically been adversarial. In recent years, there have been some notable attempts to move away from these positions. Evidence from a recent national workplace survey suggests that employers' experimentation with new work organization strategies in Ireland is impressive (see Geary, 1999). For example, 67 per cent of workplaces reported that they had made some changes to work practices, 59 per cent had team working, 15 per cent used quality circles and 71 per cent had a total quality management programme. Taken on their own, these findings would suggest that NFWO were quite widespread in Ireland, and compare favourably with most other countries. However, closer inspection of the data reveals a less noteworthy picture. First, team working was a relatively recent introduction; and second, advanced forms of team working, particularly those close to the Scandinavian model (we return to this model below), were very rare indeed.

Analysis of the Irish workplace survey data also revealed a number of factors that were positively associated with advanced forms of work organization. Most noteworthy was the importance of the financial services sector as a predictor of the existence of team working in its various forms. Other variables that produced consistently robust results, particularly in explaining team working of an advanced form, were establishments that produced customized products or services and workplaces that operated in high-tech sectors. Contrary to expectations, factors such as exposure to intense market pressures, nationality[5] and workplace size registered weak and/or inconclusive results. Perhaps most surprisingly, there is little or no evidence to support a union, greenfield site, workforce size or skilled workforce effect.

The absence of a clear, robust association between team working and intense market competition might suggest that exposure to such pressures precludes management the space to develop team working and the room to recoup the up-front costs associated with such an initiative. What seems to be crucial in explaining the incidence and intensiveness of team working in Ireland is the degree to which firms compete on the basis of product/service customization. These findings are consistent with Osterman's (1994) research in the USA where establishments that pursued the 'high-road' to competitive advantage were more likely to adopt new work practices.

We now turn to review survey evidence from continental Europe. Taking France first, the picture is unclear and equivocal. On the one hand, there is considerable evidence to suggest that the deeply embedded distrust between employees and management and the entrenched hierarchical structures have worked together to undermine any significant movement towards the introduction of NFWO (Lane, 1995). On the other hand, the moderately extensive diffusion of QCs, would seem to paint a different picture of the industrial relations landscape: in a national survey of 3,000 workplaces 33 per cent of firms were found to operate QCs (Coutrot and Parraire, 1994) – often thought to be among the highest in Europe (Goetschy and Rozenblatt, 1992). In the same survey, 11 per cent of firms claimed to have introduced 'self-regulating work groups' comprised of multi-skilled employees who had autonomy to organize their own work. The extraordinary diffusion of QCs follows on the failure of the legislatively backed *groupes d'expression* to take firm root in France and while it is now generally held that this instrument failed to increase employees' participation in a fundamental way, it did contribute towards a new rapprochement between employees and management which probably helped to foster support for QCs in more recent years (Lane, 1995).

Since the late 1980s, Italy has seen some significant attempts to restructure working practices. The re-integration of skills and the introduction of team working have been reported in particular in the chemical and telecommunications industries and some industrial districts, but these have been far from unambiguous in their implications for employee autonomy. Detailed survey evidence is rare, however, but in one survey of the Lombardy region only 11 per cent of firms reported having promoted team working where members had responsibility for organizing their own work (Regalia and Ronchi, 1991). QCs would also appear to be limited in their diffusion, but this would seem to have more to do with middle management opposition than with trade union resistance (Regalia and Regini, 1995).

In Germany, as in many other continental European countries, it is difficult to get data which can provide precise estimates of the diffusion of NFWO. Nonetheless, it is often assumed, or at least expected, that workplace innovations will be more widespread and more coherent than most other countries, apart perhaps from Sweden. Such a view was particularly associated with the early work of Streeck (1981) who argued that the classic regime features of German industrial relations – high skills, works councils, co-determination, investment in training, centralized bargaining – had given rise to a tradition of co-operation in workplace change. More recently, the Locke *et al.* (1995) study reports that QCs, team work, job rotation and flexible work structures appear to be extensively used in Germany's automobile, machine tool and chemical industries. Yet two studies reported in Fröhlich and Pekruhl (1996) for the EPOC project would suggest that the evidence for new work structures in Germany is far from compelling. Kleinschmidt and Pekruhl (1994), for example, estimated that only 7 per cent of German employees worked in team work structures. In the highly exposed mechanical engineering sector, Sauerwein (1993) found that only 2.6 per cent of firms had team work.

It is difficult to explain the limited diffusion of NFWO in Germany, but a number of factors might be suggested. First, although some German unions, most notably IG Metall, have been to the forefront in formalizing an independent view of team work, German management were not immediately convinced of its performance benefits and showed some considerable reluctance in moving towards its adoption (Turner, 1991; MacDuffie, 1995a). While this view changed in the late 1980s and early 1990s, and in particular in the car industry, the original hesitancy in introducing team work may have taken some time to overcome. Second, there is the predominance of small and medium-sized firms in Germany. Here the implementation of NFWO is unlikely to have the same resonance or appeal as it might in larger enterprises. To deploy employees around formally established team structures may seem little advance on arrangements which rely on informal practices or already existing team structures.

Third, the predominance of skilled labour in Germany with a high productivist ethos combined with more organic work structures may make team working less an imperative than it is in other countries, where it is seen as an antidote to poorer skill levels and more rigid work structures. Added to this is the emergence of a new category of employee, the 'system regulator', which by the end of the 1980s made up 5 per cent of the production workforce in the car industry, 9 per cent in the machine tool sector and 33 per cent in the chemical industry (Baethge and Wolfe, 1995). To this extent, one might fairly claim that the limited development of team work may be analogous to the limited advancement of HRM in Germany, where many of the principles normally associated with HRM have for long been codified in German labour law or in industrial relations practice: partnership between employees and management, investment in training, employment security and so on. Thus team work may be absent, but some of the benefits normally derived from team working may at least be acquired through existing work structures. On the other hand, this argument may be to present an overly sanguine view of the existing capacities of the German industrial relations system to adapt existing work structures (without necessarily having to introduce NFWO) to meet new competitive pressures. It is possible that the heavy emphasis within German enterprises on expertise, hierarchy and formal skills may work against efficient adjustment and the introduction of team working.

Finally, there is evidence to suggest that Japanese companies operating in Germany have shown some considerable reluctance in introducing NFWO widely used in Japan, such as QCs, in fear that they might be hijacked by works councils and provide an additional platform for the extension of employee influence (Deutschmann, 1992). In this context, at least, a perceived threat to management control acted as a powerful inhibitor to the introduction of NFWO.

Turning to Sweden, the pioneering role of a small number of Swedish employers, especially Volvo and Saab, in developing new work structures, are well-known. Beyond these initiatives it is, however, difficult to get a clear picture if such innovations are more widely diffused through the Swedish economy. Some commentators have intimated that the set of circumstances which led management at Volvo's Uddevalla plant to develop team work structures were unique and isolated and that the traditional Taylorist work structures in other car plants within Sweden are more characteristic of the norm. Indeed, many of the highly regarded experiments in work redesign conducted by Volvo and Saab have shown themselves to be fragile and vulnerable in the face of shifting economic and political circumstances (Kjellberg, 1992). But as in Germany, Swedish unions have shown considerable sophistication and foresight in developing an appreciation of NFWO. Where once the rallying cry of Swedish unionism was its solidaristic wage policy, recent efforts have concentrated on developing a 'solidaristic work policy', whereby a strategy for broadening employees' skills and competencies, particularly involving team working arrangements, would be closely linked to the structure of reward systems.

In the literature review conducted for the EPOC study (Fröhlich and Pekruhl, 1996) two studies are cited to illustrate the extent to which NFWO have diffused in Sweden. One survey of nearly 2,000 management respondents reported that QCs were in existence in 62 per cent of public sector companies and in 53 per cent of private sector organizations (Edling and Sandberg, 1993). Interestingly, where these new working arrangements were identified, the authors used an index to measure the degree of employee involvement and autonomy. Only 2.2 per cent of firms attained a maximum score of nine, but what was particularly striking was the degree of variation across sectors. There was considerably more innovation taking place in the private sector than in the public sector. Another study by Leion (1992) of employees' views, 2,000 in all from 249 firms, reported some significant, but modest, increases in employees' levels of autonomy in recent years. The more recent NUTEK (1996, pp. 81–2) study suggests that as many as 60 per cent of Swedish workplaces have more than 40 per cent of their employees in direct production organized in teams.

In summary, the overall picture is one of significant experimentation in employers' use of work organization strategies but within a context of considerable continuity that is not often recognized or acknowledged. Certainly, it would seem that use of new initiatives has increased in recent years in countries for which good information is available, like the UK and the USA. Elsewhere it is difficult to find evidence of sufficient quality, which allows for a statement to be made in respect of change over time. Nonetheless, the current *levels* of innovation across the countries reviewed here are considerable.

But hereafter there are problems as to whether we can say with confidence that these new practices have reached 'critical mass' in respect of the extent to which employers have adopted these new initiatives, whether these practices are of an advanced form and permit employees a significant degree of autonomy and as regards just how deeply embedded they have become in the labour process. One of the main difficulties with making such a definitive statement relates to how NFWO have been defined and measured in survey research. To reiterate, the use of popular and highly 'elastic' labels characterizes a great deal of work in this area. Studies such as that by Gallie *et al.* (1998), which use sensitive and multiple measures of work organization, are rare. But where care has been taken in instrument design two features from the resulting data stand out. First, while change is evident and the overall incidence of NFWO is impressive, less radical forms of work reorganization would seem to predominate, permitting employees limited discretion and narrowly circumscribed decision-making authority. Overall, it seems clear that the advanced forms of team work that have dominated so much of the debate are very much the exception rather than the rule. Second, in instances where employees have been entrusted with increased discretion it has not been accompanied with a relaxation in management control. Control remains as pervasive as ever, albeit organized in a different and sometimes more distant and less immediate manner. To this extent, work has been re-organized, but within a context where the various elements of worker empowerment and management control have been reconfigured and recomposed. It has not been the case that empowerment has displaced management control: it is not a story of *either/or*, but *both/and*. That is, the dynamics of change are not such that we have moved from a model of control and rigidity to one of empowerment and flexibility. Alternatives are not so neatly packaged. This has been the great benefit of Gallie and colleagues' research (Gallie *et al.*, 1998) and also of the case study research, which we examine below.

The EPOC Cross-National Survey

The EPOC survey was designed to minimize many of the limitations of previous surveys. In particular, it went beyond the simple incidence of practices such as team work to take into account such dimensions as coverage, scope and autonomy. Critically, the EPOC survey was cross-national: the same questions were asked of managers in a representative sample of workplaces in ten EU member countries within the same time span in 1996 (see EPOC Research Group 1997 for details).

EPOC identified six forms of 'direct participation' by employees in the organization of work. We focus here on the four more 'advanced' forms based on consultation with a group of workers or delegation of tasks to individuals or groups. The questions were asked in respect of the 'largest occupational group' within a workplace.

In keeping with the conceptual framework developed in the EPOC project (for further details, see Geary and Sisson, 1994), the focus was on the two main forms of direct participation defined as follows:

- 'consultative' participation – management encourages employees to make their views known on work-related matters, but retains the right to take action or not.

- 'delegative' participation – management gives employees increased discretion and responsibility to organize and do their jobs without reference back.

Both consultative and delegative participation can involve individual employees or groups of employees. Group consultation can involve temporary or permanent groups. Delegation can be to individuals or teams. This gives us four relatively advanced forms of direct participation as shown in Table 2.1.

The Diffusion of Group Delegation

Incidence Around a third of the nearly 5800 workplaces in the EPOC survey reported that members of their largest occupational group were involved in some form of formally designated team work (Table 2.2). Group delegation, it seems, was no more in evidence than the other five main forms of direct participation and was some way behind individual delegation. In terms of country, Sweden stands out, as might have been expected, as does the Netherlands. Surprisingly, Germany, where the debate about team work has been especially intense, was below the ten-country average. Significantly, too, group delegation was by no means a manufacturing phenomenon. Indeed, the largest proportion of workplaces practising it was to be found in trade (retail and distribution) (39 per cent) and public services (35 per cent). Only 29 per cent of respondents from manufacturing reported having it.

Table 2.1 *Four forms of direct participation*

Group consultation	
'temporary' groups:	groups of employees who come together for a specific purpose and for a limited period of time, e.g. 'project groups' or 'task forces'
'permanent' groups:	groups of employees that discuss various work related topics on an ongoing basis, such as quality circles
Delegation	
Individual	individual employees are granted extended rights and responsibilities to carry out their work without constant reference back to managers – sometimes known as 'job enrichment'
Group	rights and responsibilities are granted to teams of employees to carry out their common tasks without constant reference back to managers

Table 2.2 *Incidence of group consultation and delegation*

%	group consultation: temporary groups	group consultation: permanent groups	individual delegation	group delegation
ten-country average	31	30	55	36
Denmark	30	28	57	30
France	40	34	54	40
Germany	26	31	64	31
Ireland	36	28	62	42
Italy	42	21	44	28
Netherlands	26	35	59	48
Portugal	20	25	26	26
Spain	23	23	40	10
Sweden	34	29	69	56
United Kingdom	33	41	53	37

Coverage The EPOC survey confirms the importance of taking into account the number of employees covered by any such practice as team work. Overall, fewer than half the workplaces practising group delegation involved more than 50 per cent of employees in the largest occupational group (Table 2.3). The same, incidentally, is true of the two forms of group consultation. The widest coverage was to be found in Denmark, where nearly two-thirds involved more than 50 per cent of employees in the largest occupational group, followed by Portugal (58 per cent), Ireland (58 per cent) and Spain (55 per cent). In the latter three cases, there is some evidence of a 'greenfield' effect at work: the incidence of group delegation was relatively low; but where it is practised, it seems to involve a substantial proportion of employees in the largest occupational group.

Table 2.3 *The coverage of the group forms of direct participation*

	% of workplaces involving 50+ per cent of their largest occupational group in:		
	group consultation: temporary groups	group consultation: permanent groups	group delegation: team work
ten-country average	48	48	47
Denmark	51	50	66
France	50	58	45
Germany	23	28	26
Ireland	73	71	58
Italy	24	12	12
Netherlands	59	63	53
Portugal	77	56	58
Spain	49	41	56
Sweden	59	66	55
United Kingdom	52	42	47

Intensity As is described in more detail in the appendix to this chapter, the measure of intensity is a combination of the measures of scope and autonomy of group delegation. The measure of 'scope' was based on the number of rights of employees to make decisions on how their own work is performed without reference to immediate management in key areas such as the allocation and scheduling of work. The measure of 'autonomy' was based on the ability of groups to choose their own members and decide the issues they wanted to discuss.

The results, shown in Table 2.4, confirm the results of some of the national surveys such as UKWIRS. They suggest that no more than one in five of the workplaces practising group delegation approximate to the 'semi-autonomous' model that has informed so much of the debate. Even this figure gives a false impression, however, as it does not take into account the total number of workplaces in the survey. When this is done, the number of workplaces in the ten countries coming close to the model falls to around 5 per cent. Even in Sweden, the number is only around 18 per cent.

Table 2.4 *The intensity of group delegation*

| ROW % | Scores (per cent of workplaces) | | |
	low	medium	high
ten-country average	27	51	22
Denmark	13	58	29
France	32	54	14
Germany	32	46	22
Ireland	32	51	17
Italy	47	40	13
Netherlands	32	48	20
Portugal	23	48	29
Spain	65	30	5
Sweden	14	54	32
United Kingdom	32	52	16

The 'Scandinavian' versus the 'Toyota' Model The EPOC survey results were used to make the first reliable estimate of the extent of two 'ideal types' of team work identified in the earlier literature study (Fröhlich and Pekruhl, 1996): the 'Scandinavian' and the 'Toyota' or lean production approaches. These are laid out in Table 2.5.

The identification of the Scandinavian model combines the measure of the intensity of group delegation with measures of the qualifications required of

Table 2.5 *Ideal types of team work*

Dimensions	Scandinavian	Toyota/lean production
Membership	voluntary	mandatory
Selection of team members	by the team	by management
Selection of team leader	by the team	by management
Qualifications	mixed	generalists
Reward	skill dependent	uniform (seniority)
Task	complex	simple
Technology	independent of pace	dependent on pace
Autonomy	large	narrow
Internal division of labour	voluntary	largely prescribed

Source: Based on Fröhlich and Pekruhl (1996).

employees involved and the intensity of training for team work depending on the duration of the training (in terms of days) and the number of the following topics covered: data collection, presentation skills, inter-personal skills and group dynamics. Not surprisingly, the proportion matching the criteria of the 'Scandinavian model' drops even further. Indeed, only 1.4 per cent across the 10 countries conformed to it. Even in Sweden only 4.6 per cent of workplaces did so. The lowest proportions were in France and Spain (both 0.2 per cent).

The Most Important Form of Direct Participation

Around a third of workplaces, it will be recalled, practised some form of group delegation. Only 17 per cent of respondents, however, reckoned group delegation to be the most important form of direct participation at their workplace. This compares with the 27 per cent achieved by permanent consultation groups. Only in Portugal, Spain and Sweden was group delegation seen as the most important form of direct participation. It was ranked particularly low in the UK, which might be expected, but also, more surprisingly, in Germany and the Netherlands. In the light of the enormous attention team work has received, it is a sobering thought that many of the managers (around a half) practising group delegation do not regard it as important as other forms of direct participation.

This finding is perhaps hardly surprising, however, in the light of the very different scope and autonomy of the group delegation uncovered. Another contributory factor is the inclusion of the service sector. Much of the debate about work re-organization in general and team work in particular, it can be argued, has been sector blind. Team work has long been practised in many workplaces in services without having the publicity and, indeed, the labels associated with similar arrangements in manufacturing. In some cases, such as hospitals, they are intrinsic to the organization of work. A hospital manager, for example, is likely to find little that is exceptional about individual delegation or team work – these are activities in which nurses are engaged all the time. An attitude survey or problem-solving team initiative, on the other hand, may not only be new (and something for which the individual manager may have been responsible for), but also be seen as making a significant contribution to the management of change.

The Effects of Team Work

Our attention now shifts to the effects of group delegation. The survey identified eight areas of possible impact. Where respondents mentioned more than one form of direct participation, they were asked about the effects of the most important. Table 2.6 gives the results. It shows, for example, that 'reduction in costs' was cited as an effect by 56 per cent of those who said that group delegation was the most important form of direct participation.

Table 2.6 *The effects of the different forms of direct participation*

	group consultation: temporary groups	group consultation: permanent groups	individual delegation	group delegation
reduction of costs	64	61	60	56
reduction of throughput time	66	62	69	66
improvement in quality	95	94	93	94
increase in total output	48	53	44	58
decrease in sickness	31	37	22	32
decrease in absenteeism	39	39	28	37
reduction in nos of employees	30	26	26	30
reduction in nos of managers	23	22	28	31

Note: Percentages give the proportion of those identifying a given form of participation as the most important who said that a specified outcome had occurred.

In the view of the respondents, the incidence of group delegation did not have a markedly superior impact to other forms of direct participation. On only two indicators did it come out on top, namely increase in total output and reductions in the number of managers, and then only by a small margin. Moreover, given the emphasis in several studies on the role of teams in practising 'self-discipline', a particular effect on absenteeism and sickness might have been expected, but none was apparent.

Very illuminating, however, are the results for the effects of the different levels of the intensity of group delegation (Table 2.7). The greater the scope, the greater the effects for most of the forms, but more so in the case of group delegation. Respondents practising group delegation with wide scope and comparatively greater autonomy consistently reported greater effects than those achieving low scores. Indeed, there was only one indicator, sickness, where this was not the case. The contrasts are even greater when the 'Scandinavian' and 'Toyota' models of team work are contrasted. The figures for the Scandinavian model outscore those for the Toyota model on every indicator by a considerable margin, including the sickness indicator, which differs dramatically. It is also notable that the number of respondents reporting reductions in the numbers of employees and of managers is much higher than under the Toyota model. Such results prompt two conclusions. First, that the Scandinavian model was producing valued outcomes, which would be consistent with the view that such 'alternatives to lean production' (Berggren, 1993a) can combine worker autonomy with efficiency. Second, however, the costs of job losses were evident, so that such alternatives should not be seen as dissolving tensions within capitalist production systems.

Table 2.7 *The effects of the intensity of group delegation*

| | Scores on intensity | | | Type of team work | |
	Low	Medium	High	Scandinavian	Toyota
reduction of costs	46	56	68	80	45
reduction of throughput time	57	61	87	80	56
improvement in quality	96	94	98	97	91
increase in total output	39	59	85	99	27
decrease in sickness	14	42	41	53	20
decrease in absenteeism	24	45	42	55	24
reduction in nos of employees	17	32	47	38	16
reduction in nos of managers	14	29	49	52	8

Summary

In summary, the results of the EPOC survey offer robust support for some of the more balanced judgements based on the national survey evidence. The diffusion and reach of task participation are uneven, and vary, in some instances significantly, between and within countries. This is especially true when the nature and extent of the scope and the autonomy are taken into account. Overall, the critical point to emerge is that team work is very much a minority practice. Only a third of workplaces in the ten countries had any kind of formally designated team work; only around 5 per cent practised forms involving the levels of scope and autonomy associated with the textbook models and less than 2 per cent get close to the ideal type of the Scandinavian model; most lie in between this model and its 'Toyota' equivalent with a tendency towards the 'Toyota'.

At the same time, however, the EPOC results confirm the potential importance to managers of team work with wide scope and autonomy for employees. The clear message from the respondents is that the greater the scope and autonomy, the greater the effects. This is above all true of reductions in the numbers of employers and of managers. The effects are even greater when qualification requirements and training for team work are taken into account.

The Diffusion of NFWO: Explaining International Variations

There is no shortage of hypotheses in the literature as to the conditions thought necessary to promote the diffusion of NFWO. In the discussion which follows we a highlight the main ones only. We also draw on the findings of the EPOC survey where relevant.

The Nature of Competition

Many commentators and practitioners alike have reckoned that competition, and in particular international competition, is the driving force behind the introduction of NFWO, along with other strategic initiatives. For example, there are many references to the automotive and electronics industries where intense competition from Japanese companies with long-established practice of team work and other forms of direct participation is held to be the critical factor in the introduction of NFWO (see, for example, Regalia, 1995).

The EPOC results suggest that the position is much more complicated. The need to improve quality, to reduce costs and lower through-put times were certainly the dominant motives for the introduction of the various forms of direct participation. Other influences, such as the demands of employees and the requirements of legislation or collective agreements, were of much less importance. Yet the incidence of direct participation hardly varied with the level of competition, and neither was there a strong relationship between competition and the scope of participation. In surveying the US evidence, Cappelli *et al.* (1997, p. 106) argue that it is not the extent of competition which is critical but the way in which competition relates to the competitive strategy of the firm: work reform was most likely where a route emphasizing quality had been taken and also where the firm was exposed to international competition. A similar argument is advanced in respect of team working in Ireland (Geary, 1999). As we will see in analysing the case study evidence, in some circumstances competitive shocks can be important but the generic effects seem to be limited.

'Greenfield' versus 'Brownfield': the Opportunity to Start Anew

In countries like Ireland, the USA and the UK, new work practices have been associated in the main with foreign-owned companies establishing operations on 'greenfield' sites (Locke *et al.*, 1995; Sisson, 1995; Geary and Roche, 2001). The task of transforming work structures in older 'brownfield' sites with more deeply embedded organizational cultures and industrial relations processes would seem to be significantly more problematic (see Pil and MacDuffie, 1996, on institutional inertia). Innovations are pursued more often than not in an incremental fashion and very often when the need for change has become incontrovertible. In contrast, a greenfield site provides management with a significant window of opportunity to contemplate, design and successfully introduce NFWO integrated with a comprehensive system of human resource practices.

It is not necessarily the case, however, that multinational companies (MNCs) will as a matter of course go for advanced work systems on greenfield sites. MNCs, the EPOC survey confirms, did tend to practise direct participation relatively intensively, as well as taking other initiatives, but the difference was not as great as might have been expected. Also, although the numbers are very small, operations that had been set up in the last three years were virtually evenly divided between those with and those without direct participation. There were distinct country differences as well, suggesting that the nature of the industrial relations regime and/or the level of labour costs may have been important considerations. Thus, in Germany, Italy, the Netherlands and Sweden, the proportion of foreign-owned workplaces with direct participation was above average. By contrast, Spain and Portugal had higher shares of foreign-owned workplaces without direct participation, followed by France and the UK.

Systems of Organizational Governance and the Place of Human Resource Management

It is widely believed that one of the important preconditions for the successful implementation of NFWO is the priority given to human resource issues at the strategic business level and the nature of financial markets and corporate governance. A contrast is often drawn between an 'insider' and an 'outsider' system (Albert, 1991; Scott, 1991; Marginson and Sisson, 1994). The former, associated with countries like Germany and Japan, lays emphasis on long-term financial investment. The latter, found in countries such as the UK and the US, gives stress to short-term financial performance. Capitalist relations in the former, although competitive in kind, are deemed to be collaborative in orientation. The system is underpinned not only by a set of institutions that support co-operative relations between firms and financial institutions, but also by extensive employee participation in the management of the enterprise. The basis for economic success is seen to be dependent upon collaborative relations, a search for consensus and the scope to adopt a long-term view. With the outsider system, market forces are allowed to operate relatively unfettered and emphasis is placed on individual and short-term gain (cf. Appelbaum and Batt, 1994; Geary, 1994; Kochan and Osterman, 1994).

Inherently plausible and appealing though the argument is, the empirical evidence on the diffusion of direct participation is frustratingly perverse. Germany, which is often seen as one of the paradigm cases of the insider model, turns out to have below-average levels of direct participation with quite significant differences in comparison with its close neighbour the Netherlands. There are also differences between two other countries often bracketed together, namely Denmark and Sweden. While there is some evidence of a 'Southern European' pattern, there is very little for a 'Northern European' equivalent.

There is now a rich literature in industrial relations which sees the development of 'partnership' arrangements between employers and trade unions as a fundamental constituent or necessary accompaniment to the development of new business strategies based on flexible production and service delivery systems (Piore and Sabel, 1984; Kochan et al., 1986; Regini, 1995; Streeck, 1995). It may be that this concept can be made to have greater analytical purchase than corporate governance arrangements. In the case of the EPOC survey results, for example, the Netherlands and Sweden stand out on a number of counts: the incidence, scope, intensity and effects of direct participation. It is difficult to escape the conclusion that this reflects the wider context of support: an over-arching understanding or framework agreement between the social partners giving legitimacy to the project; and major public campaigns of practical support such as that run by the Swedish Work Life Fund in the first half of the 1990s. Specific institutional supports for NFWO, rather than a generic 'insider' model, seems to be crucial. This may also explain the case of Japan, where insider relationships may develop organizational trust but where there has been no specific support for extensive team working, with the focus remaining on the Toyota production system.

Case Studies of New Forms of Work Organization

Although case studies are widely acknowledged as valuable in explaining processes of change, their role has been somewhat downplayed, particularly in North American debates. It is thus important to consider what we can learn from cases. We then lay out cases exemplifying arguments in terms of exploitation, empowerment and the re-organization of control. Finally, we use these cases to generalize about the conditions that allow NFWO to flourish.

Value of Case Studies

> Case studies may provide rich insights, but one can never be sure if [*sic*] case study results can be generalized. Although case studies can be very useful for suggesting hypotheses, one must ultimately study larger samples to test those hypotheses (Ichniowski *et al.*, 1996, p. 304).

There are useful but also debatable propositions in this statement. It is true that much case evidence is based on single studies and that studies often eschew the critical question: 'what is this a case of', that is, what pattern does this illustrate or question? But cases do a great deal more than merely suggest hypotheses, as has been shown in detail with respect to an earlier tradition of case study work (Edwards, 1992).

First, surveys in this field have some important weaknesses. As indicated above, in contrast to measurements of reasonably objective features of workplace practice, NFWO are hard to measure accurately. Studies of the UKWIRS have pointed to significant discrepancies between management and worker representative assessments of workplace institutions (Cully and Marginson, 1995; Benkhoff and Peccei, 1997). It is also hard to assess causal links. Consider Osterman's (1994) conclusion that job security was not an important determinant of variations in innovative work organization across his survey. As we will see, case studies suggest the reverse. They do so because they have a sharper view of both dependent and independent variables than is possible from surveys. For the dependent variable, case analysis can consider just what something like team working really meant and how far it was embedded. For independent variables, surveys can measure the numbers of job losses but not the qualitative effect on employees' perceptions of job security.

This points to a second, and crucial, feature of case studies. Managers are happy to proclaim new approaches. Surveys can usefully identify the extent of them, and appropriate questioning can assess their depth and scope. But to understand what claims about 'empowerment' mean in practice we need to explore the dynamics of control and commitment and to explore the connections between NFWO initiatives and experience on the ground.

Third, case studies indicate causal connections between variables. We will see below just how job security promotes acceptance by workers of NFWO. Cases do not just suggest hypotheses but also reveal the mechanisms linking cause and effect.

Fourth, cases can handle bundles of variables. Instead of treating job security, say, as an independent element, case study work would examine its association with other forces. It may well be that there is no overall association between security and NFWO because in some circumstances security undermines acceptance of change (workers feel safe in their jobs and/or distrust managerial arguments) while in others it promotes it (for example, because after a period of job shedding workers now feel that they have to change to protect jobs in the future and have the confidence to do so because jobs are now relatively secure). Case study work is here genuinely explaining why certain outcomes emerge in certain conditions.

In short, at present case work has some disappointments because of its single-case format and because some case studies do not sufficiently address the lessons which can be drawn. This is not, however, a fatal flaw in case work, and one can begin to discern developments of a more constructive kind. Moreover, case work is particularly important in a field in which there is so much managerial hype and in which innovation is trumpeted but failure is quietly forgotten.

Contrasting Cases of Teams and TQM

Numerous studies illustrate an 'exploitation' view. McArdle *et al.* describe total quality management initiatives in a British electronics firm and argue that these initiatives reduced any genuine worker autonomy and tightened managerial control of the work process. They argue explicitly that TQM 'forced workers to indulge in their own work intensification and exploitation' (McArdle *et al.*, 1995, p. 170). Pollert (1996) shows that team working in a chocolate company in Britain involved tighter budgetary controls which in many ways reduced rather than enhanced the autonomy of shop floor managers; as for workers' attitudes, 'there was no indication of a change from a primarily instrumental orientation to labour' (Pollert, 1996, p. 201). Wells (1993), surveying several experiments in Canada based on team work and similar principles, concludes that these approaches tend to substitute management-dominated teams for genuine team autonomy and to exclude an independent union voice.

A twist to these studies is given by Barker (1993). This study of team work in a US printed circuit board factory found that there was coercion, but that it was generated by work teams rather than management. Given the freedom to define their own rules, teams defined performance targets which were more demanding than those formerly imposed by management and were less tolerant of those who, for example through absence, breached norms of good conduct.

A variant of these critical studies agrees that re-organization is about control rather than empowerment but suggests that experiments often fail because of a lack of managerial commitment or ability. Scott's (1994) case of a frozen food works showed that semi-autonomous work teams were undermined by a lack of management commitment to worker self-discipline. Where managers disagreed with the outcomes of self-governance, they frequently imposed their own rules about discipline and time-keeping. In Buchanan and Preston's (1992) study, cell manufacturing was undermined by inappropriate human resource policies, such as an inflexible pay system that cut across the need for cross-functional working within cells.

On the 'empowerment' side, a leading study is Clark's analysis of the greenfield site in South Wales opened by the Pirelli company. The HRM strategy included a high level of workforce flexibility, pay linked to the learning of new skills, and self-supervision. Clark argues that worker satisfaction was high and that the plant's Total Quality programme 'created a sense of involvement and empowerment' (Clark, 1995, p. 235). Clark is, however, very clear that change was a complex process with limits and contradictions. Workers felt powerless in relation to such issues as pay and staffing levels. Like other studies, Clark's points to a weakening of the influence of the trade union. Ambitions of attaining complete flexibility were also abandoned. As for self-supervision, this increased job satisfaction even though it was often accompanied by 'intensified work effort over a shift' (*ibid.*, p. 154). The picture, then, is not simply one of benefits for all. Workers generally value the new system but it meant more work effort, in line with the disciplined worker model mentioned above. The problems for unions in playing an effective role also stand out.

Contrasting views can be found within the same industrial sector. Ichniowski (1992) studied a US paper mill between 1983 and 1990. He describes the introduction of a team system of production, notes importantly that all mill workers were guaranteed job security, and argues that indicators of discontent such as grievance rates fell while productivity greatly improved.

Vallas and Beck (1996) studied four mills from 1992 to 1995. They too found extensive use of team working and TQM ideas. But they paint a less happy picture:

> with respect purely to skill requirements, manual workers have indeed encountered a rising set of skill demands, as they have had to learn the use of [new computerized systems] . . . Yet even as workers' *skill* requirements have apparently increased, we find little evidence of any expansion of craft *discretion* or *autonomy*. (Vallas and Beck, 1996, p. 353, italic original)

The difficulty is that the studies address different issues. They could both be right: workers can welcome team work, which in turn raises productivity, even though there is no true empowerment. The complexity of the situation revealed by Vallas and Beck is worth highlighting. Few studies make a clear distinction between skill and discretion or autonomy, and surveys on both sides of the Atlantic regularly report increases in workers' skills. Yet they arguably conflate the two issues. Skill refers to particular technical competence, and autonomy to the freedom to make decisions about the work process.[6] Vallas and Beck are not, it is important to note, holding up teams against an idealized standard of perfect industrial democracy, but explain in a contextualized manner how a particular innovation led to standardization and to an absence of worker autonomy. Yet they also show that – in contrast to those who picture workplace change as all-encompassing managerial control – employees' tacit skills remained important in maintaining productivity. There were limited instances of workplace resistance. Teams here were part of a re-regulation of labour which did not dissolve tensions around the control of work.

Turning now to studies which identify complex patterns of re-regulation, we can take some accounts of TQM as illustrative. A series of studies of TQM in Britain (Rees, 1995; 1998; Collinson *et al.*, 1997; Rosenthal *et al.*, 1997; Wilkinson *et al.*, 1998) all start from the assumption that TQM has the pragmatic goal of improving product or service quality and using workers' skills to do so. They suggest that managerial goals are driven by concerns with product quality and not a desire to enhance exploitation (a finding familiar from earlier studies of new technology). The managerial view in relation to the shopfloor was that workers could usefully practise discretion but there seemed to be little claim in relation to wider empowerment. Collinson *et al.* (1997) state that managers in their six firms scarcely used this term. Their goals were more pragmatic, and they recognized both the limited extent of participation which was sought in practice and the constraints on the process that were imposed by financial pressures.

As for worker views, these studies find from a range of evidence that workers generally welcome quality initiatives and that there can be some genuine increase in decision-making but that effort levels may also rise and that there is no evidence of a shift in values towards a situation of high commitment (Rosenthal *et al.*, 1997). Edwards *et al.* (1998), studying six organizations in the manufacturing and service sectors, explore the associations between aspects of worker responses. Thus an 'exploitation' view would expect that workers working the hardest and most subject to explicit performance standards would express the least satisfaction with TQM. In fact, the study reports robust positive associations which it explains in terms of a 'disciplined worker' model: workers welcome a sense of order and purpose and are willing to make extra effort if they can see the value in so doing. As for wider commitment, a comparison with earlier studies of broadly similar organizations (Edwards and Whitston, 1993) showed that there was no evidence that trust in management had risen as a result of TQM. TQM was constrained but none the less of recognized value.

Taylor's (1997) study of workers in two customer service organizations encapsulates the point. Taylor argues that what he terms tactical responsibility is enlarged by TQM, as workers are given increased autonomy on the detailed planning of tasks. But equally there is a centralization of strategic control through the use of surveillance and the setting of hard performance targets. Crucially, these two forces were not separate but were part of what Taylor terms a dialectic of control: they were necessarily intertwined and in combination reflected a new way of managing the age-old tension between the granting of autonomy and the exercise of managerial control.

Similar results emerge from studies of team work. Murakami (1995a) reports a study of team work in a GM plant in Germany. He finds that teams lead to an increase in direct participation in workplace decisions and also that team leaders (called team speakers) did not, in contrast to cases such as Pollert's (1996), become quasi-supervisors. However, half his sample of workers agreed that team work helped the firm but not them, suggesting that the legitimacy of management had not increased. A related study (Murakami, 1995a) looked at team work across nineteen car assembly plants in several countries, measuring autonomy on nine issues such as the selection of the team leader and the allocation of tasks. It found that on most issues decision-making rested more with managers than workers, with autonomy being tightly constrained.

The implication in many of these studies is that participation need not imply increased job satisfaction. Two studies have examined this issue directly. Studying modular production in the US apparel industry, Berg *et al.*

(1996) asked whether improved performance was due to better job satisfaction or improved work design. Their evidence pointed to the importance of the latter. Berg (1999) finds in the US steel industry that job satisfaction was high where 'high involvement' systems were in place. However, he finds that the association between team work and satisfaction disappears when other measures of job autonomy are added, suggesting that it is autonomy in general and not the specifics of team work which promotes satisfaction.

The overall result thus seems to be that work re-organization can promote an increase in worker–management co-operation in relation to specifics of the work process. A wider transformation does not necessarily occur. On the part of management, change experiments often have limited goals and are constrained by financial controls. Team work also often goes along with performance monitoring, so that it has to be seen as controlled participation rather than industrial democracy. As for workers, there is acceptance of discretion, but scepticism about management seems to remain. The route to increased participation need not be increased job satisfaction. Instead, there is a pragmatic acceptance of the requirements of the job and its changing demands.

This is not, however, to suggest that employee attitudes are unimportant. Consider Batstone's (1986) important paper which challenged the conventional wisdom, that Britain had poor productivity because of poor industrial relations, by arguing that the causation often runs the other way. For example, poor plant layout and raw materials handling causes breakdowns which in turn leads to employee scepticism about and distrust of the competence of managers. Faced with improved work design, workers are likely to welcome the evidence of more competence and thereby to co-operate in change. Re-organization can help in day-to-day tasks even if workers retain their distance from management more generally. It need not be seen as empowerment or exploitation, but can be recognized as making possibly small but still important contributions to the day-to-day functioning of organizations while also disrupting established assumptions about recruitment, training and promotion and the monitoring of work. We now consider what conditions are necessary for such a result.

Conditions for NFWO to Flourish

Much research has focused on the effects of NFWO. Yet it is well-established that large proportions of any new initiatives will fail. We now list a series of factors which, in our view, begin to explain the different patterns noted above.

First, the widest-ranging British study of employee involvement as a whole – which draws on case studies in eighteen organizations and a total of 778 worker responses – argues convincingly that job security was an underlying condition for employee involvement to take root (Marchington *et al.*, 1994, p. 889). In three 'successful' organizations, competitive circumstances were favourable, whereas in others where employee involvement failed there were job losses sometimes accompanied by work intensification. The same result emerges in the TQM studies. For example, Collinson *et al.* (1997) included a steel factory which had a history of down-sizing and difficult industrial relations. A period of stability allowed a new approach, embracing quality teams, to be established, and the confidence of relative job security encouraged workers to participate. Glover and Fitzgerald Moore (1998) report similar results in relation to TQM, as do Wright and Edwards (1998) in a study of team work.

A second issue concerns the production technology. Many of the accounts of failed team work experiments come from relatively labour intensive and low-skill sectors such as food manufacturing (e.g. Pollert, 1996; Scott, 1994). Team leaders became supervisors. Other negative cases come from the manufacture of products like printed circuit boards (PCBs), which although themselves hi-tech often call for the use of low-skill staff doing very repetitive tasks (Barker, 1993; McArdle *et al.*, 1995). Where workers' skills are more important and where work is less routinized there is more opportunity for concepts of empowerment to take root (Clark, 1995). Process technology seems to be particularly appropriate to team work. Wright and Edwards (1998) and Bélanger and Dumas (1998) studied aluminium smelters in Britain and Canada respectively. One reason for the successful implementation of team working in environments where it might be expected to face problems (e.g. strongly unionized plants employing manual workers with a 'macho' heavy industry culture) was that the production process already called for workers to work in teams: the idea of team responsibility had a natural affinity with this type of work organization. Cutcher-Gershenfeld *et al.* (1994), in their study of team work in Japanese-owned plants in the USA reach the same conclusion, and they stress that the 'teams' formed in lean production plants in assembly industries may have little real autonomy.

If process technology is important, how do we explain the results of Vallas and Beck (1996), that skilled workers faced standardization rather than autonomy? The starting point is crucial. These were skilled workers with some kind of craft knowledge. New computerized systems codified and restricted the exercise of this knowledge. By contrast, the aluminium workers mentioned above had no such knowledge to lose. Team work could really give them discretion (even though, as the workers repeatedly stressed, this was something that they themselves had wanted, with managers being to blame for not granting it sooner, rather than praised for acceding it at all). Second is the prior expectations of workers. The paper mill workers expected to exercise their skills and were frustrated when this was less possible.

This point about expectations is also made by Marchington *et al.* (1994). They contrast three firms. In one, there was long experience of participative management which employee involvement reinforced so as to put the programme on a positive track. In the second, participation and indeed paternalism was equally entrenched but re-structuring led to a questioning of management's commitment to such a style, so that high expectations were dashed. In the third, workers had little experience of employee involvement so that what was objectively a modest experiment had significant positive effects.

Alongside worker expectations lie management choices. As Clark (1995) explains, managers at Pirelli consciously sought a new form of employee relations, and there were clear connections with a business strategy of focusing on quality products. There was thus a reasonably coherent set of messages. By contrast, Marchington *et al.* (1994) cite cases where a tightening up of management styles tended to undermine employee involvement efforts. Collinson *et al.* (1997) show that, of their six firms, two were marked by positive associations between worker views of TQM and more general trust in management and two by a complete lack of association. In the former cases, there was a connected set of managerial policies whereas in the latter TQM was welcomed but, because of down-sizing and a tightening of financial disciplines, wider distrust remained in evidence.

The issue of managerial choice, or at least a series of actions which may not entail any coherent choices, also bears on the way in which change is introduced. Geary's (1993) account of two Irish plants illustrates the problem of dual messages: tighter control of absence, for example, alongside team working. But it also shows that, because there was no coherent vision, managerial approaches became piecemeal, with the further effect that, rather than being able to implement wholly new practices, managers had to rely on old forms of workforce co-operation. The effect of managerial initiatives will thus depend on their coherence, and this is a matter of context. We cannot say that a plan for team work, for example, is or is not an example of an advanced or high involvement work system. Much will depend on how coherently the plan is implemented and also, as noted above, on the expectations which workers have of it.

As well as market and technological conditions and manager and worker expectations, the state of industrial relations is an important influence. In a case reported by Hendry (1993), in one of the cases studied by Rees (1998) and in the Wright and Edwards (1998) study, management made a conscious effort to work with and through existing shop steward organizations, and in these cases that once-familiar figure of British industrial relations, the convenor (senior shop steward working full-time on union business and paid by the company), played an important role. In cases studied by Rees (1998) and by Collinson *et al.* (1997), management were trying to reduce union influence and here much more difficulty was experienced in making TQM initiatives stick. Plainly, union channels are not the only possible ones, and Rees reports a case of a non-union firm where TQM worked effectively; among the reasons, he argues, was the existence of an effective employee representation system. But it does seem that attacking existing union structures runs against TQM's effectiveness.

That said, however, the conditions under which unions can play an influential role seem limited. In Britain (Geary, 1995) and North America (Wells, 1993) many initiatives by-pass unions or involve major challenges to existing job grading structures and seniority provisions. A union which is well-established but which is also able to engage constructively with management may be able to shape the outcome. But in many other cases managers may see the union as an obstruction or an irrelevance. In the words of a Rover UK manager, 'the unions were invited to the party but they didn't seem to want to come' (Storey, 1992, p. 250).

Finally, there are national-level contextual factors. If we stay with the case of unions, Murakami's (1995b) comparison of GM plants in Germany (Opel) and Britain (Vauxhall) implies important differences. At Vauxhall, team leaders were appointed by management, team autonomy was slight, and team work was introduced in an adversarial industrial relations climate. At Opel, there were the above-noted team speakers, and the works council was able to insist that they be elected. Teams were not seen as a challenge to existing union structures. The point is strengthened by a comparison between Vauxhall and Opel in Spain (Ortiz, 1998). In the latter case, unions welcomed team work because it brought benefits such as reduced boredom and better health and safety; they were able to do so because they had strong institutional security within the industrial relations system. By contrast, at Vauxhall union power rested on the shop steward, whose influence in turn rested on control of day-to-day production issues. Team work threatened to remove such issues from union channels and was thus seen as a threat.

A second feature of the national context is the structure of firms and of corporate control. In the Anglo-Saxon countries there has been intense debate about 'short-terrorism', which is said to discourage firms from the long-term investment in human capital that NFWO entail. In the case of the USA, Appelbaum and Berg (1996, pp. 198–205) demonstrate that the deregulation of financial markets and the growth of new money markets increased the number of take-overs and led to an emphasis on immediate shareholder value. But, they stress, such trends do not prohibit team work, for they would suggest a decline and not a growth in its use. There are conditions, these authors argue, in which task participation will be encouraged, including firms with a history of innovation (so that the benefits will be apparent and thus stock markets will not mark down the costs of the necessary investment), technically dynamic sectors, and monopolies. None the less, the climate of countries driven by immediate shareholder value is likely to make it hard to introduce advanced forms of team working widely.

In short, studies which stress the negative aspects of work re-organization may be correct to the extent that the above conditions are absent. The survey evidence suggests that developed team work remains rare, and that the extent of 'transformation' is likely to be small. Equally, however, it can take root in some situations, though even here, as we have stressed, it is likely to mean a qualified re-regulation of work and not a shift towards high commitment.

Such findings support the obvious expectation that in some countries NFWO will be relatively compatible with the industrial relations climate, and we saw above that the EPOC results point to important differences between countries in the extent of direct participation. It is rather hard to go further than this, however. When it comes to exploring the nature and depth of NFWO, we lack detailed comparative research. What does 'team work' actually mean in France, say, and is it the same thing as in North America? Do issues of skill, autonomy and work intensification, which have featured heavily in Anglo-American debates, have direct counterparts in other countries? It is very hard to say.

Implications

We noted above the importance of workers' expectations as a filter, so that objectively similar processes have different outcomes. There are two general implications. First, work re-organization, like any other workplace activity, has to be related to its context. Similar programmes have very different results, depending on the context of their introduction. Second, any particular outcome will reflect the combination of a range of forces. We cannot say that prior experience of participatory management will necessarily encourage advanced team work, for in some circumstances it creates expectations which cannot be realized, so that workers without the experience will be much less critical.

A quantitative approach might still argue that, 'other things being equal', experience of participation will encourage further development. But the key point is that other things are not equal. Workplace initiatives come in packages and are inserted in existing sets of relationships. The effects of certain influences will depend on other forces. This is not to say that no causal statement can be made. On the contrary, some of the studies reviewed above attempt to explain the relevant interactions. What is needed to verify the ideas contained in them is not a survey but other cases where the situation differs in relevant respects. For example, it has been asserted above that, where unions are well-established, NFWO initiatives which operate alongside the marginalization of unions will tend to fail. A test of this thesis would seek out firms which seem to have NFWO along with attacks on unions and thus assess whether the thesis is wrong or in need of some form of elaboration or qualification.

In terms of where case study work goes, two issues stand out. The first is the need for comparative study so that causal conditions can be identified. Part of such study needs to be internationally focused for, as discussed above, the meanings and contexts of NFWO are likely to vary between countries in important ways. Second, obtaining good data on employee responses will be crucial to assessing the complex effects of NFWO.

Conclusions

Interest in NFWO has certainly increased and, as the EPOC survey shows, is no longer limited to North America or Britain but has become widespread across Europe. However, it is now well-established that diffusion of new work practices remains limited (Pil and MacDuffie, 1996). We have tried to go beyond measures of the extent of new practices, to consider their depth and significance and the conditions allowing them to emerge. A key finding is that team work and 'involvement' take different forms. We have stressed the difference between teams under lean production, where autonomy remains tightly constrained, and those under the 'Scandinavian' system where workers enjoy broader discretion. The evidence suggests a concentration towards the former. The conditions permitting the development of the latter include organizational factors (the commitment of management to genuine involvement), the economic context of the firm (ability to offer job security and a degree of insulation from short-term pressures) and the industrial relations context of the country (with 'social partnership' being more fully developed in some countries than others). On the basis of these conditions, the concept of diffusion, with its implication of one new way of organizing work which slowly spreads, seems too strong. In many environments, team work is unlikely to take root. In addition, the idea that it will be extended even where conditions are favourable is too unidirectional. Springer (1999) for example argues that the German auto industry, once the home of quality of work life experiments, has seen a 're-Taylorization' of work. According to Springer, this is because involvement is stressed only where there are tight labour market conditions. With more emphasis on product market competition, the focus has been on production efficiency.

We should also avoid too strong a reliance on a limited array of models. These are only ideal types, that is, analytical representations of the world. It is not the case that pure models exist in the real world. In practice, firms develop their own approaches, depending on their own histories and goals. 'Country effects' can also be identified as important: the nature of trade union organization, the legislative supports for employee voice, the structure of corporate finance and control, labour market conditions and the importance attached to employment security. But there are also important differences within countries which suggest that, within the constraints of a particular industrial relations regime, employers have more or less scope and incentive to adopt NFWO. Within country factors that can be identified as being of significance are: union strength, unions' ability to develop and articulate an independent view of NFWO, the extent and influence of work councils or similar employee participation bodies, the form of competitive pressures and the nature of the production process or service delivery system. As an international study of the auto industry concluded, even lean production, which is often seen as a reasonably clear-cut model, varies significantly not only between countries but also within them and also between plants of the same company (Kochan et al., 1997).

The degree of success of work re-organization within the workplace is also crucially dependent on the place and influence exercised by employees and their representatives in its introduction and regulation. We have stressed the importance of employee expectations in mediating change programmes, so that apparently 'strong' forms of worker involvement can be treated with scepticism where employees have previously exercised traditional skills to which they are committed, while 'weaker' forms, introduced where discretion was previously low, can be welcomed. We have also underlined the importance of the provision made for job security and the coherence of the management change programme and its consistency with its overall human resource management agenda.

As to the effects of re-organization, our central argument is that it has middling and complex effects. The common tendency to see it as being either exploitative or transformative is to exaggerate its intentions and consequences; our claim is that it rests within more mundane and modest efforts to re-regulate labour. Nor is it simply a matter of seeing it as a zero-sum game. There are elements of new work organization which are of benefit to employees and may be welcomed, but there are also aspects which impose new demands and which may not be seen to be so advantageous. But the balance of costs and benefits is not simply six of one and half a dozen of the other: where work is substantially re-organized, there is a dynamic of change rather than a juggling of existing patterns. Team work can entail autonomy and responsibility, freedom and control. It is indeed a new dialectic.

Our theoretical perspective helps to explain these conclusions. To start with the final empirical conclusion, NFWO are a contemporary representation of the continual need for management to balance the needs of exercising control and encouraging creativity. They thus contain inherent tensions, as the theme of a dialectic indicates: NFWO do not resolve the contradictions of the employment relationship, but express and manage them in new ways. The complex effects of work re-organization are thus to be expected. So are the uncertain moves towards it, and moves away from it. Management do not generally embrace employee involvement unless they see a need for it or a benefit to it. As is now well-established, the Swedish firms practising team autonomy and long cycle times during the 1960s and 1970s did not transfer these practices to their non-Swedish plants, where labour market conditions were different. Arguments for re-Taylorization point in a similar direction. At the same time, some Japanese firms are reported to be moving away from the extremes of lean production because of the problems of recruiting and retaining employees in tight labour markets.

The specifics of a 'cycles of control' approach evidently need to be modified. The approach explains managerial concessions of 'relative autonomy' as a response to either organized employee pressure or tight labour markets. It is thus not clear how one can explain the emergence of 'high involvement' or 'high commitment' approaches when labour movements in most countries have been weakened and when unemployment has been high. But the broad idea of cycles, together with that of tensions within any given managerial approach, can be sustained. First, our evidence clearly shows that the extent of workplace transformation has been limited. It is not the case that significant work re-organization has been widespread or deeply implanted; hence, the extent of any trend running counter to the cycles theory can be questioned. Second, firms' labour strategies are driven by many considerations, of which the factors stressed by the cycles theory are only two. As Kochan *et al.* (1986) argued some time ago, increased competition in terms of quality rather than price has allowed some firms to adopt a strategy based on quality and value-added rather than cost minimization. In these conditions, a policy of employee involvement may make sense. Third, therefore, the aim of charting a cycle across a whole economy may be even less appropriate than it was in the past, for firms behave in different ways according to their competitive situations. Fourth, it is now a commonplace in the HRM literature that 'soft' elements such as involvement and training go along with the 'hard' ones of performance measurement and output targets. The case studies cited above illustrate the point. It is not the case now – if it ever was in the past – that firms rely either on direct control or on responsible autonomy. They use both.

The problem with the cycles theory was that it moved too directly from a general statement about the capitalist labour process – namely, that management can use strategies based on control or autonomy – to a specific argument that they in practice use one or the other and that they are driven between them by forces on the labour process and the labour market. Once we recognize that strategies are combined and that they are shaped by other forces, a more subtle analysis is possible. We have attempted above to identify a series of these other forces and to explain their role. But the cycles theory is correct in seeing labour control strategies as shifting and as having inherent tensions. We have shown that NFWO do not simply escape the problems of Taylorism. They have their own contradictions: specific ones, such as balancing individual responsibility against loyalty to teams, or reconciling work team autonomy and the need to meet externally imposed targets; and more generic ones around the balance between control and autonomy and the extent to which management can insulate autonomy in the labour process from the pressures emanating from capitalist competition. NFWO are a re-regulation of work, not the end of regulation.

Finally, what are the prospects for new ways of working? A view based on transformation would identify a relatively linear development, with more firms adopting new work·practices. A cycles view stresses fluctuations around the timeless issue of how to persuade workers to work. Evidently, we need to use elements of both: team work is different from conventional Taylorism, and yet it also contains the contradictions of control and autonomy. In the immediate future, some firms are likely to face conditions which permit the extension of team work, and to that extent some further spread of new work practices is likely. However, among these relatively advanced cases there may also be some shift towards a more controlled approach, as the idea of re-Taylorization suggests. As to the wider extent of team work, the unknown issue is where the benefits cease to outweigh the costs. There is now a large literature claiming to find that high performance work systems improve corporate performance. Yet, as more firms adopt the systems, the benefits may weaken while the costs are also relatively high. Recall the point that these systems are most appropriate in technologically advanced settings. The more that they are applied outside those settings, benefits will be less and costs, in terms of training staff, re-structuring management and so on, will be greater. Other imponderables include the economic prosperity of countries and the role of labour movements. Some form of team work is likely to remain on the agenda for a considerable time, but whether it becomes as emblematic of a whole period of capitalism in the way in which Taylorism represented the period from the 1920s to the 1970s is much less certain.

Appendix: The EPOC Survey

The EPOC survey into direct employee participation was commissioned by the European Foundation for the Improvement of Living and Working Conditions. A standard questionnaire, translated with the help of industrial relations 'experts', was posted to a representative sample of workplaces in ten EU member countries during the summer and autumn of 1996. The size threshold was 20 or 50 employees depending on country. The respondent was either the workplace general manager or the person he or she felt was the most appropriate. The main subject of the questions was the largest occupational group. Total responses numbered 5786, ranging from 298 in Portugal to 826 in Germany. The overall response rate was 17.8 per cent (ranging from 9.4 per cent in Spain to 38.8 per cent in Ireland). Responses have been weighted to be representative of the sampled population.

The precise wording of the key question on group delegation was as follows: Has the management given to formally introduced work teams the right to make decisions on how their work is performed on a team basis without reference to an immediate manager for one or more of the following?

allocation of work	job rotation
scheduling of work	co-ordination of work with other internal teams
quality of work	improving work processes
time keeping	attendance and absence control

Subsequent questions asked about:

the involvement of employees in participative structures (whether it was voluntary or compulsory);

the composition of the team (whether it was decided by management or team or both);

and the issues discussed (whether they were decided by management or team or both).

Respondents were also asked whether:

the team had a leader and how he or she was chosen (by management or team or both);

the team was able to propose changes in the organization and/or planning of work (if so, whether frequently, sometimes or rarely);

and management or team or both decided to implement any changes.

The 'intensity' of participation reported in Table 2.4 embraces measures of 'scope' and 'autonomy'. The measure of scope was based on the number of rights of employees to make decisions on how their own work is performed without reference to immediate management in the areas of:

allocation of work	scheduling of work
quality control	time keeping
attendance and absence control	job rotation
co-ordination of work with other internal teams	improving the work process

The measure of autonomy was based on the ability of teams to choose their own members and decide the issues they wanted to discuss.

Notes

* 'Ballad of a Thin Man', copyright © 1965 by Warner Bros. Music, copyright renewed 1993 by Special Rider Music. All rights reserved. International copyright secured. Reprinted by permission.

1. Although quality circles are sometimes seen as a purely consultative form of employee involvement, they need not be in that employees can be given the discretion to redesign some parts of the work process. The same often holds for TQM programmes.

2. Consider, for example, the work of Scarborough and Terry (1997) on the UK car industry. Their survey of seven plants of the major car producing companies (Ford, Peugeot-Talbot, Rover (BMW), Vauxhall (GM), Toyota and Nissan) revealed a strikingly uniform picture in respect of the introduction and operation of team-based work organization where supervisory roles were significantly altered or done away with. At this level at least, the changes point to a significant transformation in the way work had been re-organized. Their more detailed case study investigation of Rover, however, revealed a more mundane and complex picture: elements of a new model of work organization had been introduced and the workplace regime had changed in a manner which challenged many traditional job controls and demarcations, but many of the model's key features had remained under-specified, its introduction had been piecemeal and views as to its form and operation were contested and the focus of much dispute.

3. The most recent UK workplace survey was renamed *The 1998 Workplace Employee Relations Survey.*

4. This interpretation receives further support from a study from the National Centre on the Educational Quality of the Workforce (EQW, 1995) which, in reducing the size threshold for sample selection to twenty employees, found that the incidence of high performance work practices was lower than that found by Osterman (1994).

5. While there was no association between teams and whether a workplace was foreign- or Irish-owned, among the former group US-owned establishments were significantly more likely to have introduced team-working (see Geary and Roche, 2001).

6. Note that Braverman's 'de-skilling' thesis is about the latter, despite its label. Claimed tests of Braverman which ignore this obvious point are not tests at all (Armstrong, 1988).

3 THE IMPACT OF NEW FORMS OF WORK ORGANIZATION ON WORKERS*

Eileen Appelbaum

There is widespread agreement in both academic and popular reports that the pace of experimentation with innovative workplace practices has accelerated in recent years in the industrialized economies (Marchington *et al.*, 1993; Appelbaum and Batt, 1994; Osterman, 1994; Freeman and Rogers, 1995; Lawler III *et al.*, 1995; Harley, 1999). However, the notion that new work systems are emerging, in which workers have greater discretion over the work process, is a matter of considerable controversy. What some see as an acceleration in the adoption of fundamental changes in work organization is viewed by others as a deliberate effort by management to intensify the work process or, more benignly, as merely a quickening of the pace of management fads and fashions (Barley and Kunda, 1992; Ramsay, 1996). Yet, despite the tendency by corporate executives to favour quick and low-cost solutions, many organizations have embarked in the last decade on costly and difficult changes in how work is organized and managed.

A parallel development during this period has been a heightened emphasis in many firms on maximizing shareholder value, often at the expense of other company goals. This has led corporate headquarters to turn plants or work sites into profit centres that are evaluated primarily on their contribution to corporate share performance. This emphasis on short-term profits threatens to derail the slow, difficult and resource-intensive task of fundamental restructuring of work systems to enhance performance. It favours instead cost-cutting measures that yield more immediate improvements in the bottom line, whatever their ultimate effect on morale or competitiveness (Appelbaum and Berg, 1996). Attempts by some firms to combine outsourcing and downsizing with the introduction of high performance practices have demoralized workers and fueled cynicism about management's intentions.

While the process of change faces obstacles and is impeded by a narrow focus on short-term profits, both theory and evidence support the view that firms in a wide range of industries in industrialized, and even some industrializing, countries have begun to implement a new, more participatory, organization of work. These more participatory work systems are often referred to as high performance work systems (HPWS), where it is understood that the practices are adopted in order to foster high performance, but that it is an empirical question whether they in fact succeed in this aim.

What Is a High Performance Work System?

High performance work systems are characterized by three components – (1) a work organization that provides employees with the opportunity to participate in decisions, and human resource practices that (2) increase workforce skills and (3) create incentives for workers to participate effectively. Firms adopt these workplace practices to improve operational performance at the plant or work site. Unlike past attempts to humanize work or improve the quality of work life, these practices are not designed with the goal of increasing worker control or autonomy or job satisfaction. Whether these practices result in such worker outcomes is an empirical question, but achieving these outcomes is not management's primary motive.

Work Organization

Organizing the work process so that non-managerial employees have the opportunity to contribute discretionary effort is the central feature of a high performance work system (HPWS). High performance work systems decentralize the gathering and processing of information to non-managerial employees, who then use this information to solve problems and make operational decisions. To contribute to operational performance, front-line workers need to have the authority to solve problems and influence changes in organizational routines. The precise venues in which front-line workers gather information, process it, and act on it vary between different organizations. This may account for the fact that no dominant combination of practices characteristic of an HPWS has emerged, and it may explain the emergence of different HPWS models. To be effective in improving performance, however, workers need to have the responsibility, authority and opportunity to solve problems and make decisions that affect work processes. High performance work systems are rarely about worker empowerment, despite the hyperbole surrounding these workplace practices in the business press, but they are about sharing power on the shop floor.

The scope for decision making by workers in an HPWS would be limited if non-managerial employees lacked opportunities to communicate and co-ordinate their ideas with workers, managers, and experts in their work groups and in other parts of the organization. Workers with problem-solving and decision-making responsibilities need to be able to call on the expertise of professionals or other specialists in addressing problems they identify, and to communicate proposed solutions to other workers and managers. This type of communication is another important dimension of an HPWS. Co-ordination and communication among employees in an HPWS, including front-line workers, replace many of the hierarchical interactions that occur in a traditional work organization. This contrasts sharply with Taylorist work organization, which, as Aoki (1988, p. 16) observed, minimizes the need for such communication.

Communication, autonomy, problem solving and decision making by front-line workers can exist within a variety of organizational settings, but many managers believe that they are enhanced when they are embedded within groups or teams. Thus, self-directed work teams, which are involved directly in the production process, as well as 'off-line' problem-solving or quality improvement teams not directly involved with production, are often elements of an HPWS.

Thus a more participatory organization of work, in which employees have the opportunity to participate in substantive decisions, is typically character-ized by four dimensions that distinguish it from a more traditional, Taylorist organization of work. They are: (1) the extent of worker autonomy and control over decisions affecting work tasks; (2) the extent of communication that front-line workers have with other workers and managers in their work group and with workers, managers and experts in other parts of the organization; (3) the extent to which employees work in self-directed teams; and (4) the extent to which employees participate in problem-solving or quality improvement teams. These dimensions can be used to characterize where a particular establishment falls on a continuum from highly participatory to highly traditional forms of work organization.

Workforce Skills

Even if employees have the opportunity to use their initiative, creativity, and knowledge in the interest of the organization, their efforts will only be effective if they have the appropriate skills and knowledge. Workers who have only a concrete knowledge of their jobs, who are only expected to carry out routine functions, and who know little of the broader objectives of the organization are not in a strong position to make a contribution beyond the performance of their assigned tasks. Workers in an HPWS need better skills and knowledge across a broad front – including basic skills, technical and occupationally specific skills, and leadership and social skills – in order to be effective decision makers.

Staffing practices and more rigorous selection and recruitment procedures can enable a business to obtain employees with the appropriate knowledge, skills and abilities to function effectively in a HPWS. Selective staffing is generally expected to lead to a better-educated or more proficient work force. Training is also likely to play an important function in a high performance work system. Firms can increase workforce skills by increasing the amount of formal training or structured on-the-job training in technical skills, problem-solving skills, and team-building skills.

Selective recruitment and training are often complementary practices since additional training is less expensive and more effective when workers are already well-prepared. Typically, high performance plants are more selective in hiring and provide more training to workers. Training and selection can be substitutes, however, if an employer is willing to pay wages high enough to recruit workers with the skills it requires or to attract experienced workers from other firms.

The effective deployment of both off-line and self-directed work teams associated with an HPWS requires firms and workers to invest in firm-specific worker skills. Firm-specific skill requirements increase because firms share business and financial information with employees and because front-line workers are expected to be knowledgeable about the firm's products and markets. Workers are also expected to develop the ability to meet with customers and to be sufficiently knowledgeable about how the organization operates to help solve customer problems. Workers need to have a deep understanding of their own organization and of the customers' needs.

The same is true if workers are to address shop floor problems effectively. The team-building, problem-solving and decision-making activities they undertake, as well as their co-ordination and communication with co-workers, must be carried out in a manner consistent with the organization's corporate culture. In addition, team members must be able to carry out supervisory tasks, such as assigning tasks and dealing with absences, and do routine maintenance tasks. Of course, some of these skills have general as well as firm-specific characteristics.

Workers in self-directed production teams are also required to increase their technical skills in order to perform multiple tasks, carry out statistical process control, and do quality inspections. These skills may be specific to a firm and investments in them may increase the 'asset specificity' of workers' human capital – that is, the extent to which their knowledge and skills are valuable in the employing firm and the degree of difficulty they have in transferring these skills to other settings. Workers need incentives and motivation to make these investments in firm-specific skills as well as to contribute discretionary effort to the production process.

Incentives

The purpose of work reform and participation is to elicit effort from employees that cannot easily be monitored. How can an organization provide incentives to motivate employees to use their imagination, creativity, enthusiasm, and intimate knowledge of their particular jobs for the benefit of the organization? Firms can provide three main types of incentives to encourage workers to expend discretionary effort – financial or extrinsic rewards, intrinsic rewards, and a long-term stake in the company.

Incentives are usually construed – perhaps too narrowly – as pay practices adopted by management to align the interests of workers with those of the company. In an HPWS, this is often sought by making pay contingent on work group or company performance. Indeed, during the last several decades, firms have tried a wide variety of ESOPs (employees stock ownership plans), profit sharing, gain sharing, merit pay, and other compensation policies that in one way or another give workers a financial stake in the success of the company. The problem with these schemes is that they are subject to externalities – rational individual workers have no incentive to change their behaviour if their individual contribution has no discernible effect on the overall profit. This free-rider effect undermines the motivational effects of such pay schemes. Furthermore, profits depend on many factors besides worker productivity and effort. Firms with exemplary productivity can fail if they do not sell their output, and hard-working dedicated workers will not be productive if they must work with outmoded equipment. Should the incomes of lower level workers be at risk as a result of factors over which they have no control?

Individual piece rates and commissions tie compensation directly to individual output and are still widely used. On the other hand, piece rates tend to encourage quantity over quality and they create individual interests that may conflict with the broader objectives of the team or organization.

These arguments logically favour gainsharing or group incentives (such as team-based piece rates), which reward workers for tangible improvements that result from identifiable efforts of a relatively small group of workers. The norms and peer pressure inherent in small group dynamics may counteract the externality problems (Kandel and Lazear, 1992).

Incentives for high performance work organization are not necessarily limited to financial rewards. Indeed, a search for intrinsic job rewards from work that is meaningful and challenging was the foundation of most work reform efforts from the 1930s through the 1970s. The notion that workers will be more productive if they are challenged in their work has exercised a powerful grip on this field. High performance systems generally increase the intrinsic rewards of work, and thereby enhance worker satisfaction and commitment.

Many scholars and practitioners believe that discretionary effort is far more likely to be forthcoming when 'employees have a vested interest in the long term performance of the organization and the expectation that they will benefit from their long term perspective' (Doty and Delery, 1997, p. 38). Workers are more likely to make the necessary investments in skill attainment, to expend the additional effort to gather and share information, and to participate in decision making when their claims to be stakeholders in the enterprise are recognized by the firm and when they have a reasonable expectation of employment security. In this context, profit sharing, quality incentives, and other forms of pay-for-performance may be understood, as they are for managers, as recognition by the company of the worker's stake in the firm. For workers, investments in skills are costly in terms of the effort, time and resources necessary to acquire them; and the payoffs to these investments can only be realized in a long-term employment relationship. Thus, incentive pay practices can be effective in motivating employees to supply appropriate levels of discretionary effort when they are implemented along with other HRM practices intended to increase *mutual* trust and commitment. Indeed the importance of trust has been a staple of the work reform literature for many years.

EILEEN APPELBAUM

Employee Outcomes and High Performance Work Systems

The demands on front-line employees in high performance work systems extend far beyond performing their assigned tasks and can encompass responsibility for the operational performance of the establishment where they are employed. Workers may experience this as an increase in stress or as greater intrinsic rewards from the job. The outcome for workers depends on a variety of factors. These include the nature of technology and the production process, the level of trust and mutual commitment among workers and managers in the workplace, whether workers have the training to be effective in their new roles, whether their pay rises commensurately with their additional responsibilities, whether their jobs are secure, and so on.

Indeed, outcomes for workers may well be mixed. There are often complementarities among the workplace practices adopted by firms, in the economist's sense of that term. That is, two practices are complementary if doing more of one of them reduces the cost or increases the return to doing more of the other. For example, raising the educational criteria for hiring new workers reduces the cost of training workers. This provides firms with an incentive to introduce the two practices together. The existence of such complementarities implies that firms should implement bundles of workplace practices simultaneously. It may very well be that some of these practices will have contradictory effects on outcomes, such as stress or job satisfaction, that are important to workers.

Overview of the Chapter

This chapter addresses three issues associated with the diffusion of high performance work systems. First, what is 'new' about these work systems? Second, what are some of the contradictory effects that the case study literature suggests these workplace practices may have on workers? And third, what can we learn from recent surveys of workers about how they are affected by new work organization and human resource practices?

The next part examines what is 'new' about the current wave of diffusion of new work systems. Certainly, the work organization and human resource practices characteristic of an HPWS have a long history or obvious antecedents. Briefly, the argument I develop is that earlier rounds of experimentation with job enrichment, employee involvement and joint labour–management efforts were driven by management's attempts to address worker alienation, dissatisfaction and unrest. In contrast, the current round of workplace reform is the result of management's urgent need to reorganize the production process in order to meet world-class performance standards for variety, customization, quality and delivery times.

One result is that the focus of employers has been almost entirely on improving plant, business unit or work site performance. Not surprisingly, very little management attention has been directed to the effects of changes in the organization of work on workers. With plant performance, rather than employee motivation, as the rationale behind the transformations underway in key sectors of the economy, most recent research has tended to neglect workers' views of the changes. Yet it is entirely possible that jobs that have been restructured to meet management-defined changes in the requirements of organizations will have a negative effect on the incumbents who hold these jobs. Certainly, the suspicion persists among more sceptical observers of management practice and the labour process that managers are adopting more sophisticated workplace practices in order to obscure the interests of workers or promote their own careers, and are achieving any performance gains through an intensification of work. Conversely, sociologists and organizational psychologists note that many of the workplace changes can be expected to increase the intrinsic rewards from work and may, therefore, increase job satisfaction.

The observation that workplace change in the last two decades has been employer driven and that multiple practices with potentially divergent effects on workers tend to be adopted at the same time suggests that outcomes for workers may be equivocal. Certainly, the case study literature suggests that changes in work systems have diverse, and sometimes negative, impacts on workers.

In the following part, I examine four tensions, or paradoxes, with respect to the effects of high performance work systems on workers that are suggested by recent case studies. Workers may experience (1) an increase in discretion regarding work methods and task assignments, but a decrease in control over the pace or amount of work; (2) an increase in both the intrinsic rewards from work and in stress; (3) an emphasis by managers on increasing the organizational commitment of workers to the neglect, and possibly to the detriment, of job satisfaction; (4) a greater marginalization of unions or an increase in their effectiveness.

The final part reviews recent empirical studies that report workers' experiences with HPWS practices. The emphasis on recent studies reflects our view that changes in work organization during the last decade largely reflect very different motives on the part of managers than earlier workplace reforms. The studies reviewed report on large-scale surveys of workers, on case studies that include surveys of employees at the work site, or on meta-analysis of ethnographic or case studies. Thus the emphasis is on studies in which workers, whose expectations regarding changes in work organization may be more pragmatic than those of either managers or researchers, have the opportunity to report their views of their own experiences. For the most part, the outcomes about which workers care most – wages and employment security – have not been studied. In addition, very few studies examine directly how the clusters of practices associated with new forms of work systems are experienced by front-line workers. There has, however, been some important empirical analysis of workers' experiences with particular practices associated with HPWS in a number of industrialized economies. I examine these studies for insights into the tensions described above.

Workplace Reform: Is It Different This Time?

Attempts to reform workplace practices and make work more meaningful and less alienating for workers are almost as old as the mass production technologies and the routinized jobs associated with the Taylorist work system itself. The history of academic research and company practice relating to work reform and employee participation dates back to the late 1920s. In the earliest period, reformers and managers argued that it was deficiencies in workers and the social needs and personal problems that workers brought to the job that prevented the full utilization of human resources and improved organizational performance. The human relations movement proposed that companies adopt a paternalistic approach to employees, counselling them on personal problems and manipulating workers' desires to work co-operatively in small groups to encourage them to work harder. There was little opportunity for workers to engage in problem solving or to make decisions. Moreover, management interest in work reform was sometimes based on a desire to discourage unionization. While the ideas of the human relations movement had a strong effect on managerial ideology, they never became rooted in managerial practices and, by the 1950s, this type of work reform had died out.

Beginning in the 1950s in the UK, Norway, the USA and elsewhere, the focus shifted from the deficiencies of workers to problems with the design of work. While the motivational potential of small work groups continued to be an important component, research and practitioners focused on the link between the design of work and production technology. Influential research by the Tavistock Institute in England emphasized the need to co-ordinate the social needs of the workforce for integrated jobs that allowed them to use their capacities and skills with the technological demands of the production process. This was the socio-technical systems (or group relations) approach. Some reformers emphasized job characteristics and argued that jobs could be redesigned to motivate workers by promoting self-actualization and by making work more satisfying, interesting, and fulfilling. Work humanization in Europe, and Quality of Work Life programmes in the USA were introduced in this period. More motivated workers, it was assumed, would be more productive and would raise organizational performance. Others emphasized a reorganization of work that increased the participation of workers through autonomous work teams and that conformed to the technological requirements of the production system. Workers in such a work system were also expected to be more highly motivated, but the performance gains were expected to come from a better alignment of the work system and the technology and the greater responsibility of workers. During the late 1960s and 1970s, quality circles also became popular. These were off-line groups that met to solve particular problems, often having to do with quality. Quality circles were not directly integrated into the production process, but provided a means through which workers' ideas and suggestions could be incorporated into the operation of the plant or work site without requiring a fundamental reorganization of the work process.

These organizational reforms also tended to be short-lived. After an initial success, interest often waned as the agenda of easily solved problems grew smaller and meetings became less frequent. The link from worker motivation or satisfaction to organizational productivity or performance proved to be rather tenuous. The effects of these workplace reforms on organizational performance, though usually positive, tended to be modest. And, while they were often popular with workers and unions, managers tended to abandon them when business turned down.

The current wave of work reorganization, with its emphasis on the participation of front-line workers in problem-solving and decision-making activities, began in the mid-1980s and then accelerated in the 1990s. Some observers have responded with a sense of déjà vu or a discussion of management fads. Indeed, not everyone is convinced that something new is happening. Critics see the Fordist model of mass production technology and Taylorist work organization being replaced by an even more oppressive neo-Fordist production system (Barker, 1993; Parker and Slaughter, 1993; Graham, 1995). Some argue that information technology provides managers with new powers of surveillance and enables them to intensify work effort, creating stress for workers (Sewell and Wilkinson, 1992; Sewell, 1998; Knights and McCabe, 1998a, b). In this view, managers are simply giving workers token amounts of participation and responsibility in order to manipulate them into accepting an intensification of work. Nothing much has changed – old ideas have simply been 'rebranded' by management gurus, consultants and business school professors are being recycled (Harley *et al.*, 1999).

Earlier waves of experimentation with more participatory work systems were abandoned because managers felt that the weak effects of improved job satisfaction or commitment on productivity and performance did not justify the company's investments in training and time spent in meetings or in problem-solving activities. Will that happen again? Is this just the latest wave of workplace reform, destined to ebb rather than grow in importance over time? Two considerations suggest that the answer may be 'no'. First, many analysts argue that effective implementation of more participatory work systems require broader organizational changes and co-ordinated changes in human resource policies. Second, earlier waves of workplace reform occurred during a period when mass production technologies and Taylorist work organization were in their ascendancy, yielding dramatic increases in productivity in various goods-producing industries, especially for companies that produced long runs of standardized products for a mass market. The development of information and computer technologies has altered the logic of production and the nature of competition in a variety of goods- and service-producing companies.

Researchers in a wide range of disciplines – economics, industrial relations, human resource management, strategic management – have emphasized the importance of embedding work organization changes that increase employee participation in changes in a broader system of complementary workplace practices (Katz *et al.*, 1985; Kochan *et al.*, 1986; Kochan *et al.*, 1989; Cutcher-Gershenfeld, 1991; Arthur, 1992; Holmstrom and Milgrom, 1994; Huselid, 1995; MacDuffie, 1995b; Milgrom and Roberts, 1995; Becker and Gerhart, 1996; Delery *et al.*, 1997). They have also emphasized the importance of relating changes in work organization to the company's efforts to solve real business problems, such as improvements in on-time delivery, reductions in product development cycles, better customer service, and so on. Theoretical considerations suggest that there may be synergies among the work organization and human resource practices that make up a high performance work system, with the greatest gains in plant or establishment performance occurring when plants adopt clusters of complementary practices. Thus, in contrast to earlier waves of work reform, the adoption of coherent systems of workplace practices may enhance the potential for productivity and performance improvements.

The logic of the argument that firms that adopt a coherent set of workplace practices should have superior performance is compelling. Empirical research on the effects of systems of workplace practices on performance is rather recent, however, and there are still only a few studies of this relationship. These studies (most notably MacDuffie, 1995a; Pil and MacDuffie, 1996; Delery *et al.*, 1997; Ichniowski *et al.*, 1997; Becker and Huselid, 1998a, b; Appelbaum *et al.*, 2000) do find evidence of complementarities. These studies suggest that bundles, systems, or configurations of internally coherent practices can be identified, and that such systems of practices have a greater effect on establishment performance than do individual practices.

The second reason for suspecting that this period of workplace reform and increased employee participation may be different than earlier rounds is that participation can increase performance only under certain technological and market conditions. If tasks are uniform and stable, and if there are well-known solutions to problems that arise, then a traditional, routinized and hierarchical work organization would be most effective. But if tasks vary frequently because of changing products or production technologies and increased product variety, then more participatory work systems may be more appropriate. In the last decade, information and computer technologies have had a profound effect on the standards of competition in many industries, increasing the premium for quality, timeliness, and customization. These changes in the competitive environment have led managers in many establishments to rethink the role of workers in the production process and have led to the implementation of more participatory work systems. These conditions contrast sharply with the market environment that characterized the earlier decades of the twentieth century.

Thus the novelty in the current round of work reform and implementation of more participatory work systems is twofold: first, firms are adopting *clusters* of work organization and human resource practices; second, the managers who adopt these practices are motivated by an urgent need to improve firm performance in order to maintain revenues and profits. This contrasts sharply with previous rounds of workplace reform earlier in this past century, which were primarily intended to address (and defuse) worker alienation and dissatisfaction with work as well as the increased militancy of unions. Mass production technologies and Taylorist work organization – sometimes referred to as the Fordist production model – were still able to deliver rising wages and profits, and firms often found that the benefits of organizational transformation did not repay the costs. This equation appears to have changed in industries affected by computer and information technologies, where firms now compete on the basis of product variety, customization, strict conformance to quality specifications, and on-time delivery.

Four Tensions: The Potential for Contradictory Effects on Workers

The potential for contradictory effects on workers arises from two sources. First, high performance work systems are adopted today in order to meet the needs of management without much concern for the needs of workers. It is entirely possible, therefore, that workers' needs are not being met. Moreover, in the view of some observers, the effects of high performance work systems on workers are actually pernicious – a means of manipulating workers into collaborating in the intensification of work and accepting an increase in stress. Second, the tendency for firms to introduce clusters of complementary practices without specific regard for the effects of these practices on workers may result in these diverse practices having contradictory effects on workers. A review of the case study literature suggests four such potential tensions.

First, high performance workplace practices generally increase worker autonomy over and involvement in methods of work and task assignments. However, this increase in discretion over the assignment of tasks and methods of work may occur in tandem with a loss of control over the pace of work as inventory buffers are reduced between workers or between stages of the production process. Klein (1991) found that the adoption of just-in-time inventory practices and the elimination of buffers reduced workers' control over the pace of work and scheduling of breaks in some (but not all) settings. This is especially true in the case of team production, where performance gains are expected to result from the increased autonomy of the work group and worker regulation and co-ordination of the work process. The redesign of jobs in relation to team-based production (Appelbaum and Berg, 1997) increases worker discretion over the work process – how much say they have over what happens in their jobs, whether they take part in discussions about decisions that affect their jobs, and how much influence they have in deciding methods of work and tasks. Jobs are more integrated, and work teams tend to have responsibility for relatively complete parts of the production process. However, worker control over the pace of work may be reduced. Elimination of inventory buffers between departments in the auto industry appears to have had this effect (Parker and Slaughter, 1988; Berggren, 1993a; Lewchuk and Robertson, 1996). Workers' job discretion may also be limited if teams serve to increase conflict among workers or as a social control mechanism rather than as a means of increasing worker autonomy (Barker, 1993; Graham, 1995; Vallas, 1999).

The second tension, closely related to the first, is that workers in restructured workplaces report both higher levels of intrinsic rewards from work and, at the same time, higher levels of stress and anxiety than do those in traditionally organized jobs. Workers in a HPWS have increased autonomy and control over the work process, and work teams have greater authority to deal with quality issues and greater responsibility for problem solving than do traditional groups of workers. As a result, workers in these work systems often find that their work is more challenging, requires them to be more creative, and makes greater use of their skills. They frequently have more training as well. Thus they tend to report far higher levels of intrinsic rewards from their jobs than do other workers. However, there is some evidence that these workers also experience higher levels of job-related stress (Turnbull, 1988; Dawson and Webb, 1989; Appelbaum *et al.*, 1994). To the extent that workloads have increased as a consequence of work restructuring, and where the elimination of buffers means that workers are required to maintain an excessively fast pace of work, the increase in the intensity of work results in higher levels of stress (Parker and Slaughter, 1988; Elger, 1990; Berggren, 1993a). Berggren (1993a) examined Japanese auto transplants in the USA and argued that performance gains in these plants were the result of an intensification of work. Specifically, he pointed to management's relentless performance demands; substitution of long working hours and mandatory overtime on short notice for work-in-process inventories; recurrent health and safety problems, despite an emphasis on safety and avoiding accidents, as a result of the intense pace of work; and strict conduct, attendance, and discipline codes. Berggren remarked on the contradictory character of the work experience in these plants, where workers support quality circle activities and appreciate the social qualities of the team concept, but also see teams as a way to get workers to pressure each other to work harder. Self-directed work teams may also find they have been assigned supervisory or maintenance responsibilities without having been given the time or resources to carry them out, with a resulting increase in the intensity of work and in job-related stress.

In part, however, higher stress may be related to the greater responsibility for identifying and solving production problems – the same challenges that make work less routine and increase the intrinsic rewards from work. In a case study of the Scottish division of a multinational electronics firm, Dawson and Webb (1989) found that '[t]he stresses of such a system are not to do with direct pressure for production volume, but those resulting from the responsibility for solving production faults, while watching the 'daily rate' production targets slip further behind' (Dawson and Webb, 1989, p. 230). There is also a paradoxical pressure concerning the appearance of 'not working' while engaged in such attempts to fix the process. The extra stress, they suggest, may result from the fact that 'employees are not merely encouraged but *expected* to identify process problems, intervene in production to rectify them and suggest changes in the organization of production to prevent their occurrence' (*ibid*, p. 236).

The third tension, closely related to the first two, is related to the motives of managers in introducing HPWSs. As managers adopt changes in work organization in order to improve performance, they frequently introduce practices intended to increase the organizational commitment of their employees. Performance gains from new work systems depend on the willingness of workers to use their imagination, creativity and knowledge for the benefit of the organization (Bailey and Merritt, 1992). This type of work effort cannot easily be specified in a job description or elicited through monitoring and close supervision. Managers try to motivate such behaviour by adopting human resource policies expected to lead employees to identify with the organization and to accept its goals as their own. They promote a unitary view of the firm in order to motivate discretionary effort by workers on the organization's behalf. As Lincoln and Kalleberg observe:

> When an organization finds the means to elicit the commitment of its members, it has at its disposal a very powerful mechanism of control. Indeed, the new interest in organizational commitment as an employee work orientation appears to stem from the realization that the problem of control in organizations is in large measure solved when the commitment of its members is high. (Lincoln and Kalleberg, 1990, p. 23)

Whereas organizational commitment measures the worker's identification with an organization and acceptance of its goals and values, job satisfaction is an indicator of the worker's perception of the quality of his or her work experience. As early as the 1930s, researchers associated with the human relations movement in the USA were criticizing the narrow jobs that characterized Taylorist work organization on the grounds that workers have psychological needs that are not met by fragmented and routinized jobs. Herzberg (1962) concluded that jobs with more variety and complexity improve job satisfaction. This straightforward relationship between job satisfaction and job attributes gave way to a more complex model of job satisfaction (Hackman and Lawler, 1971; Hackman and Oldham, 1975;

Hackman and Oldham, 1976; Hackman and Oldham, 1980). The theory originally focused on the design of individual jobs, but was later applied to work groups or tasks (Hackman, 1987). The job characteristics approach emphasizes the effects of job design on the psychology of workers. In contrast, the sociotechnical systems (STS) approach (Trist and Bamforth, 1951; Emery and Trist, 1960) focuses on optimizing the relationship between the technological requirements of particular production processes and the social needs of workers in order to improve performance. The emphasis is on the effectiveness of self-directed or autonomous work teams.

What all of these earlier efforts at work reform had in common was a line of causation that ran from more satisfied workers to increased organizational commitment to enhanced performance. Earlier efforts to reduce the alienating effects of mass production on workers emphasized job redesign that led to higher levels of both job satisfaction and organizational commitment, with the two worker attitudes being very highly correlated. Today, managers who introduce more participatory work systems emphasize incentives to motivate workers to participate in training and decision making as an important component of an HPWS. Job redesign intended to increase job satisfaction is not a consideration. As a result, the positive association between satisfaction and motivation may no longer hold. This may be particularly the case if job stress increases. Alternatively, increased worker autonomy in an HPWS may result in both higher commitment and higher satisfaction.

The final tension or paradox relates to whether high performance workplace practices marginalize unions or increase their influence with workers and managers. Management often sees the introduction of practices such as work teams, quality improvement teams, incentive pay, and information sharing as a means not only of increasing worker loyalty to the company and developing an alignment of worker and company interests, but as a means of reducing the power of unions and weakening their influence over work and shop floor practices. Much of the early resistance to the introduction of modern workplace practices by unions in countries such as the USA, the UK and Australia was a reaction to efforts by management to undermine the legitimacy and effectiveness of unions. However, union responses to work reorganization have changed in the USA in the last decade as workers' positive experiences with HPWSs have accumulated.[1] Management may view the introduction of changes in work practices as an opportunity to marginalize the union, but workers generally want their unions to engage management over the nature, extent, terms and conditions of workplace changes (Rankin, 1990). Many unions now recognize the opportunities for positive gains for their members – more training, profit sharing or higher compensation, employment security – when firms choose to compete on quality rather than cost and to rely on the capabilities of workers to succeed in this competitive strategy. High performance work systems provide the organizational infrastructure for this strategy.

Unions may also benefit organizationally from participating in the introduction of HPWSs. Managers in both union and non-union settings have discovered the difficulty of transferring responsibility, authority and accountability to front-line workers. This can be accomplished more easily when managers are able to negotiate with worker representatives over the introduction of new workplace practices – an advantage which unions can provide (Collinson *et al.*, 1996). Furthermore, managers at the plant or work-site level may lack the knowledge to introduce participatory practices. Where unions have the resources and expertise to play an active role in the process of organizational change, they often become more visible to their members. Some American unions have found that their influence, both with their members and in negotiations with management, has increased as a result. This positive effect may be more usual in the USA, where unions may be seen as participating in decisions that formerly were strictly the prerogative of management. In the UK and Australia, however, where work organization has traditionally been subject to collective bargaining, recent agreements over the implementation of employee participation and other high performance practices have sometimes reduced the union's traditional collective bargaining role to one of consultation (Geary, 1994), and may have reduced the influence of unions vis-à-vis management in the eyes of their members. These challenges to unions may be less important in other European countries, where institutional and legal structures support the rights of unions or works councils to negotiate over changes in work organization.

Evidence of Impact on Workers

While there are very few surveys that directly examine the effects of high performance work systems on workers, a number of surveys carried out in the last decade in the USA, Canada, the UK, Europe and Australia provide evidence on particular practices and their effects on workers. One exception is a recent survey of more than 4,000 employees in the steel, apparel and medical electronic instruments and imaging industries carried out by the author and her colleagues that examined many of the issues raised here (Appelbaum *et al.*, 2000). In this section, we review the survey evidence.

Worker Discretion

Evidence of an increase in worker discretion over the last decade comes mainly from the Employment in Britain survey, a nationally representative survey of employees carried out in 1992 (Gallie and White, 1993; Gallie, 1996). The study was designed to allow comparability with earlier British surveys. The survey examined the relationship between an index of task discretion[2] and worker skills, and found a strong positive correlation between task discretion and increasing skills (Gallie, 1996). It also compared responses to two questions – do you decide normal daily tasks and do you initiate new tasks on your job? – for 1984 and 1992. Professional and managerial employees scored far higher than any other workers, and only a minority of skilled or unskilled manual workers had discretion over their job tasks; but manual workers experienced the largest increases among the occupational groups in discretion over both normal and new tasks (Gallie, 1996). The survey also found that the proportion of people that had principal say over the amount and pace of work increased from 67 per cent to 77 per cent between 1984 and 1992 (Gallie and White, 1993). Workers who participated in quality circles were more likely than other workers to feel that they personally would have either a great deal or quite a lot of say over decisions, at their place of work, that changed the way they did their job (47 per cent compared with 28 per cent of those not involved in a quality circle). The survey also examined the extent of direct supervision of British workers. Overall it found that in substantially less than half the cases, including less skilled manual and service jobs, workers reported that supervisors had a great deal of influence over how hard they worked, which tasks they did, which methods they used, and the quality standards to which they worked. Roughly a third of workers reported that tight supervision had increased and a similar proportion reported that it had decreased over the previous five years.

Two US studies of workers in self-directed teams combined a case study methodology with surveys of workers (Appelbaum et al., 1994; Batt, 1995; Batt and Appelbaum, 1995). These studies provide evidence that employees who work in self-directed work teams have significantly higher levels of discretion over work than do workers in traditional work systems. A survey of sewing machine operators found that, in contrast to the bundle system where the operator's tasks were directed by a supervisor, between two-thirds and three-quarters of module operators reported that they participated in setting production goals, participated in selecting work methods, undertook routine maintenance, scheduled time away from work (vacations, absences), and got adequate time from management to meet and solve problems; 88 per cent reported that they had the authority to stop production to deal with quality problems and a similar percentage said that they met to solve production problems. There was a positive and significant association between working in a module and the extent of participation in decisions that affected the workers' jobs, the opportunity to discuss major decisions before they occurred, having a lot of say about what happened on the job, and having influence over such things as how the garment was assembled, tasks or work assignments, procedures, and quality improvement. In contrast, the extent of these practices were all negatively correlated with bundle sewing (Appelbaum *et al.*, 1994).

A survey of employees at a regional telecommunications company also found important differences in the amount of discretion that workers in self-directed teams had (Batt, 1995; Batt and Appelbaum, 1995). Self-directed teams in network craft jobs enabled installation and repair crews to take responsibility for serving customers in a geographic area. Workers in teams reported significantly more influence over tasks or work assignments, tools or procedures, and the pace or speed of work than did workers in traditionally supervised crews; and they more often had adequate authority to meet customer needs. In contrast, customer service representatives found that automatic call distribution systems and office rules constrained employee discretion in teams as well as traditional work organization. While personal influence is low for workers in both team and traditional settings, customer service representatives in teams reported significantly greater influence over tasks and work assignments, tools or procedures, and pace or speed of work (see also Drago, 1986). Batt (1995) and Batt and Strausser (1997) also found a dramatic decrease in direct supervision of self-directed teams compared with traditionally managed groups.

A recent analysis of the relationship between job discretion and a large number of high performance workplace practices, using the 1995 Australian Industrial Relations Survey and the 1998 UK Work and Employment Relations Survey, found a small but positive relationship in each data set. While the effects of the individual practices tended to be small or insignificant, the overall effect from all high performance practices together was a significant increase in discretion (Harley *et al.*, 1999).

Intrinsic Rewards

Gallie and White (1993) examined opportunities for self-development in relation to changes in skills. A third of workers who experienced a skill increase agreed strongly that their job gave them the opportunity to learn new things, and 82 per cent felt that job responsibilities had increased. Among workers whose skills were unchanged, the proportions were 13 per cent and 38 per cent, respectively. The survey found that changes at work that increased skills and responsibility offered better opportunities for self-development, but it also found that increases in skill demands and responsibility were associated with increased stress. Of those in jobs where skill demands had increased, 67 per cent reported an increase in work-related stress, compared with only 32 per cent in jobs where the skill level had remained the same.

Cordery *et al.* (1991) reported the results of a longitudinal study of the implementation of autonomous work groups (self-directed teams) among process workers at a greenfield site and at an established site of a unionized mineral processing plant in Australia. The self-directed teams had collective decision-making responsibility for daily operational decisions, and multi-skilling was built into the jobs of team members. Three groups of workers were compared – workers in self-directed work teams in the new plant, workers in self-directed work teams in the traditional plant, and other production workers in the traditional plant. Workers in self-directed teams in both settings reported higher intrinsic rewards and higher job satisfaction and job commitment than did traditionally managed workers.

In our survey of workers in three manufacturing industries, participatory work organization – measured by an index comprised of participation in self-directed work teams, off-line problem-solving teams, extent of autonomy, and communication with workers, managers and professionals outside the work group – led to higher intrinsic rewards from work. For the sample as a whole, each of the components of the participation scale raised intrinsic rewards. However, participation in a sewing team or module in the apparel sector reduced intrinsic rewards for these workers (Appelbaum *et al.*, 2000). Among telecommunications workers, network craft workers who worked in teams reported significantly higher intrinsic interest ('significance') in their jobs compared with those in traditionally supervised crews (Batt and Appelbaum, 1995).

Harley *et al.* (1999) found no relationship between their overall index of high commitment management practices and intrinsic rewards; nor did any of the components of this index, including teamworking, have an effect. However, information on the thirteen high commitment management practices that make up the overall index was obtained from interviews with managers, whereas the report of the extent of intrinsic rewards from work came from the employee survey. As a result, it is not possible to relate the intrinsic rewards from work reported by a worker to whether that worker participated in a team, making these results difficult to interpret.

Hodson (1996) examined the relationship between work organization and workers' efforts to attain dignity and self-realization. These are difficult outcomes to measure in a worker survey because what he terms 'workers' strategies of autonomous activity' are situationally specific. Hodson used a meta-study of 108 workplace ethnographies to distinguish five forms of workplace organization – craft control, direct supervision, assembly line, bureaucratic control and worker participation. Work organization has a U-shaped or, more precisely, a backward J-shaped effect on job satisfaction, pride and insider knowledge – all of which, he argued, make work meaningful and lend it dignity. The effect on each of these variables was positive and significant for craft control, turned negative for direct supervision, assembly line, and bureaucratic work organization, and then turned positive and significant again for worker participation. The effect of work organization on the effort bargain also follows the same U-shaped pattern; however, only worker participation has a significant effect on work effort. Hodson concluded that workers appear to work harder in participative organizations of work but also experience greater pride and job satisfaction and possess greater insider knowledge.

Pace of Work and Stress

A large number of case studies contend that management's aim in introducing teams and other participatory practices is to increase its ability to monitor and discipline the workforce. These studies argue that management successfully uses teams to shift at least some surveillance from managers to co-workers, and achieves performance gains through the application of peer pressure as teams create and enforce group norms that lead to work intensification. An analysis of 90 ethnographic case studies found that team organization of work increased group discipline (Hodson et al., 1994).

Empirical support for the view that lean production results in an intensification of work can be found in a Canadian survey of union workers in the independent automotive components sector (Lewchuk and Robertson, 1996). The researchers did not use the worker survey to classify firms according to the system of work organization employed. Instead, they assigned companies to one of four work organization systems – Traditional Fordist, Lean, Change or Exploitative – based on their own assessments following interviews with labour and management and site visits at each plant.

The lean plants were generally the worst, exceeding even the exploitative plants in terms of the percentage of workers (a large majority in every case) reporting excessive work loads, increasing work loads, increase in work pace, and tying with the exploitative plants on work pace being too fast. Workers at the exploitative plants (defined as 'productivity was increased . . . by driving labour harder') were least likely to have reported having difficulty changing job features or to have reported distaste going to work at least half the time; only 20 per cent reported that it was difficult to get time off. These surprisingly positive responses from workers at firms classified as exploitative raise serious doubts about the adequacy of the authors' classification scheme. If their classification scheme is accurate, the survey results are an indictment of lean production. Workers in plants classified as lean were significantly more likely than those in traditional plants to report overly heavy workloads, too few people, too fast pace, too little time; increases in workload, physical load, work pace, and less time to do work assigned; more difficult to get time off and less free to go to the washroom; unlikely to have received training in the last three months and unlikely to keep pace until age 60. Levels of stress and health risks in lean plants were not significantly different from those in traditional plants, but some of these levels had increased significantly compared to two years earlier.

Geary (1994) suggests caution in interpreting reported increases in how hard people are working. He points out that new work organization may result in a more balanced production flow, and may reduce the pressure on less skilled workers. A reduction in equipment downtime and an improved ability to stay on schedule may reduce, rather than increase, the amount of involuntary overtime. And workers may not feel aggrieved by putting in more work effort if they feel their workplace is better managed, that their job security is improved, and that there is a financial payoff to them, as well as to the firm, for improved performance. A 1995 survey of 280 employees in six UK organizations with identifiable total quality management (TQM) programmes found that 57 per cent reported that they were working harder and that they liked doing so, while only 19 per cent were working the same or harder and disliked doing so (Collinson et al., 1996). The study found that workers subject to output targets and those who are most aware of the monitoring of their work were most likely to be favourable towards quality initiatives and to express trust in management.

However, the Employment in Britain Survey suggests that these findings may not be generalizable and may be too sanguine (Gallie and White, 1993). In the national sample, those employees who experienced markedly higher levels of work effort experienced the highest stress levels. The survey found that 72 per cent of those in jobs where work effort levels had increased also felt higher stress levels. This was true of only 26 per cent of those in jobs where work demands were largely unchanged and of only 20 per cent of those in jobs where they had decreased.

Our survey of workers in three manufacturing industries specifically examined the relationship between more participatory work systems and work intensification or stress (Appelbaum *et al.*, 2000). Workers were asked how often they had too much work to do or too many different demands on their time. They were also asked about involuntary overtime and conflict with co-workers. The survey found no relationship between speed-up and the extent to which the work system was participatory. Moreover, it found that workers in more participatory settings were less likely to be required to work overtime involuntarily and were less likely to experience conflict with co-workers. In general, more participatory work systems had no effect on overall job stress, with the exception that for workers in the steel and medical sectors, increased communication with workers, managers and professionals outside their work group raised job stress slightly.

Organizational Commitment and Job Satisfaction

Lincoln and Kalleberg's (1990) landmark study of job satisfaction and organizational commitment in the USA and Japan, based on a survey of manufacturing workers in the early 1980s, examined the effects of workplace practices in 'commitment-maximizing' organizations, on organizational commitment and job satisfaction. The study found that participation in a quality circle (QC) significantly increased organizational commitment and job satisfaction for both US and Japanese workers. Even after adding task characteristics to the model, participation in a QC continued to have a significant positive effect on organizational commitment and job satisfaction for both samples of workers. In addition, job complexity, teamwork and autonomy also had significant positive effects on both of these worker attitudes in the two countries, with the exception that teamwork did not affect the job satisfaction of US workers.[3] In the full model, which included social bonds among workers and intrinsic and extrinsic rewards from work, autonomy and QCs continued to have a significant positive effect on commitment and satisfaction for US workers. For Japanese workers, QCs were no longer significant and, net of the effects of the other variables, teamwork then had a significant negative effect on job satisfaction. Autonomy, however, continued to have a significant positive effect. Thus, this study found strong effects of both substantive participation (teamwork, autonomy) and consultative participation (QCs) on job satisfaction and organizational commitment.

Most subsequent studies have found that substantive participation in decisions through self-directed work teams with high levels of group autonomy has a stronger effect on worker attitudes than do consultative participation through quality circles or other parallel or off-line teams. In a review of studies of different forms of employee involvement, Cotton *et al.* (1988) concluded that self-directed work teams generally produce improvements in both productivity and employee attitudes whereas, overall, quality circles have little effect on either. In a review of empirical studies between 1990 and 1996, Cohen and Bailey (1997) also concluded that substantive participation was a better predictor of outcomes than was consultative participation, and that autonomy was associated with higher job satisfaction.

But these conclusions with respect to the effects of substantive participation on worker attitudes appear to be overly optimistic and to be influenced by the positive effects on job satisfaction and commitment found in studies carried out in the 1960s and 1970s. Studies of more recent 'natural' or 'quasi' experiments that occur when self-directed teams are compared with employees still in traditional work settings suggest that the effects of substantive participation on job satisfaction, while generally positive, are more mixed. Substantive participation often has no effect on organizational commitment, and positive effects appear to diminish over time.

A longitudinal study over three years of the implementation of autonomous work groups at several sites of a non-union British confectionery manufacturer found a substantial positive and lasting effect of work design and autonomy on job satisfaction (Kemp *et al.*, 1983; Wall *et al.*, 1986). However, the study did not find a positive effect on organizational commitment, and voluntary labour turnover increased with the introduction of autonomous work groups. Similarly, in the longitudinal study of work groups in unionized mineral processing plants in Australia, Cordery *et al.* (1991) found that workers in autonomous work groups in both the greenfield and established plants were significantly higher on measures of both job satisfaction and organizational commitment, although there was a drop-off over time in the levels of organizational commitment.

Ondrack and Evans (1987) compared survey responses of Canadian petrochemical workers employed in greenfield plants that used self-directed work teams, in older plants that had been converted to teams, and in traditionally organized plants. They found no significant differences in job satisfaction between the self-directed teams and traditional work organization. Batt and Appelbaum (1995) also found that working in a self-directed team had no effect on job satisfaction for any of their groups of workers. With respect to organizational commitment, self-directed team had no effect for either group of telecommunications workers; while for apparel workers, working in a self-directed team had a significant negative effect.

Griffin (1991) investigated the long-term effects of an overall work redesign (along the five dimensions suggested by Hackman and Oldham, 1980) on job satisfaction, organizational commitment, and performance of bank tellers at banks located in seven US metropolitan areas. The work redesign took place in conjunction with the implementation of an on-line computer network. Griffin's results suggest that changes in job design initially increase job satisfaction and organizational commitment, but that these effects tend to dissipate over time. Performance effects, in contrast, take much longer to occur but tend to persist.

Many studies of self-directed work teams, in both manufacturing and services, have found a positive relationship between autonomy and satisfaction (Cordery et al., 1991; Pearson, 1992; Cohen and Ledford, 1994; Batt and Appelbaum, 1995; Seers et al., 1995; Cohen et al., 1996; Appelbaum et al., 2000).

There have been very few empirical studies of quality circles or other off-line teams (Steel and Shane, 1986). Generally such studies find that consultative participation has little or no effect on job satisfaction or organizational commitment. Thus, studies cited in a review by Ledford et al. (1988) found that quality circles had no effect on job satisfaction. Batt and Appelbaum (1995) found that off-line teams had no effect on job satisfaction or organizational commitment for apparel or telecommunications workers. Steel et al. (1990) compared responses of participants and nonparticipants in quality circles at a US mint over a 14-month period and found that participation had no effect on job satisfaction. Two studies found that quality circles 'buffer' disruptions within organizations so that QC members experience less deterioration in job satisfaction (Mohrman and Novelli, 1985; Marks et al., 1986). However, in a longitudinal study of the effects of quality circles, Adams (1991) found that job satisfaction declined over time both for workers who participated and those who did not, and that there were no significant attitudinal differences between the two groups. Griffin (1988) found that participation in quality circles increased job satisfaction and organizational commitment 18 months after implementation, but this effect disappeared by 36 months. Other studies (Mohrman and Novelli, 1985; Head et al., 1986) have found that attitudes of former quality circle members are not better, and may sometimes be worse, than those of nonparticipants.

One study of organizational commitment examined the effects of *individual* influence and participation (Cappelli and Rogovsky, 1994). Using path analysis, the authors found a direct relationship between influence on the work process and organizational commitment that did not operate through job characteristics. They also found that several of the job characteristics, including autonomy, had a positive effect on organizational commitment.

In our study of workers in three manufacturing industries (Appelbaum *et al.*, 2000), the survey found that the opportunity to participate scale had a positive effect on job satisfaction for steel workers only, and no effect for workers in the other two industries. The positive effect was due to the effect of increased autonomy on satisfaction for these workers. Organizational commitment was also higher for steel workers in more participatory work systems, again because of the effect of autonomy. For apparel workers, participation in a sewing team reduced both job satisfaction and organizational commitment.

Thus, except for the positive effects of autonomy on job satisfaction, the link between substantive participation in self-directed teams and work attitudes appears weak; and most studies find that consultative participation in quality circles and other off-line teams have no effect on either job satisfaction or organizational commitment. However, self-directed teams generally have positive performance impacts (see studies reviewed in Cohen and Bailey, 1997). This result provides support for the main argument of sociotechnical theory – that it is the work team's capacity to make on-line decisions and on-going improvements in the process that leads to the improved performance of the team. For workers, the main benefits are greater autonomy and intrinsic rewards.

Strengthen or Weaken Unions

Management's use of practices such as employee involvement, information sharing and profit sharing to create a more co-operative industrial relations climate raises the question of whether these efforts to build organizational commitment undermine workers' attitudes towards unions. Several studies have examined whether unionized workers can be simultaneously committed to both their employer and their union. Studies of US and Canadian workers have consistently found evidence of dual commitment – i.e. a high correlation between the commitment of workers to their company and to their union (Angle and Perry, 1986; Thacker and Rosen, 1986; Conlon and

Gallagher, 1987; Magenau *et al.*, 1988; Beauvais *et al.*, 1991). However, with the exception of a co-operative union-management relationship, organizational and union commitment are affected by different factors. Studies of dual commitment in the UK and Australia raise questions about the generalizability of these results. Guest and Dewe (1991), in a study of dual commitment among British electronics workers, did not find a strong effect of positive industrial relations on either organizational or union commitment. A study of white-collar clerical and customer service employees in a government agency in Melbourne, Australia (Deery *et al.*, 1994) found no evidence of dual commitment and, further, that workers who considered the industrial relations climate to be more positive were significantly more committed to the organization and significantly less committed to the union.

Surveys of rank and file union workers in the USA who participated in Quality of Work Life (QWL) programmes have generally found that participation either has no effect or is associated with a more positive view of the union's effectiveness and satisfaction with the union (Kochan *et al.*, 1984; Thacker and Fields, 1987; Verma, 1987). A 1987 survey of members of three different bargaining units within the same union local venue, which examined the relations between participation in a QWL programme and loyalty or commitment to the union (Eaton *et al.*, 1992), found that QWL participants were less likely than non-participants to view such programmes as a threat to the union and that participation in a QWL programme was associated with higher levels of loyalty to the union.

A 1994 US worker survey provides evidence on a related question (Freeman *et al.*, 1997). The survey examined the effect of employee involvement (EI) programmes on the attitudes of union and non-union employees towards the company and towards unionization in a random sample of private sector employees. Non-union workers were queried about their views on employee representation generally, and unions specifically. For the entire sample, 63 per cent of those who participated in an EI programme reported feeling 'a lot' of loyalty toward their company, compared with 49 per cent of those at companies with no EI programmes. Employees without unions were asked to imagine that employees chose their own representatives to meet with management and discuss problems. Compared to their current system, 60 per cent of EI participants thought this would be more effective, as did 70 per cent of those with no EI programmes. However, when asked how they would vote if a union representation election were held, only 23 per cent of EI participants, compared with 39 per cent of those with no EI programmes, said that they would vote for the union. The percentage who would have voted against the union were 67 and 47 respectively. Union members were asked to describe their personal experience with the union at their company. Among EI participants, 42 per cent responded 'very good' and 8 per cent responded 'bad' or 'very bad'. At firms with no EI programmes, the responses were 21 per cent 'very good' and 6 per cent 'bad' or 'very bad'. This suggests that participation in an EI programme increases employee loyalty to the company and, among employees in unionized companies, leads to better personal experiences with the union.

A related finding comes from a survey based on a random sample of employed persons in a Midwestern American state (Hodson *et al.*, 1993). The researchers found that employees who participate in an EI programme were more likely than other workers to express solidarity and unity with other workers, and to have greater concerns about organizational injustice. Increased job autonomy and participation were related to more, rather than less, worker solidarity.

Conclusion

Organizational change in industrial economies moves forward under the impetus of market opportunities and technological possibilities. The logic of competition in many industries has led managers to re-evaluate the role that workers can play in the work process and to adopt high performance workplace practices. Complementarities among business strategy, technological competence, and a range of modern work organization, human resource and industrial relations practices imply that market success in these industries requires the adoption of clusters of practices, or HPWSs.

Because workplace change is management driven and motivated by a need to improve plant or establishment performance, and because clusters of complementary practices tend to be introduced as a package, the impacts of HPWSs on workers may be somewhat contradictory. There are still very few surveys of workers that inquire about their experience with new work systems, so the evidence is rather thin. In addition, surveys like the Australian Workplace Industrial Relations Survey (AWIRS) or the Work and Employment Relations Survey (WERS) in the UK, although large and nationally representative, suffer from the fact that managers are asked about workplace practices whereas workers are only surveyed about their feelings and attitudes. When associations between work organization and, say, autonomy or stress are made, it is managers' characterization of work organization and the individual workers' experience with stress that are compared. It is not possible to determine whether the worker reporting stress is actually engaged in high performance practices. Surveys such as those reported by Appelbaum *et al.* (2000), which focus on particular industries and combine a worker survey with a case study methodology, are able to relate the participation of individual workers in particular workplace practices to individual perceptions of worker outcomes. The evidence of this latter study is reassuring – high performance work systems pay off for workers as well as firms. The approach suffers, however, from the fact that the sample of firms and workers in the study may not be representative, and so the results may not generalize.

It is difficult to draw definitive conclusions from the survey evidence about what HPWSs do *for* workers. The weight of the survey evidence, though by no means unanimous, suggests that they do not do much that is negative *to* them. An analysis of the 1995 AWIRS and the 1998 WERS, for example, concludes that in both Australia and the UK, benefits and disbenefits tend to be minor on balance (Harley *et al.*, 1999); while Appelbaum *et al.* (2000) find positive payoffs.

In short, the jury is still out.

Notes

* This paper was prepared as part of a larger study, chapter conducted jointly with Thomas Bailey, Peter Berg, and Arne Kalleberg, of the effects of changes in workplace, human resource, and industrial relations practices on firm performance and worker outcomes in three industries, steel, apparel, and medical electronic instruments and imaging (Appelbaum *et al.*, 2000). In particular, the description of high performance work systems and the discussion of what may be new about adoption of these practices is based on that joint work. I want to thank my colleagues, especially Arne Kalleberg, for helpful comments on an earlier draft. I also thank Stephanie Scott-Steptoe for administrative and logistical assistance, Terrel Hale for library search services and for accessing the materials used in this paper, and the Alfred P. Sloan Foundation for generous financial support.

1. Surveys suggest that union workers prefer wider job rotation and team, rather than supervisor, authority over the work process. Babson (1996) compares surveys of unionized auto workers at body and stamping facilities at a Ford Escort and a Mazda plant. Despite the nominal designation of workers at the Mazda plant as 'Team Members', Babson found no teams with decision-making authority at the plant, and a

traditional supervisory structure. In contrast, he found that the Ford Escort plant had introduced a team-based production system. A survey of workers at the Ford Escort plant found that, compared with the way things were done before the team concept, 70 per cent liked their current job better and only 18 per cent said it was worse. Overall 73 percent reported they had benefited from the team concept, while only seven per cent said they had been hurt by it. Workers at the Ford plant reported that they wanted even more control over what went on in the plant. Babson contrasts this to an internal union survey of 2,400 workers at the Mazda plant in which 73 per cent of respondents reported that their jobs had been unilaterally changed by supervisors or engineers without consultation, and 67 per cent of these reported that the changes made their jobs harder. The surveys are not directly comparable, but Babson found them consistent with his own observations. In a survey of workers at a unionized regional telecommunications company in the US, Batt and Appelbaum (1995) found that over 75 per cent of workers in traditional work groups said that they would volunteer for teams if given the opportunity. By contrast, less than 10 per cent who are now in teams said that they would like to return to traditional supervision.

2. The items in the index were: 'I have a lot of say over what happens in my job', 'My job allows me to take part in making decisions that affect my work', 'How much influence do you personally have deciding what tasks you have to do?' and 'How much influence do you personally have in deciding how you are to do the task?'

3. In this analysis, teamwork referred to whether the worker 'has to work closely with others in order to do the job well,' and not to participation in a semi-autonomous or self-directed work team. Autonomy referred to employees' discretion over work (freedom in carrying out job tasks, control over speed of work, use of their own judgement).

4 WORKPLACE INNOVATION AND THE ROLE OF INSTITUTIONS

Paul R. Bélanger, Paul-André Lapointe and Benoît Lévesque

Over the past two decades, problems of workplace productivity and alienation and growing international competition have sparked an explosion of literature on the various forms of innovation in the workplace. This research has further established a link between local innovations and national models of economic development, thus raising the question of the need for a degree of functional coherence or fit between innovation in the workplace and national models. The economic crisis of the 1980s certainly highlighted a number of institutional rigidities and stimulated the search for organizational innovations in production units. But, in the 1990s, due to what might be labelled 'institutional blockages', the diffusion of these local organizational innovations was extremely slow.

In order to understand this trend, it is necessary to place local innovations, be they organizational or institutional in nature, in their wider institutional contexts. In this chapter we argue that organizational innovations, far from being a simple matter of adjusting human and material resources, come into conflict with the collective agreement and the social roles institutionalized therein. Moreover, when these organizational and institutional structures are reciprocally adjusted at the level of the firm, local innovations often come into conflict with the macro-social institutional system and the strategies of the major social actors (employers, unions and government). In other words, the nature and evolution of the institutional system within which the firm is located, as well as the strategies of and the relationships between the major social actors, have a strong influence on the character of workplace innovation.

Drawing on the theoretical traditions of the Regulation School, the first part of the chapter sets out a theoretical framework that distinguishes between organizational and institutional structures and spaces at the macro level (the social system of production) and the micro level (the firm). The discussion ends with an examination of the crisis of Fordism and the emergence of a new productive paradigm. The second part of the chapter analyses the tensions between the firm's organizational and institutional structures. Here it is argued that organizational innovations clash with institutional rules, thereby provoking tensions and dilemmas for unions that are participating in the management of the workplace. The final part of the chapter focuses on the relationship between the firm and the social system of production. The diffusion of innovations at the micro level is constrained by the macro-social institutional framework, a framework that the social actors still do not seem to be prepared to modify. In order to illustrate the tensions between institutions and social actors, we discuss the experience of the province of Quebec in Canada.

Theoretical Framework and the Dynamics of Change

In order to develop a better understanding of the changes in production and work that have occurred over the last two decades, it is necessary to distinguish between organizational and institutional structures and between the macro- and micro-social spaces in which changes occur, an approach that highlights the numerous tensions that affect the process and type of changes. This section discusses four themes: the social system of production; the firm and its structures; the relationships between these two socio-economic spaces; and the crisis of Fordism and the dynamics of innovation.

The Social System of Production

One of the fundamental characteristics of a social system of production, as espoused by the French Regulationist school of thought, is the necessary existence of coherent and consistent relationships between the elements that make up the system, that is, the regime of accumulation, the model of work organization, the mode of regulation and the social actors.

The regime of accumulation concerns the basic elements of any production system – what to produce, how to produce and for whom to produce. It refers to the nature of goods and services produced, the mechanisms for allocating production resources among firms, the method of production and the distribution of the results of production. In other words, the regime of accumulation relates to norms of production and consumption.

The model of work organization, or 'production paradigm' (Lipietz, 1989), refers to the prevailing forms of division of labour within and between firms.

The mode of regulation refers to the set of laws, norms and routines, embodied in institutions, that ensures that the regime of accumulation is reproduced by forcing or encouraging the various actors to adopt appropriate behaviours. Hollingsworth and Boyer define these various structures as follows:

> the following institutions or structures of a country or a region are integrated into a social configuration: the industrial relations system; the system of training of workers and managers; the internal structure of corporate firms; the structured relationships among firms in the same industry on the one hand, and on the other firms' relationship with their suppliers and customers; the financial markets of a society; the conceptions of fairness and justice held by capital and labor; the structure of the state and its policies; and a society's idiosyncratic customs and traditions as well as norms, moral principles, rules, laws, and recipes for action. (Hollingsworth and Boyer, 1997, p. 2)

The mode of regulation thus includes labour laws and economic policies, and it structures the actors' behaviour and strategies. Of all of the institutions that constitute the mode of regulation, such as the education or health system, it is the capital–labour relation* that most directly relates to firms and work since it represents 'the set of juridical and institutional conditions governing the use of paid work as well as the reproduction of workers' conditions of life'. (Boyer, 1986, p. 18; our translation)

When the mode of regulation, the regime of accumulation and the model of work organization function together coherently, a model of development (or social system of production) is created. These configurations vary in time and space because social relations and social struggles play a fundamental role in their constitution and evolution. The Fordist regime of accumulation is thus characterized by the harmonious coexistence of mass production and mass consumption, while the capital–labour relation ensures that real wages increase at the same rate as productivity. For workers, wage increases represent the trade-off for their acceptance of Taylorism, thus defining the essence of the Fordist social compromise. Regulation generally functions through the collective agreement, the legitimacy and scope of which are defined by labour legislation and by the welfare state which, through a variety of support and assistance programmes, ensures the stability of workers' income.

However, the various institutions that constitute a mode of regulation, as well as the social compromise underlying them, cannot be understood without referring to the way in which they were created. In this respect, there has prevailed a strong tradition making use of either the notion of ideology, as in Dunlop (1958), or the institutionalization of values, as in Parsonsian functionalism. Far from being the expression of common values, we suggest that institutional forms are social compromises that result from the social struggles and social relations specific to each society. Thus the institutional rules of the game are established through a series of relatively detailed and elaborate compromises arising from the relations between social forces, social classes and social movements.

This was the case of the New Deal in the United States, for example. These compromises over the respective fields of action of capital and labour are legitimized by a broadly shared worldview that is defined in terms of technical, economic and social progress (Offe, 1985; Lipietz, 1989). Thus the sometimes violent social struggles over the direction of societal development are channelled into institutionalized modes of conflict resolution, thereby reducing any challenge to the model of development. This is what makes it possible to establish a degree of coherence among institutions and to define the contours of societal configurations (Maurice *et al.*, 1982) or national trajectories (Boyer, 1986; 1993; Boyer and Hollingsworth, 1997).

There is, then, a hierarchical relationship between the elements of a social system of production. Social relations generate institutional compromises, which in turn regulate behaviour at the organizational level. But these elements are not subject to the same temporality: organizations change rapidly and their forms can vary widely, whereas institutions display greater inertia. Indeed, within a particular institutional configuration, a wide range of organizational forms can be tolerated, although such diversity introduces greater instability and causes considerable tensions that can lead to a major crisis. Institutions are characterized by long-term temporality; they ensure social stability and form its hard core since the rules of the game tend to allocate power in a society. To summarize, this approach suggests the existence of a dominant model that is relatively stable over a given period of time, but which is subject to strong pressures during periods of crisis, as we will see below.

PAUL R. BÉLANGER, PAUL-ANDRÉ LAPOINTE AND BENOÎT LÉVESQUE

The Firm and its Organizational and Institutional Structures

Whereas the social system of production constitutes the macro socio-economic dimension in a given country, the firm represents the micro dimension and there is usually a degree of coherence between these two. For example, the production paradigm is generally embodied in the firm and operates to produce specific goods and services. Moreover, this production space is structured by the institutional forms of the capital–labour relation. However, the firm enjoys a relative autonomy. Not only does it adapt the dominant principles and rules, but there is also space for the emergence of new organizational principles.

In this sense, the firm can be regarded as an organization, that is, a particular correlation between technical means, human resources and production goals, bringing together different means of dividing and co-ordinating labour between a 'plurality of agents' (Coriat and Weinstein, 1995). The organization can thus be perceived as a system of action in which co-operation and agreement are only achieved through struggles over a 'fair day's work' (for example, the effort bargain; see Edwards, 1986) and in relations between employees and supervisors. However, these struggles are framed by rules derived from the social system of production, i.e. the rules of the industrial relations system governing the capital–labour relation: wage norms, standards of production and work organization, and the rights and responsibilities of workers. Other rules specify the relationships with other actors (shareholders, firms, consumers, users, local communities, etc.). This body of rules allocates power and responsibility within the firm. With the set of decision-making procedures, these rules constitute the firm's political system (Touraine, 1973), which is, in the Weberian sense, a legitimate mode of representation of interests. In brief, not only is the firm an organization, it is also an institution.

The politico-institutional system generates decisions about both the internal environment (its organizational dimension) and the external environment (for example economic and financial strategies). This duality is apparent in both the strategic action literature (for example, Kochan *et al.*, 1986) and the Regulationist School (for example, Leborgne and Lipietz, 1988). Thus, at the institutional level, the firm is defined by a dual relationship: labour relations (union–management relations) and inter-institutional relations (relationship with other firms, consumers, governments, universities and communities). In this sense, the institutional level also constitutes a system of action, a site of struggles where the principal issue is the capacity to influence the firm's decisions. Defined in this way, the politico-institutional system is more complex than what is generally suggested in the industrial relations literature. In particular, it suggests a degree of autonomy between the organizational and institutional dimensions of the firm, as each dimension has its own issues, actors, and system of action.

Just like the capital–labour relation, firms take on different forms depending on the historical period. For each period, it is possible to identify one or several dominant models of firms (or Weberian ideal-types) based on the principal regularities and routines observed in actual firms. On this basis, it is possible to conceive of a Fordist model of the firm characterized by mass production and Taylorist work organization as well as by institutional rules dominated by management prerogatives that sometimes restrict the collective agreement. In particular, the institutional system of the Fordist firm is characterized by a strict division of power: management retains the exclusive right to make strategic decisions related to the firm's economic, marketing and financial affairs, as well as decisions related to work organization, so long as it complies with negotiated work rules. The Fordist compromise rests on a double exclusion: the exclusion of employees from decisions about their own work and the exclusion of unions from the management of the firm. This division of responsibilities is quite clear: management is responsible for the economic performance and unions are limited to social concerns about the consequences of this production system.

Macro- and Micro-Social Spaces

The distinction between the organizational and institutional dimensions makes it possible to move from a societal (or macro-social) analysis to a micro-social analysis of a particular firm. In the macro-social space, the national-level social actors determine the social structures, that is their institutional and organizational forms. These involve national rules such as the industrial relations system, property rights and the banking and financial network. These rules materialize in firms, which generally observe them, and together comprise the dominant model. But, alongside the dominant model, there are also particular models that differ to varying degrees. Although these models may be compatible with the institutional rules, there are some cases, like that of Saturn for example (Rubinstein *et al.*, 1993), where the difference is greater because they entail either new rules or new power relationships. Thus the actors within a firm may comply with societal rules, or they might invent new rules or constitute pockets of innovation compared to the generally accepted society-wide rules. These innovations may relate to the firm's institutional dimension (its political system) and/or to its organizational structure. Thus it can be said that the dominant model of the firm co-exists with configurations specific to particular firms.

This distinction between the societal and local spaces is significant. In periods of crisis – or, at least, change – macro-social regulations are shaken, thus leaving more room for innovative experiments. In other words, the gap between a particular configuration of a firm and the dominant model may grow wider. The micro-systems, or local firms, can then become sites for new social forms to emerge, for at this level there is a proximity effect, which stimulates a specific collective dynamic that can modulate, adapt or even reject the dominant forms, and to seek innovative institutional solutions for a firm's survival or social cohesion (Gilly and Pecqueur, 1995). This raises the question of the diffusion of these pockets of innovation and, more generally, of the transformation or transition from one institutional configuration to another. However, before examining this question in more depth, it is first necessary to consider the crisis of Fordism and identify the contemporary dynamics of innovation in production.

The Crisis of Fordism and the Emergence of a New Production Paradigm

In the Fordist era, internal tensions gradually developed that undermined the reproduction of the regime of accumulation, ultimately leading to a double crisis in the 1970s and 1980s. First, there was a crisis of work, or worker alienation, provoked by workers' rejection of Taylorism and the attendant working conditions. Second, a crisis of efficiency resulted from both the rigidities of Taylorism, which made it difficult for employers to adapt the production system to more diversified and uncertain markets, and from its weakness in mobilizing workers' know-how to improve quality and productivity (Lapointe, 1995). This double crisis of Taylorism, especially the crisis of efficiency, intensified firms' weaknesses in the face of a slowdown in economic growth, which was widely attributed to globalization and new forms of competition based on quality and diversity (Piore and Sabel, 1984; Streeck, 1991). A new production paradigm was thus essential in order to overcome the internal contradictions of the previous paradigm and this sparked a wave of innovation.[1]

However, in the 1980s, as unemployment rose, bargaining power shifted to management. As unions were weakened, the crisis of work was largely overshadowed by the crisis of efficiency. The search for a new paradigm was thus increasingly defined in terms of flexibility, quality and productivity. Moreover, because of the weakening of unions, the new paradigm was defined almost entirely on the basis of managerial initiatives and unbridled neo-liberalism and flexibility (Bélanger, 1995). Thus, there were strong pressures to abolish all rules, which were now deemed to be obstacles or rigidities hampering managerial freedom.

Under the banners of flexibility, variety, quality and efficiency, a range of organizational innovations, supported by the computerization of the production process, were thus introduced. In the area of production management, various techniques were used to diminish work-in-process stock, to shorten set-up times and product cycles, to improve supply management and to increase the firm's sensitivity and response to customer needs (Coriat, 1990; 1991; 1997). In the area of quality-management, firms set up quality-assurance programmes and quality improvement groups involving worker participation. There was also considerable industrial rationalization.

In the area of work organization, the new production paradigm was linked to the principles of flexibility, autonomy, involvement and participation. Flexibility spurred the reduction of job classifications, the promotion of 'multi-skilling' and the elimination of barriers between production and maintenance. Flexibility also resulted in changes in compensation systems with pay being linked to individuals' skills or ability to perform several tasks, and varying according to individual, group and firm performance. Organizational innovations also included the 'delayering' of the hierarchical structure and the devolution of a number of managerial functions to employees, resulting in increased worker autonomy and responsibility. In some cases, employees were organized into teams and given collective responsibility over their work.

These developments gave rise to the notion of 'empowerment', seen by some analysts as a shift from control to commitment (Walton, 1985).

As a result of changes in production and quality management, production systems became more fragile and increasingly dependent on human resources for their smooth operation. Given the lack of buffer stocks, the functioning of the production system increasingly relied on employee initiatives and co-operation in response to unexpected events. This work re-organization also entailed a greater devolution of responsibilities to workers. It was therefore necessary to ensure that the new autonomy would be devoted to increasing production. Employees also accepted higher production goals because they appreciated the new autonomy characteristic of the new forms of work organization (Freeman and Rogers, 1999), thereby reducing the importance of trade-offs in exchange for greater involvement. As noted above, one of the dimensions of the crisis of Taylorism was the rejection of monotonous work and authoritarianism. *Work in America* (1973) provided a clear account of the crisis within the production system that gave rise to demands related to quality of life, dignity and recognition of worker know-how. The result was a range of experiments with work re-organization centred on greater worker autonomy (Lapointe, 1995). Even when team work is initiated by management in the context of 'lean production', workers do not necessarily wish to return to traditional Taylorism (Wells, 1996; Freeman and Rogers, 1999). Although this reaction is too often explained in terms of fear of losing a stable and well-paid job (Cappelli, 1999; Osterman, 1999), workers do appear to want to escape the constraints of Taylorism and to participate more fully in their work (Freeman and Rogers, 1999).

There are several ways to foster employee involvement in the management of production. One way, predicated on new forms of human resource management, offers job security in exchange for employee involvement and seeks to reduce work-related conflict by redefining the firm as a community. Such an image of the 'pacified' firm, for example IBM in the USA (Ouchi, 1981; Peters and Waterman, 1982) or Cascades in Quebec (Aktouf, 1991), can also threaten the legitimacy of trade union representation, depicting unions as relics from the past. Another strategy to increase employee involvement entails 're-engineering'. This strategy dispenses with the notion of job security as a trade-off in favour of a systematic attack on the firm's organizational and institutional rigidities (Hammer and Champy, 1993; on this managerial discourse, also see Boltanski and Chiapello, 1999). According to this strategy, the only trade-offs workers receive for increased commitment are intrinsic to the work itself, in terms of increased autonomy and skills. A third strategy, more prevalent in unionized firms, seeks to involve the union in management and in negotiating various trade-offs. Here, organizational innovations are likely to clash with older principles of collective regulation.

Tensions in the Firm

The introduction of the organizational innovations discussed above has repercussions at the institutional level of the firm. The body of rules and the distribution of power, as well as the compromises underlying them, are called into question, which gives rise to tensions on three issues: (1) the modification of work rules and the trade-offs to be conceded to employees in order to forge a new compromise; (2) the role and legitimacy of the union, especially when it participates in management; and (3) the system of governance or, more precisely, the tensions among the different groups vying for influence in the running of the firm.

Work Rules and Trade-Offs

Organizational innovations clash with work rules designed to secure job control, especially those rules relating to the definition of jobs, the internal and external movement of the workforce based on seniority, and task-based wage systems. Such rules aim to control work load, provide a degree of job security, and eliminate arbitrariness and favouritism in workforce movements. However, the focus on flexibility and team work significantly undercuts these rules, and work intensification and job cuts emerge as real threats for workers. What new forms of protection and trade-offs can counteract these threats?

In North America, collective bargaining has led to the consolidation and strengthening of a complex body of work rules. Although this pattern of work organization imposed many internal rigidities, employers were willing to pay this price in order to secure virtually complete freedom to use layoffs, usually temporary, to adjust to market fluctuations. In return, these work rules, based on seniority and recall rights, ensured a degree of job security. A range of factors have combined to undermine employment security. Efforts to achieve greater flexibility through employee involvement are aimed squarely at increasing productivity, with obvious consequences for the size of the workforce. Restructuring and process re-engineering, which encourage firms to refocus on their core competencies and abandon non value-added activities, raise the spectre of increased contracting-out of work (Lévesque *et al.*, 1999). The economic context of increased competition in a context of free trade places yet further pressures on employment.

Although flexibility and other organizational changes undermine employment, they are necessary to ensure the survival of firms in the context of increased competition. Yet, for these innovations to have a significant and lasting impact on the performance of the firm, increased commitment on the part of workers is crucial, and this seemingly requires some form of trade-off in terms of job security. The dilemma is clearly one of contradictory requirements: how to introduce changes that undermine employment while providing some form of guarantee on employment security so that workers will buy into the changes? Viewed from another angle but with similarly contradictory ramifications, in seeking short-term gains by intensifying work and reducing employment levels, management compromises the achievement of the very conditions (like training and job security) that can ensure worker commitment and the long-term survival of organizational innovations.

How can these contradictory requirements be simultaneously achieved? The answer lies in the overall dynamics of the relationships between social actors. For example, the German and Japanese models, which have been successful in reconciling internal flexibility and job security, have inspired a range of experiments in North America. These trade-offs are supposed to form the basis for a new compromise, that is, employee and/or union involvement in return for job security and gain-sharing, and, in some cases, union participation in management. Thus a new compromise on employment has taken shape in some firms. In exchange for agreeing to internal flexibility, other organizational innovations, and increased involvement in work, workers have obtained stronger job guarantees and unions have secured a degree of participation in decision-making. Some analysts, emphasizing the economic and utilitarian aspects of this compromise, have described it as a 'productivity coalition' or a 'mutual gain enterprise' (Windolf, 1989; Kochan and Osterman, 1994). Others, more sensitive to the dynamics of power and co-operation in firms, have seen new forms of industrial democracy and partnership in this compromise (Verma and Cutcher-Gershenfeld, 1993; Bélanger et al., 1994). A third group, which remains more wedded to the old forms of work regulation, has perceived it as an assault on workers' gains and a strategy for weakening unions (Wells, 1993; Parker and Slaughter, 1994).

In order to obtain this compromise, unions have to be able to exercise a degree of bargaining power, which shifts the analysis to the macro level and raises a serious problem. In the context of high unemployment and economic globalization, most countries have seen a huge shift of bargaining power in favour of employers as well as a decline in the rate of unionization. In brief, unions are becoming weaker and are less able to negotiate trade-offs in return for employee involvement. In the United States, employment is becoming increasingly insecure and real wages are stagnating and even declining, while, paradoxically, the diffusion of organizational innovations continues in firms and is accompanied by a degree of employee commitment and improvement of performance. In short, because unions have grown weaker, employer concessions are not required. The American model is thus now characterized by involvement without trade offs, in the context of a weakening of unionism and collectively negotiated rules. The fear of job loss and the intrinsic satisfaction derived from the new pattern of work are thus working in combination to foster the acceptance of innovations and enhanced commitment (Cappelli, 1999; Osterman, 1999).

Union Participation in Management

What position then should unions adopt as regards workplace innovation? North American unions first tended towards two equally ineffective positions – opposition and passive acceptance. Neither of these was suitable for promoting workers' interests. Opposition meant exclusion from the change process, thus allowing management to introduce changes unilaterally, without consultation or negotiation. Passive acceptance, while offering the benefit of union participation, leads to a dependent form of participation, unguided by a distinctive union programme. Such a posture is likely to weaken the local union and isolate it from its members. Through trial and error, unions have gained a better understanding of the issues brought to the fore by innovations. In particular, when they have been able to draw on external resources (e.g. the training and expertise provided by central union bodies or dialogue with other unions) and to mobilize their internal resources (stewards and members), unions have been able to fashion positions in favour of involvement based on their own vision of workplace change. In these cases, unions seek to shape the innovations so that they better reflect workers' interests. Even though specific to each workplace, the general union strategy regarding workplace innovation typically includes the following demands: a sharing of the benefits of involvement; job protection; safer and more skilled work; the recognition and use of worker know-how; participation in the design and introduction of changes as well as their negotiation in collective agreements (Betcherman, 1995; Lapointe and Bélanger, 1996). Union participation in management may appear to run counter to union traditions (Parker and Slaughter, 1994), but only if trade unionism is defined in its most defensive and adversarial form. A proactive trade unionism can, on the contrary, enhance worker involvement.

A weak union movement will have little chance to force a compromise because management is free to pursue a logic of neo-liberal competitiveness. A strong union movement has a choice between two paths: it can block innovations by assuming a defensive posture centred on the distribution of profits and opposition to new rules; or it can adopt an autonomous, proactive position, putting forward its own counterproposals in order to reach a new institutional compromise where employee involvement is 'exchanged' for the acquisition of new partnership rights (Bélanger and Lévesque, 1994a) or industrial democracy (Coriat, 1990).

Once a union has made a choice between these different paths, the participation process itself gives rise to a host of other issues. Drawing on our own research (Bélanger *et al.*, 1994; Grant *et al.*, 1997; Lapointe, 1997; 1998; 2000) and those of others (Bourque and Rioux, 1994; 1997; Harrisson and Laplante, 1994; 1996) into Quebec firms that have gone further in developing these new forms of union participation, it is possible to specify the contours of an emerging model.[2] First, work rules aimed at constraining managerial action and ensuring some protection for shopfloor workers are significantly weakened. The principal goal of collective bargaining shifts to the organization of work and the economic and financial management of the firm. The nature and mechanisms of labour–management relations change, becoming more focused on co-operation and problem-solving around integrative issues (economic and financial management and work organization). Indeed, the traditional mode of bargaining that focused on wages and other issues is not well suited to the new issues, such as employment, and to organizational innovations, such as flexibility and cross-trades co-operation. For these new issues, the signing of a collective agreement only marks the beginning of a process that requires ongoing co-operation. In other words, the emerging model entails a high level of labour–management co-operation and of union participation (Walton *et al.*, 1994).

The mode of negotiation is also changing. Periodic negotiations are being replaced with negotiation on a continuous basis, which is necessitated by changes in the organization and management of work. Problem-solving processes are being grafted onto the grievance procedure. Sector-based negotiations are being replaced with decentralized negotiations at the level of the establishment in order to take into consideration the specific changes in each workplace.

Union action is also being transformed. Whereas unions used to be concerned chiefly with negotiating and supervising rules constraining managerial action, they are now also participating in decisions through networks of joint committees, where they are more likely to have a direct influence on the decision-making process. Within these committees, the distribution of power and the decision-making processes vary widely, thus creating significant differences in real power exercised by these committees.

These changes are also altering the way the firm is governed. The former strict division of roles and responsibilities is being replaced with a new sharing of power. Unions are now concerned with the firm's economic performance, for which they feel partly responsible since they have a hand in the decisions. Workers and unions are also now finding themselves performing duties that used to belong exclusively to management.

Participation therefore leads to a modification of traditional roles. By participating in management, unions embrace, to a certain extent at least, the goals of productivity and quality that traditionally belonged exclusively to management. Since this participation seeks to protect employment, particularly when threatened with closure, the maintenance and development of employment are associated with firms' economic performance. It follows, therefore, that long-term job protection cannot be ensured by collective bargaining alone but also requires participation in strategic decisions (Rubinstein *et al.*, 1993). However, such strategic engagement creates a tension between this new role for unions and their more independent role as the representative and defender of workers (Shaiken *et al.*, 1997).

Union participation in management can also entail a confusion of roles between union and management with the attendant possibility of co-option in which the union becomes management's spokesperson to workers (Wite, 1980, Green, 1996). Unions thus face a difficult dilemma. How can they take part in strategic management without being ensnared in the logic of management, a logic that subordinates social performances (employment, wages and working conditions), and thus workers' interests, to the demands for return on investment and profitability of capital? The solution is found, in part, in the development and promotion of an alternative logic of management, an independent logic that subordinates the profitability of capital and shareholder earnings to social performance and workers' interests (Lapointe and Bélanger, 1996; Lazes and Savage, 1996).

Union participation gives rise to other paradoxes. Can real participation that actually has an influence on decision making be compatible with a weakened union 'partner'? This paradox can only be resolved by constructing new bases of union power, principally on the basis of the fragility of the new organizational systems and on the capacity to mobilize workers in this organizational context (Eaton, 1995; Lapointe and Bélanger, 1996).

Genuine union participation therefore depends on an autonomous logic, the exercise of countervailing power, and the availability of resources and expertise. But how can these conditions be met without adequate institutional support? What is required, for example, is a law promoting union participation and guaranteeing rights and thus independence, as the Wagner Act did for the obligation to recognize and negotiate with unions (Turner, 1991; Green, 1996).

Participation also creates contradictions within the larger union structures. Union participation in management makes the local issues specific to each firm primordial, a situation intensified by management investment policies that put units of the same firm into competition with each other. The result is an inward-looking, workplace-focused style of union action, on the pattern of Japanese-style enterprise unionism (MacDuffie, 1995c) and in which there is a fragmentation of the union movement as local unions distance themselves from their wider affiliations. Moreover, higher-level union bodies are not always in agreement with the diffusion of local union experiments with participation and seek to hold them back and even to curb them, as in the UAW's response to Saturn in the USA (Wever, 1995; Shaiken *et al.*, 1997; Heller *et al.*, 1998).

In workplaces where unions participate in management, contradictions also develop between the leaders and members of the local unions. The new approaches to bargaining and union–management relations result in a rapprochement between union representatives and management. These approaches stress co-operation, trust, an understanding of the other party's interests and viewpoint, and relational and affective proximity, all of which appear to be essential conditions for establishing and maintaining union participation in management. To the extent that union leaders become closer to the firm's management, they may grow more distant from their members. Thus union leaders appear, rightly or wrongly, to be too close to management and incapable of maintaining the independence they need to represent adequately the interests of rank-and-file workers. Daily problems in the workplace – work intensification, favouritism, health and safety problems, movements between work stations or between shifts, pressures to increase productivity – do not vanish because unions participate in management, and may in fact be exacerbated in the struggle for survival in the face of threatened closures. These problems are often ignored and subordinated to the joint efforts made by management and the union to protect jobs. Nevertheless, given the democratic nature of unions, those leaders who are deemed to be too close to management can be replaced by other, more critical leaders who are more attuned to the daily problems of members. A dynamic that might result in a democratization of work is thus introduced.

An overwhelming majority of North American unions have taken on a participatory role on the basis of an instrumental calculation, that is, in order to achieve goals deemed to be vital in the context of a highly unfavourable balance of power. However, once introduced, instrumental participation touches off a dynamic process that brings to the surface numerous tensions and contradictions and which, under the pressure of workers' demands, can lead to democratic participation. Thus, a fragile – and sometimes even reversible – process of democratization at work is put in place (Lapointe, 2000).

The System of Governance of the Firm

Contradictions also occur within the governance system of the firm. These contradictions spring from two sources: the domination of investors and shareholders in the internal system of governance and the decentralization of organizational structures.

Investor and shareholder pressure on firms to increase their short-term returns make it difficult to create the conditions required for changes at the level of local production units, thereby reducing the chances of survival for workplace partnership experiments (Voos, 1994; Weinstein and Kochan, 1995). Such pressures often conflict with efforts by local management. While innovation programmes require investments in training or technological change, corporate management, shareholders and investors may be more interested in reducing costs, through downsizing, in order to generate immediate profits. Numerous partnership experiments have thus been derailed, as illustrated by the recent reversals of some of the major success stories in the USA following unilateral management decisions to carry out mass layoffs, even though some of the firms were making profits. These layoffs were announced and carried out to attract and retain shareholders increasingly preoccupied by short-term returns. The cases of unionized firms like Xerox, Levi Strauss and Corning, as well as non-unionized firms like IBM, provide telling examples of this phenomenon (Cappelli, 1999; Osterman, 1999). Comparative research, particularly on Germany (Wever, 1995), suggests that this situation would not occur if institutional constraints at the macro-social level were to constrain the behaviour of managerial actors.

As large firms decentralize, local production units are converted into profit centres. Although these units enjoy greater autonomy in the use of resources allocated by the head office, they face increased pressure for short-term profitability and are evaluated solely on that basis. This generates further pressure to introduce organizational innovations, to promote labour-management co-operation and to increase employee commitment. Indeed, these latter objectives become pre-conditions for the achievement of short-term profitability, which is in turn the only way to ensure the production unit's long-term survival. Thus a curious logic is developed in which the firm's long-term interests require the satisfaction of the short-term interests of shareholders and investors: today's high returns guarantee tomorrow's investment and job protection. However, this logic runs counter to workers' short-term interests because the quest for short-term returns is too often undertaken at the cost of work intensification, deteriorating working conditions and a lack of training. Moreover, the promises of job protection often vanish in the wake of restructuring and layoffs ordered by head office in order to respond to financial pressures.

These contradictions and paradoxes at the heart of workplace innovations make the current changes fragile and unstable. Contemporary innovations, generally local in nature, often clash with the macro-social institutional system. The achievement of both organizational and institutional innovations is highly challenging for local actors, union and management alike. These local actors are the real artisans of change who, without a universal model of change (Kochan and Osterman, 1994), must use organizational 'boot-strapping' (Sabel, 1995) to meet the requirements of the market and the head office. They have to reconcile contradictory goals and resolve the tensions created by the changes. They create new local institutional rules, but these remain extremely fragile.

The diffusion of these 'pockets of innovation' (Streeck, 1992) is difficult in the absence of favourable social conditions. On the one hand, the pockets of innovation may come up against the dominant forms of practice and therefore remain isolated while, quite ironically, still being regarded as centres of excellence (Boyer and Orléan, 1994). Innovations thus remain a deviant minority, even though their delinquency continues to be advanced as a model in management textbooks. On the other hand, a local innovation can be diffused if the societal level collective actors see a social advantage in it and make it part of their respective agendas, or are urged to do so by the state. This was the case of the high-wage policy initiated by Ford and diffused only after the negotiations under the New Deal in the 1930s in the USA.

Institutional Blockage

Tensions develop between local innovations and the macro-level institutional framework when the latter remains unchanged. However, these tensions are not sufficient to stimulate a reform of the institutional framework. We first examine these tensions between local and societal levels, and then use the case of Quebec to illustrate the role of unions, employers and the state in the possible transformation of macro-societal institutions of labour regulation.

Tensions between the Micro and Macro Levels

As workplace innovation develops, a gap emerges and then gradually widens between the conditions needed within firms to sustain innovations and the lack of institutional conditions at the societal level to ensure that these needs are met. Indeed, the macro-social institutional conditions sometimes act as obstacles or barriers to the development of local innovations, making the 'institutional deficit' even deeper. The main sources of tension are rooted in labour–management co-operation, union participation in management, employment and training.

The consolidation of workplace union–management co-operation necessitates a degree of institutional support, but such support is not always available. For example, in the USA and Canada, labour laws were built on the assumption of a conflict of interest between labour and management and legalism has been the preferred method to deal with this conflict. The legal framework does not provide any mechanisms for co-operation in either the workplace or at the level of the firm. In addition, employers and unions disagree profoundly over the reform of labour legislation. The Dunlop Commission, which was set up by the Clinton Administration, failed in its attempt to foster a compromise under which the union movement would accept greater workplace flexibility in return for a reform of labour laws that would facilitate unionization (Osterman, 1999).

These tensions between the micro and macro level are occurring in a context where collective expression in the workplace is required by the new production models and demanded by workers. But the union movement is not always able to promote this role and is often simply absent. This is particularly true of the United States (Freeman and Rogers, 1999) and has given rise to a debate over the need for legislation to introduce 'works councils'. According to some analysts, this could lead to a division of labour between the works councils and the unions. The works councils would be concerned with the more integrative issues, those related to work organization and the management of production, whereas the unions would concentrate on distributive issues, such as wages and sharing of gains (Bluestone and Bluestone, 1992). Such a division of labour is, however, open to criticism, since work organization can just as easily be considered a distributive issue that might generate considerable conflict over issues such as work intensification. Others believe that works councils could compensate for the lack of union representation in the United States (Freeman and Rogers, 1999). Still others are opposed to the idea of works councils because they see it as an attempt to implement forms of management-dominated unionism similar to the American Plan in the United States in the 1920s. The German experience is instructive in this respect, for it shows that the dual system of representation can operate to the benefit of workers when strong unions play a hegemonic role within the works councils (Rogers and Streeck, 1995).

Furthermore, co-operation at the local level cannot really develop without support from the central union and employer confederations. Access to external resources provided by their parent bodies, such as training and expertise, are crucial to the ability of local unions to participate in the management of the firm (Lévesque *et al.*, 1997). Without these resources, local unions are either less willing to participate (because of the complexity of the issues and the dilemmas related to participation), or their participation is more fragile and susceptible to the managerial logic of competitiveness, thus threatening to weaken them (Lapointe, 2000). On the other hand, the support of local participation experiments by national unions poses a major dilemma. The decentralized bargaining associated with these experiments further risks undermining union bargaining power, which has historically depended on taking wages and other working conditions 'out of competition'. Reducing the scope of co-ordinated bargaining might result in an overall deterioration of conditions for unionized workers. In contrast, overly centralized and co-ordinated bargaining is detrimental to local experiments (for the US example of the relationship between the United Auto Workers (UAW) and its local union at Saturn, see Shaiken *et al.*, 1997; Heller *et al.*, 1998)

Employment security is usually considered an essential condition for sustainable local innovations. Contradictions emerge here due to the differential treatment of different categories of workers. In exchange for union acceptance of organizational flexibility and increased employee involvement, management agrees to provide stronger job guarantees. However, these guarantees are difficult to maintain in the context of unstable markets and increased competition. Firms that protect employment during periods of economic downturn are relatively disadvantaged compared to their competitors that are quick to effect layoffs. If the institutional framework is not supportive of employment protection, firms that adopt this strategy are penalized (Levine and Tyson, 1990). In order to sustain local innovations in such a context, firms might only give job security to workers who form the central core of the firm's operations. To deal with fluctuations in production levels, they use a secondary workforce (e.g. part-time, fixed-term or self-employed workers) or subcontracting (Weinstein and Kochan, 1995). Thus, although partnership admittedly increases the protection of some employees, it also generates growing precariousness for others. It thus divides workers into winners and losers (Kern and Schumann, 1989). This situation also contributes to the isolation of the union movement from other social movements insofar as unions are identified with partnership arrangements that promote this kind of dualization of the labour force. In this sense, improvements in job security won by unions may no longer be synonymous with a social progress for all workers. Unless the deadlock over reduced work time and work sharing can be broken, this contradiction cannot easily be resolved within the firm; it requires a societal choice and appropriate legislation. The issue of training also highlights the institutional hiatus between firms engaged in the partnership process and the existing social framework. Organizational innovations require additional training. Although training is intrinsically a public good, namely one that benefits society as a whole, it is largely the responsibility of individual firms. Managers thus worry about investing in training workers who might leave and work for a competitor. Either they spend very little on training or seek to retain their workforce through the use of career ladders, high wages or job security. However, by focusing solely on the core workforce, this alternative intensifies the dualization of the labour market. The remedy for this dualization and the improvement of the general level of workplace skills still requires broader institutional measures that spread the costs among all the actors in the socio-economic system.

Lastly, the structure of the financial markets clashes with the requirements of local innovation. The predominance of capital oriented towards the 'fast buck' runs counter to local experiments, which require a more patient approach. To establish the necessary conditions for local innovation (training, participation and job stability) and to provide the time for organizational learning and the mastering of the innovations, short-term investments are required, though they might only yield a return in the long term. In contrast to the situation that prevails in Germany and Japan, the American situation does not favour this at all (Kochan and Osterman, 1994). In this respect, the case of Quebec, to which we turn below, offers a great advantage because of the scope afforded to 'patient' capital, including union investment funds, state investment corporations, and the co-operative movement (Bourque and Lévesque, 1999).

All of these tensions demonstrate the interconnectedness between the micro level, which exerts pressures for change on the macro level, and the macro level, which can limit the diffusion of new local institutional arrangements. To solve this institutional blockage, the actors at the societal level have to take the lead. As our theoretical framework suggests, institutions are only transformed by the actions of social actors. Moreover, there is a very close link between the positions of social actors and the form and degree of the institutionalization of labour relations in a given country. Hyman (1997), for example, explored the link between union ideologies and institutional forms in a number of European countries. In the United States, where institutionalization is relatively weak, the regulation of labour relations is restricted to the processes of union recognition and collective bargaining and to the subjects of negotiation, which it tends to specify in detail. In fact, in some states, the union recognition process has been made so difficult (Green, 1996) that firms can avoid the union–management component of their governance system. Moreover, employers remain steadfastly opposed to any labour law reform that might facilitate unionization. This situation contrasts with that of Germany, where institutionalization is much 'denser' given the dual system of co-determination (unions for collective bargaining of wages and work councils for work organization) and laws on employment protection and training (Wever, 1995). These differences flow from the model of relationships between the social actors. In particular, the more a confrontational logic predominates, the weaker the institutions and the greater the number of industries in which firms are left to compete as best they can. Conversely, the more a logic of co-operation prevails, the more institutionalization is extended to public goods such as research and workforce training (Streeck, 1991).

Social Actors and Institutional Inertia: the Quebec Case

Despite the growing convergence between nations resulting from the globalization of markets and economies, there is still scope for distinct national models (Hollingsworth and Boyer, 1997). As Boyer (2000) puts it, 'The age of nations is not finished'. Indeed, social actors and institutions retain the capacity to shape and modify the impact of forces – markets, technologies and organizational paradigms – operating at the global level. Thus, different national trajectories are being consolidated, despite comparable organizational paradigms, and this can be seen in the institutions and relations between social actors at the societal level. In other words, although there is a marked convergence between industrial societies towards a new organizational paradigm, the tensions created by the diffusion of this paradigm at the micro and macro institutional levels vary from one context to another.

In North America, because the Fordist institutional framework, strongly influenced by the Wagner Act, is common to both the United States and

Canada, the institutional tensions are similar. However, because the different systems within North America are strongly influenced by the relations between social actors at the societal level, the resolution of these tensions may well lead to different outcomes, which will in turn have a major influence on the diffusion of organizational innovations and on social and economic performance. The weakness of unionism in the United States, for example, means that organizational innovations are spreading widely, but without the benefit of either partnerships or trade-offs. Given the adamant opposition of employers, who presently dominate labour relations, it is highly unlikely that the institutional structures will be transformed in the foreseeable future in a way that would strengthen unions (Osterman, 1999; Cappelli, 1999). In Quebec, the situation is completely different. The nature of the relations between the societal-level actors may in fact prove to be quite favourable to a change in the institutional framework that would encourage the diffusion of firm-level partnerships. A large body of research (see Ichniowski *et al.*, 1996, for a good summary) suggests that such a diffusion would in turn contribute strongly to the deepening of organizational innovations and the improvement of economic and social performance.

The new organizational paradigm has been widely adopted in Quebec firms, but new institutional arrangements, and especially partnerships, are much less common.[3] As regards the macro-institutional framework, there has been little change, though it should be noted that this framework is much more supportive of unionization than is the American regime. It is within this dual gap that the tensions and contradictions occur, a problem that the intervention of the social actors might well help resolve.

In Quebec, there are a number of factors that would seem to favour a modification of the macro-institutional framework so as to support the diffusion of new organizational and institutional arrangements. The nature of societal-level social relations, especially relations between employers, unions and the state, is one such factor. Support for the diffusion of local innovations should be aided by one of the highest levels of union density in North America, by supportive public policies, and by a range of consensus-building mechanisms. However, as we will see below, these positive factors have not been sufficient to provoke institutional change.

In 1999, union density in Quebec stood at 35.4 per cent. Although this represented a fall of several percentage points since the beginning of the 1990s, union density remained higher than in the neighbouring province of Ontario (26.4 per cent), in Canada as a whole (29.8 per cent) and the United States (14.1 per cent). Indeed, union density in the United States has been in sharp decline since the mid-1970s when it stood at nearly 30 per cent (Murray and Verge, 1999, Table 1, 21). The continuing strength of union representation in Quebec is undoubtedly due, at least in part, to the social compromises and institutional framework in Quebec. For example, the 1977 reform of the Quebec Labour Code involved three fundamental changes that were clearly supportive of unionization: obligatory first-agreement arbitration when the parties are unable to reach a settlement on their own; automatic recognition when more than 50 per cent of those in the bargaining unit sign a membership card during a unionization drive; and a ban on the use of replacement workers during strikes. In addition, the 1979 Act Respecting Occupational Health and Safety contributed to the development of workplace partnerships by creating labour–management committees charged with the joint management of health and safety issues (Rouillard, 1989).

The major union confederations have also adopted positive and proactive positions vis-à-vis organizational and institutional innovations in the workplace.[4] In the first half of the 1990s, the Quebec confederations held various conferences and issued strategy documents aimed at their members that announced their support for work reorganization and union participation in management (Bergeron and Bourque, 1996; Lapointe and Bélanger, 1996).

The union scene in Quebec is also distinctive because of the existence of an organization that plays a significant role in the economy – the Fonds de Solidarité des travailleurs du Québec (Quebec Workers' Solidarity Fund), under the control of the FTQ (Fédération des travailleurs et travailleuses du Québec). Created in 1983, at a time when unemployment had surged to around 12 or 13 per cent, this union investment fund specializing in venture capital set out to protect and create jobs, particularly by investing in firms that were threatened with closure. Funded on the basis of voluntary contributions from union members (for whom it serves as a pension fund), the Fund mutualizes the risks incurred by workers when they invest in companies. The workers, who buy shares in the Fund, also benefit from significant tax deductions, running as high as 80 per cent of the value of the shares they purchase. In addition, in each of the firms in which it invests, the Fund signs a shareholder agreement giving it a seat on the board of directors and an employer contribution to the training of employees in economic affairs. This contribution finances the economic education that the Fund provides to employees of the firm (Fournier, 1991; Grant and Lévesque, 1997). Since it was created, the Fund has become a key economic and financial actor in Quebec. Its links with the co-operative movement and provincial crown corporations, as well as the size of its asset portfolio and its proactive strategies, have made it a pivotal agent of economic development in the province. With assets of more than $3 billion and around 385,000 shareholders, the Fund is involved in nearly 1,500 firms.[5] In this way it has undoubtedly contributed to a reorientation of unionism by encouraging partnerships and by making unions more sensitive to economic and financial issues.

Lastly, the Quebec union movement is deeply involved in politics, where it plays an influential role. It enjoys a special relationship with one political party, the Parti Québécois, which was in power between 1976 and 1985 and has governed since 1994. As a result, the role of the state and labour legislation are quite favourable to unions. The union movement also enjoys close relationships with other social movements and community organizations (Lapointe and Bélanger, 1996). In short, then, the union movement is a major social actor that is strongly entrenched in Quebec society.

Quebec employers, who are organized into two province-wide associations,[6] are relatively tolerant of unions. A good example of this stance occurred in the early 1990s when the CPQ (Conseil du Patronat du Québec), having been authorized by the Supreme Court of Canada to contest the law against strike replacements, decided not to pursue the case in order to preserve the climate of co-operation in the province. In addition, Quebec employers have often expressed a positive attitude towards unions in many of their publications (Bourque, 2000). Even more significant, however, are the various forms of consensus-building in which employers are intimately involved.

In fact, there is a wide range of consensus-building bodies at both the provincial and sector levels in Quebec. At the provincial level, the two most important are the Economic Summits and the Advisory Council on Labour and Manpower. Over the past twenty years, the government has organized five economic summits in which both unions and employers have taken part. Initiated as a way of stimulating consensus-building among the principal employer and union organizations in order to foster economic development and job creation, these summits have brought about a rapprochement between the actors and have led to the adoption of joint positions on a number of strategic issues. This was the case, for example, at the November 1996 Summit on the Economy and Employment, which produced a common declaration recognizing the legitimacy of the actors and the need for co-operation in the workplace. Union representatives agreed that profitability and flexibility were needed to help promote employment, whereas employer representatives recognized that employment was a major objective and that the success of organizational innovations depended on the involvement of unions.[7]

The second provincial level consensus-building mechanism of note is the Advisory Council on Labour and Manpower. Chaired by a government appointee and made up of representatives of the major union and employer organizations, the council's role is to foster consensus-building between the actors and to provide advice to the government concerning its proposed legislation and other initiatives in the field of labour relations and labour market policy. The council also has the mandate to produce policy papers aimed at the actors in the world of work. In 1997, on the basis of extensive consultations between employer and union representatives, the council issued an important document on organizational innovations. That document affirmed that training, employment protection, partnership and union participation in management were indispensable for the success of organizational innovations.[8]

The sector-level bodies, and more particularly the Sector Consultative Roundtables (*Tables de concertation sectorielle*) and the Sector Labour Force Committees (*Comités sectoriels de main-d'oeuvre*) also play an important role in consensus-building. Although both are organized along the lines of the same economic sectors, the former focus on promoting economic development while the latter concentrate on training. These consensus-building bodies, thanks to the participation of government representatives, bring together employer and union representatives from the sectors concerned. Based on joint projects and a consensual decision-making process, the mission of these bodies is to promote labour force training, technological updating, organizational innovation and labour–management co-operation as ways of improving the economic and social performance of firms (Charest, 1999; Bourque, 2000). These intermediate-level bodies therefore break with the Fordist logic of competition between firms, interest representation based on the firm, and conflict-based labour relations.

The state plays a crucial role in establishing the conditions that encourage the diffusion of workplace innovations. Not only does it encourage union–management co-operation and the development of unionism, it also uses the financial muscle of the corporations under its control. A particularly important role is played by the Quebec Industrial Development Corporation (recently renamed Investment Quebec), a crown corporation that provides venture capital to firms. During the first half of the 1990s, the Corporation came to the rescue of some thirty firms that were in financial difficulty, though making its assistance conditional on the signing of a 'social contract'. Under these agreements, the parties agree to sign a long-term collective agreement (i.e. for six years) and undertake to establish a joint-management committee, to introduce a quality and flexibility programme, and to increase employee training. Some of the firms where social contracts have been signed have proved to be stellar examples of successful organizational innovation and partnership, and have served as models for other firms undergoing change. The social contracts also led to an amendment of the Labour Code eliminating the previous three-year maximum limit on the duration of collective agreements (Bourque, 2000). Because of its policy of providing special loans allowing workers to buy shares in their firms, the Corporation is also associated with the creation of Worker-Shareholder Co-operatives (known as CTAs after their French name, *les coopératives de travailleurs actionnaires*).[9] Where CTAs exist, workers as a group hold a block of the firm's shares (generally between 10 and 30 per cent) and therefore have a seat on the board of directors (Lévesque, 1994).

Lastly, in terms of capital markets, there is a considerable amount of 'patient capital' available in Quebec, i.e. investors who are willing to defer returns on investment to the long term. This allows innovative firms to escape the tyranny of the quarterly profit statement. What makes this possible is the considerable socialization of Quebec capital, as represented by union investment funds,[10] the strong role played by the co-operative movement in the financial sector, and the presence of large crown corporations. The latter have a range of specific objectives: some, like Hydro-Québec, the provincial power utility, act as custodians and managers of certain natural resources; others, like the Quebec Deposit and Investment Fund, are involved in financing government activities and investing in privately held firms; still others, like the Quebec Industrial Development Corporation and the General Investment Corporation of Quebec, invest in publicly listed firms in the private sector. Taken together, these organizations control a considerable amount of capital and play an important role in the economic development of Quebec (Bourque and Lévesque, 1999).

Despite these many positive conditions at the level of Quebec society, macro-social institutional changes that would promote new local institutional arrangements have been slow in coming. What are the factors that explain this institutional resistance?

First, Quebec's proximity to the United States, where neo-liberalism predominates, and the interpenetration of the North American economies have a strong dissuasive effect on any radical transformations that might disturb economic relations. The Quebec government has thus preferred to let local actors negotiate their adaptations to market forces at the level of the firm. Moreover, there are few incentives, at least for employers, to transform the macro-institutional framework. Indeed, it has become evident that organizational innovations designed to increase quality and productivity can work, to some extent at least, even without institutional reforms, as is the case in the United States.

As for the social actors, the level of mobilization in favour of institutional change is clearly insufficient. In comparison with the massive battles fought to reform the Quebec Labour Code in the 1950s and 1960s, or for the recognition of industrial unionism in the United States in the 1930s, the major social actors of today have not really thrown themselves into the struggle for real change. On the one hand, employers suffer from a serious problem of representation. Employers' associations can make pronouncements in favour of a new socio-productive model and union participation in management; but individual employers[11] are opposed to institutional arrangements that would provide a greater degree of workplace democracy because they are not interested in footing the bill, either in terms of the concessions involved (job security, wages and training) or of the sharing of power. On the other hand, in the context of growing insecurity and inequality, unions are faced with pressures to fight for a share of the gains from productivity increases and for job security, which runs the risk of reviving calls to defend past gains and revitalize traditional rules. These pressures result from a disenchantment with workplace innovations, which, although they are supposed to generate positive effects for workers as well as for employers, often leave workers with the impression that they have been left out in the cold. When this occurs, union support for workplace innovation crumbles and the demands for institutional changes that would support these innovations evaporate.

Lastly, it should be stressed that workplace changes are highly complex. There are persistently significant differences between the actors about the nature of innovations and the conditions associated with them. This complexity is an obstacle to the emergence of a minimal consensus over the transformation of the wider institutional framework.

Conclusion

The two analytical distinctions at the core of this chapter – between macro- and micro-level spaces (i.e. the socio-productive system and the firm) and between organizations and institutions – provide the tools for a better understanding of the dynamics of the innovation process. They also highlight the complexity of workplace change because of the tensions associated with these innovations and the dilemmas they create for the social actors at both the level of the firm and society as a whole.

Workplace innovations are rooted in an overarching organizational paradigm that combines flexibility, autonomy and quality, while at the same time reflecting and illustrating globalization and the growing proximity of nations and national economies. However, this new paradigm is not adopted simply because it is more efficient. Its adoption in the workplace and, especially, its impact on the improvement of social and productive performance depend instead on the specific institutional context and the strategies of social actors.

When introduced in the workplace, the new organizational paradigm generates tensions and dilemmas over the concessions to be made to workers (in terms of training, employment, working conditions and pay) and over the role of local unions that must reconcile apparently contradictory demands. How, for example, can increased job security be reconciled with protection against work intensification? How can participation in management be reconciled with the independent representation of workers? Lastly, tensions and dilemmas also emerge within management by creating a division between those managers focused on the achievement of shareholder interests and those more concerned with implementing local innovations and the conditions required for their success.

The major issue is not so much the diffusion of organizational innovation as it is the implementation of the conditions associated with their diffusion and their sustained impact on the improvement of economic and social performance. These conditions basically concern the concessions to give to workers and the question of partnership. However, the resolution of this major issue cannot take place solely in the workplace and the firm. Local actors need the support of societal-level actors and a change in the macro-institutional framework. As long as this framework remains unchanged, it constitutes a barrier to the concessions and partnership needed at the local level. First, the existing institutional framework does not require employers to provide any employment protection or training, conditions that are key to the success of local innovations. Second, the framework rests on adversarial relations between local actors, whereas co-operation is essential for innovation to occur. Third, the institutional framework continues to underpin a financial system that allows, indeed encourages, the domination of shareholders and investors, whose short-term perspective has a deleterious effect on local innovations.

The resolution of these contradictions requires the involvement of societal-level social actors, who need to redefine the rules of the game so as to promote concessions and partnership and thereby contribute to the sustained improvement of economic and social performance at local level. In this respect, our analysis of the Quebec model sheds light on these broader issues. In Quebec, many of the conditions favouring a change in the institutional framework are in place: a strong and proactive trade union movement, a high level of union–employer co-operation, a large amount of socialized capital, and a government that is sympathetic to the union movement. However, as a result of institutional inertia, experiments in partnership at the local level are much less widely diffused than organizational innovations, and are plagued by extreme fragility.

We have advanced a number of hypotheses to explain this apparent paradox of an institutional system caught between pressures from below (that is workplaces and establishments) and from above (that is societal-level social actors). Can this inertia be explained by the fact that organizational and workplace change occurs more rapidly than institutional and societal change? Although this time lag is undoubtedly part of the answer, it is also necessary to consider the complexity of the changes to be implemented, the international context (especially, at least in Quebec's case, its proximity to the prevailing model of development in the US), and actor strategies. Researchers must now turn to these various factors in order to gain a fuller understanding of the continuing challenges of social innovation in the workplace.

Notes

* The term *rapport social* has no easy equivalent in English. It is rendered here and throughout this chapter as the 'capital–labour relation' as it is in a recent English text by Robert Boyer, one of the major contributors to the regulation school. In a different text by Boyer, it is translated as 'wage–labour nexus'!

1. This process can be broken down into three phases, each strongly influenced by the overall context of social relations. The first phase saw the emergence of a new organizational paradigm and the loosening of rigidities. The context of this phase was marked by new forms of competition, economic globalization and the introduction of new microelectronic technologies. During the second phase, the locus of action was the firm, within which organizational innovations generated tensions with the existing institutional forms. The third phase saw tensions shift towards the interface between the firm and the production system when the new institutional and organizational arrangements developed in the firm came into conflict with the macro-institutional level.

2. This interpretation is also partly based on the models of the 'Mutual Gains Enterprise' (Kochan and Osterman, 1994) and 'American Team Production' (Appelbaum and Batt, 1994).

3. There are no recent large-scale studies of the diffusion of organizational and institutional innovations in Quebec firms. Nevertheless, some research has confirmed the spread of organizational innovations. For example, Maschino's (1992) survey of more than 200 establishments revealed that, in 1991, organizational innovations had occurred in 61 per cent of those establishments. A recent study of the ground transportation equipment sector (Lapointe *et al.*, 2000), concludes that there has been a strong diffusion of organizational innovations but a weak diffusion of partnerships. Lastly, many case studies have demonstrated the widespread diffusion of organizational innovations and the very fragile nature of partnerships (e.g. Grant and Lévesque, 1997; Lapointe, 1998; Bourque, 1999).

4. In contrast to the USA and the rest of Canada, where a single large union confederation dominates, Quebec is characterized by plural unionism. Union membership is split among four large confederations and a large number of independent unions. The Fédération des travailleurs et travailleuses du Québec (FTQ), which brings together those unions in Quebec that are affiliated with Canadian and American unions, is the largest confederation, representing 37.3 per cent of union members in the province. The three other confederations, which have no affiliation with unions in the rest of Canada or in the United States, are the Confédération des syndicats nationaux (CSN), the Centrale des syndicats du Québec (CSQ) and the Centrale des syndicats démocratiques (CSD). These three confederations represent, respectively, 23.9, 9.9 and 3.8 per cent of union members in Quebec. Despite this pluralism, there is a strong tradition of inter-union 'common fronts' in Quebec.

5. Fonds de solidarité des travailleurs du Québec, 1999, *Prospectus simplifié*, 16th edition; *Rapport annuel* and *Répartition des actionnaires*, Statistiques au 30 septembre.

6. The *Conseil du Patronat du Québec* (CPQ) (Quebec Employers' Council) and the Alliance of Manufacturers and Exporters of Quebec.

7. Sommet sur l'économie et l'emploi, 1996, *Les faits saillants*, Québec, Secrétariat du Sommet, 3 November.

8. Conseil consultatif du travail et de la main d'œuvre, 1994, *Document d'orientation; Document de réflexion sur une nouvelle organisation du travail*, 1997.

9. The CTAs are unique to Quebec, although they resemble in some ways the Spanish anonymous firms and the Employee Stock Ownership Plans in the USA. For a comparison of these different models, see Lévesque (1994) and Comeau and Lévesque (1993). Between 1985 and 1990, some

twenty-odd CTAs were created. Beginning in 1991-2, the CTAs received a fresh boost with the joint involvement of the Industrial Development Corporation of Quebec, the Regional Development Co-operatives and the unions, especially the CSN (Coté and Luc, 1994). Although the CTAs hold shares in small and medium-sized businesses, they are also shareholders in some large firms.

10. In addition to the FTQ's Solidarity Fund, the CSN created its own investment fund, *FondAction*, in 1996, which now has assets of $70 million (Bourque, 2000).

11. It needs to be pointed out here that there are a number of divisions among employers. Senior managers, and particularly the headquarters' managers in multi-establishment firms, are more likely to oppose partnerships and concessions to workers because they are more exposed to the demands of shareholders and investors. On the other hand, managers of individual establishments are more likely to be open to partnerships and concessions because they are more aware of the conditions required to ensure the survival of the local establishment and the improvement of its performance over the long term.

5 North American Labour Policy under a Transformed Economic and Workplace Environment

Richard P. Chaykowski and Morley Gunderson

Whether changes in North American labour markets and industrial relations systems are characterized as either a transition or a transformation, they are having profound implications for the labour policies that govern that system. The source of the changes occurring in labour markets and in industrial relations systems is clearly rooted in the underlying environmental changes taking place, foremost among these being the globalization of product and capital markets, rapid technological innovation and the diffusion of new technologies globally, as well as significant changes in the structure and composition of labour forces themselves. Of course, along with (and partly in response to) these pressures for innovation, there have occurred a wide range of changes in institutional arrangements affecting labour markets and industrial relations, as well as shifts in government policies. That these transformations have been underway worldwide for some time, that the nature of the change is very complex, and that the degree of the change continues to vary considerably across regions of the world, is now well understood.[1] What appears much less well understood are the implications for economic, social and political outcomes and how we ought to adapt our institutional arrangements in this context.

One important feature of post-World War II economic development has been the rise of regional trading blocs, especially in Europe, North America and Southeast Asia. The development of regional economic blocs typically built upon naturally evolving trade relationships and, in many cases, formal economic agreements among nations were undertaken only once regional trade was fairly well developed, although the trade agreements often served to strengthen economic integration over time. While developments in many of the major trading blocs have some important parallels, they remain quite distinct overall. For example, the North American trading bloc has so far only encompassed economic matters, whereas the arrangements governing economic union within the EEC are embedded in a far broader and deeper set of socio-political arrangements. We would, therefore, expect that the pressures on labour markets and industrial relations systems in North America, as well as their effects, differ from the pressures and outcomes occurring in Europe or the Pacific Rim. Even so, some aspects of the globalization process are creating common pressures (e.g. on unions or for increased workplace flexibility) that clearly transcend regional economic blocs, and these effects often emerge at the industry level or firm level.

In the following survey, we outline the challenges for labour policy, especially industrial relations, under a progressively transformed economic and workplace system. Our discussion is confined to developments in North America and, within that, we focus primarily upon Canada and the USA, primarily because of the broad social similarities as well as the historically very high degree of economic integration between the two countries.

Our particular emphasis is on highlighting the policy trade-offs that are involved in the current environment. Emphasis is placed on adjustments that occur through both the external labour market (e.g. often involving layoffs, job search and unemployment) as well as through the internal labour markets of firms (e.g. through their workplace practices and human resource policies). In fact, a theme of the chapter is that greater co-ordination of the external and internal adjustment policies is necessary in order to face the emerging challenges. The implications are explored for a wide range of labour policy initiatives including: collective bargaining law as conventionally embodied in labour relations acts; labour standards legislation in such areas as minimum wages, hours of work and overtime, and termination policies; human rights and anti-discrimination laws including those pertaining to pay and employment equity; health and safety and workers' compensation laws; pension and retirement policies; unemployment (now employment) insurance; training and adjustment policies; and income maintenance policies. Obviously, a comprehensive treatment of all of these policies is beyond the scope of this chapter; as such, they are used to illustrate the main points with respect to the restructuring of policy initiatives. Finally, particular attention is also placed on the role of government in diffusing workplace innovation.

The complexity of the process of transformation that Canadian and American policymakers confront and the public interests at stake are illustrated by the federal policy initiatives to reform federal labour relations in Canada in 1996 (i.e. Task Force on Review of the Canada Labour Code) and by the work of the national Dunlop Commission on labour relations in the USA in 1994.[2] In Canada, the labour movement remains relatively strong, and the labour relations policy initiative was confined to marginal changes to the legislation covering workers in the federal jurisdiction.[3] In this case, the objectives were limited and the strength of the labour movement was sufficient to ensure that legislative reform occurred and in a manner which did not necessarily compromise its interests. In contrast, the US initiative would have potentially affected a much larger proportion of the labour force than the Canadian initiative; it also took place against a backdrop of a labour movement functioning within the context of an increasingly de-unionized labour market and an apparent inability to create a sufficient bipartisan base of support for labour law reform within Congress. But the fundamental policy dilemma in both countries is that the consequences of labour market and workplace adjustment are giving rise to a growing need for labour policy initiatives at the same time as it is becoming increasingly difficult to create political and social consensus around national issues, as the fiscal imperatives are creating greater pressures to constrain costly policy initiatives, and as employers express their needs for flexibility. As traditional institutional arrangements become increasingly mismatched with the economic environment in which they are embedded, the challenge is to restructure the policies to meet the changing needs of all of the actors in the industrial relations system – employers, employees and governments.

In the following section, the primary background environmental factors affecting the industrial relations policy initiatives are briefly outlined. This is followed in the third section by a discussion of their implications and the challenges for labour market policy. In the fourth section, we concentrate on developments at the workplace level by considering the implications of the transformation of workplaces and the diffusion of workplace innovation for policy. We conclude with some general observations on industrial relations policy and the role of government in the new economic and workplace environment.

RICHARD P. CHAYKOWSKI AND MORLEY GUNDERSON

Environmental Factors and Outcomes Influencing Labour Policy Initiatives

The background environmental factors that are generating the transformation of the North American industrial relations system have been analysed in more detail in various sources.[4] As such, they are only briefly summarized here, with particular attention to those features that have the most important implications for labour policy. It is also important to emphasize that the background factors are intricately inter-related – so that it is, generally, not possible to attribute cause and effect uniquely to any one environmental factor.

On the demand side, pressures are emanating from a variety of inter-related sources. Globalization of product and capital markets, trade liberalization and technological change (especially associated with digitalization and the information economy) are leading to dramatic economic restructuring. Trade liberalization has occurred globally through such mechanisms as the General Agreement on Tariffs and Trade (GATT) and the World Trade Organization (WTO), but has been more advanced within the three regional trading blocs. In North America, the process of economic integration has evolved over the entire period of its modern history. In the latter twentieth century, the presence of US-based firms in Canadian industry became substantial, and American parent companies dominated in several key Canadian industries, such as auto manufacturing, chemicals, and oil. The Canada–US Automotive Products Trade Agreement (Auto Pact), not surprisingly, constituted one of the first major institutional steps towards North–South economic integration; while in the 1990s, the airline industry was opened through 'Open Skies' discussions.[5]

But it was the Canada–US Free Trade Agreement negotiated in the late 1980s and the subsequent North American Free Trade Agreement between Canada, the USA and Mexico that formalized the notion of a North American trading bloc that, in 1995, totalled 7,500 billion US$, of which the US economy alone accounted for roughly 90 per cent. Similarly, the trading bloc contained a combined labour force of approximately 181 million, of which the USA accounted for around 73 per cent. Perhaps more importantly, Canada and the USA represent each others' largest single trading partner; while Mexico is highly trade-dependent upon the USA, bilateral trade between the USA and Mexico is substantial but remains far less than the extent of Canada–US trade.

Technological change has contributed to a transformation in both the range of consumer products (e.g. computer software, medical services) in demand as well as in production systems (computer-aided design and manufacturing robotics). The former effect has played a supporting role in the rise in demand for the output of service-related industries and, therefore, in the long run industrial restructuring (especially the shift away from manufacturing towards services experienced in Western industrialized countries in the last several decades of the twentieth century). For organizations and workers, the effects of technological change have, however, been most profound in the workplace. Worldwide, technological innovation has stimulated and facilitated the evolution of production away from the once-dominant mass production system towards new production systems.

Labour market outcomes and workplace developments have reflected these demand-side developments. The shift towards a 'service economy' has resulted in the creation of jobs that are both 'high-end' ones associated with 'good jobs' (e.g. professional or managerial jobs that are of high skill and rewarded with high pay) as well as the 'bad jobs' in personal services. In some industries, mergers and acquisitions have been prominent, as firms restructure to attain the economies of scale or market niches to survive in the international marketplace and, in so doing, have often opted for a smaller core of full-time workers. Mass layoffs and worker displacement have led to substantial income losses and prolonged periods of pronounced unemployment.[6] Macroeconomic circumstances have contributed to the difficult labour market environment. Severe recessions in the early 1980s and 1990s have left a conspicuous legacy, with unemployment rates ratcheting up during each recession and yet not falling back during the subsequent 'jobless' recoveries. Restrictive monetary policies have restrained inflation but, along with the restrictive fiscal policies, they have also fostered the sustained unemployment. Although the aggregate unemployment rates have fallen considerably over the course of the economic boom that began in the late 1990s and carried into the new decade, there continues to be considerable worker displacement created as industries and firms continue to restructure.

While the degree of earnings and income inequality increased in most OECD countries through the 1980s and 1990s, it increased the most in the USA and the UK (Gottschalk and Smeeding, 1997).[7] In the USA this is, increasingly, viewed as a troubling trend, first because it has been an extension of a long-run trend in which earnings and income inequality have increased over the latter several decades of the past century and, second, because the USA has persistently ranked among the top Western industrialized countries in terms of the extent of inequality (Levy and Murnane, 1992;

Karoly, 1993; Gottschalk and Smeeding, 1997). Two specific aspects of this concern are the persistence of poverty and the possible 'hollowing out' of the American middle class (Duncan *et al.*, 1993; Gottschalk, 1997). In contrast, the increase in inequality in Canada has been quite limited relative to the US experience, and poverty rates have been relatively stable (Gottschalk and Smeeding, 1997; Osberg and Xu, 1999).[8] One of the institutional factors identified as contributing to the increase in US inequality has been the rapid de-unionization of the workforce – a factor not yet evident in Canada (Freeman, 1996; Fortin and Lemieux, 1997).[9] In contrast to both Canada and the USA, the degree (level) of inequality is quite pronounced in Mexico, and the level and extent of social safety net available in Canada and the USA is not available (see Commisison for Labor Cooperation, 1997).

On the supply side, the nature and composition of the workforce itself have been changing dramatically. The North American population is aging as the baby-boomers (the leading edge is now in their 50s) are impeding promotion opportunities and now also constitute an expensive component of the workforce, especially because of seniority-based wage increases, pension costs, and health and disability costs. They often also experience severe adjustment consequences if they are displaced from jobs where they have accumulated industry and firm-specific skills that are not readily adaptable to new forms of employment.

Women continue to enter the labour force in large numbers in both Canada and the USA, continuing a trend that has accelerated since the 1970s. In Canada and the USA, the two-earner family is now the norm and not the exception. Considerable ethnic diversity prevails in the workforce of both Canada and the USA, especially with respect to the new entrants. Immigration continues to represent a major source of labour-force growth in both of these countries.

In the public sector, governments have been under significant pressure to reduce deficits. While this can be done either by raising taxes or reducing expenditures, raising taxes has conventionally been unpopular in the USA and is, increasingly, a political 'non-starter' in Canada, leaving the reduction of expenditures as the main method. During the 1980s and 1990s in Canada, this has been manifest in several ways: reductions in government programmes; attempts to shift programme costs to other levels of governments;[10] attempts to shift costs to the private parties; privatization and subcontracting;[11] and the increased use of user-fees (Thompson and Ponak, 1992; Thompson, 1995). While the economic boom of the mid to late 1990s has afforded both American and Canadian governments the opportunity to achieve balanced budgets, it has not (yet) translated into a significant reversal of the overall trend towards fiscal austerity. While some have argued that many of these changes (such as decentralization, deregulation or privatization) have occurred in order to restructure government to achieve efficiencies, others maintain that these policies thinly disguise the real motive of simply shedding government expenditures.

Institutional changes have also been prominent among many OECD countries, most noticeably the decline of unionization in many countries, but especially in the United States. In the mid 1960s, union density rates were fairly similar in Canada and the United States; both were at approximately 30 per cent of the workforce that could potentially be unionized. While the overall rate in Canada has remained in the range of 30–35 per cent, in the USA it has declined to under roughly 15 per cent overall and the decline of US private sector unionism has been even more dramatic (now at around 11 per cent). In the face of this de-unionization of the labour force, there has been a complete failure of the American labour movement to achieve desired legislative reforms.[12] Consequently, unions in Canada have to bargain with a watchful eye to the South, especially because the United States is our major trading partner, and multinationals have increased discretion to shift their operations to non-union environments. This also has implications for earnings inequality, since the higher degree of unionization in Canada has helped reduce inequality relative to the United States (see Lemieux, 1993, 1997; Chaykowski, 1995b and Chaykowski and Slotsve, 1996).

Finally, the process of globalization has clearly stimulated a broad rethinking of the role and nature of nation states in the twenty-first century as well as altering the political landscape within countries (e.g. Rosencrance, 1996; Courchene, 1997; 1999). Interestingly, as globalization advances, economic regionalism is also increasingly prominent in several areas of the world (e.g. Catalonia in Europe; Ontario and the US states contiguous to the Great Lakes; British Columbia increasingly focuses on Asia-Pacific economic linkages; and the south-western US states and Northern Mexico) (Courchene, 1998). Within Canada, this economic regionalism is often reflected in emerging economic links on a North–South, as opposed to an East–West, basis. Regionalism in North America is also reflected in the political domain: in Mexico, the Chiapas region has distinct political challenges. In Canada, the Western provinces increasingly have a Western political focus; Quebec is preoccupied with issues of political separation; and the Atlantic provinces increasingly focus on Atlantic alliances.

Influenced by the new policy environment, there have also been significant shifts in the political agenda within Canada and the US. Many states in the USA have undertaken an extensive overhaul of their welfare systems, and some have argued that a new policy agenda is required if the USA is to gain ground in the fight against the persistent problem of poverty (see Blank, 1997). In Canada, decentralization has been prominent, with increasing powers being passed to the provinces (especially in the area of training), but also, at the same time, a greater responsibility for financing major social programmes (such as health and education) has also been devolved to the provinces.

Implications of the New Environment for North American Labour Market Policy

Labour Market Policy and the Shift in Political Leverage

Just as global competition and market imperatives are compelling employers to develop new strategic responses, unions also face similar challenges and choices with respect to various areas (see Chaykowski, 1995a; Lipsig-Mummé, 1995): organizing challenges; co-operative strategies; alliances with other interest groups; international initiatives to deal with the challenges that are occurring at the international level; and political strategies. Given that employers and unions are under pressure to develop strategic responses to survive, it would seem natural that governments are also under pressure to adjust their labour policy framework in order to ensure the attainment of desired policy objectives. In fact, the myriad of inter-related changes that are occurring in the economic and political environment are having profound implications for labour policies.

As indicated in the introduction, most of the changes are giving rise to a need for policy initiatives to deal with the adjustment consequences that are occurring. This is the case, for example, with respect to layoffs and job displacement and retraining needs, as well as with the prospect of growing income polarization and wage inequality. Meanwhile, the increasingly diverse workforce has given rise to pressure for initiatives, such as anti-discrimination laws and pay and employment equity initiatives, to facilitate the integration of diverse groups into the labour market.

At the same time as there is an increased demand for new initiatives, however, there is also growing pressure to reduce costly labour market regulations that can increase costs and reduce flexibility and competitiveness. That pressure from employers is also backed by their increased bargaining power in the political arena. This has occurred because employers now have a more credible threat of locating their plants and investment in countries (or different jurisdictions within countries) that are more 'open for business'.[13] This leverage stems from various factors: reduced tariffs mean that they can locate in low-cost countries and export into high-cost countries; physical capital in the form of plant and equipment is increasingly mobile, with flexible factories that are now linked by advanced communications and transportation systems, and less tied to local markets and raw resources; and financial capital is more mobile on a global basis (Thurow, 1992).

Jurisdictions can compete for that investment and the associated jobs in a variety of ways:[14] subsidies and tax breaks; public infrastructure; and reduced regulations, including labour regulations. This can lead to the downward harmonization of labour laws and policies to the lowest common denominator (i.e. a 'race to the bottom'). But there are forces that can mitigate this phenomenon and some regulations can save on labour costs elsewhere: workers' compensation, for example, can save on liability claims through the courts, since workers essentially have given up their right to sue employers in return for workers' compensation benefits (Chaykowski and Thomason, 1995).[15] One problem is that costs are often shifted back to employees, however, in the form of lower compensating wages for the benefits associated with such programmes as workers' compensation, unemployment insurance or pensions.[16] Public expenditures on a social safety net can also be 'good investments', saving on other public expenditures that might otherwise be necessary to deal with costly social maladies (such as crime and ill-health) that can be the by-products of not having an adequate social safety net. While cost saving elsewhere in the system and cost shifting can reduce the cost to employers of some labour policies and regulations, the fact remains that the net effect of most labour policies and regulations is to raise costs.[17]

To the extent that jurisdictions compete for business investment and jobs associated with that investment, employers have greater political bargaining power to resist these initiatives. In contrast, labour has experienced reduced political bargaining power. As noted above, organized labour in the USA operates under the prevailing threat of de-unionization and has little prospect of affecting labour policy in its favour. Moreover, its traditional alliance with the Democratic Party appears to be weakening with time, as union influence declines generally and as the Democratic Party itself seeks broader political alliances. In Canada, the traditional labour party (the New Democratic Party) suffered a significant loss of support at the national level in the 1990s. In some key provinces (notably Ontario) the New Democratic Party has also experienced a rift with some of the major unions as a result of its attempt, while in power in the early 1990s, to achieve fiscal restraint through a 'social contract' that was viewed by the labour movement as an attempt to set aside existing collective agreements (Hebdon and Warrian, 1999).

In the new economic context, the costs of new labour law initiatives are unlikely to be shifted forward to customers, since increased internationalization of trade means that consumers can purchase from markets where labour regulations do not add much to product costs.[18] Cost shifting backwards to capital is also not likely, given the greater international mobility of capital.

Individual workers, however, are increasingly likely to bear the brunt of the costs of labour law initiatives because the costs can be shifted backwards to them in the form of lower compensating wages in return for the benefits of such policies. Among individuals, cost shifting backwards to skilled labour is becoming somewhat less likely, given the mobility of professional and skilled labour. The backward cost shifting is therefore, unfortunately, most likely to occur for unskilled labour because it is the most immobile factor of production, hence unable to 'escape' the tax or cost-shifting. This could compound their already deteriorating labour market position – that is, they are more likely to bear the brunt of the adjustment consequences from any skill-biased technological change and import competition from countries with lower-wage labour.

Challenges For Labour Market Policy

In this section we outline key policy challenges confronting governments in North America (especially Canada and the USA) that arise in the context of the changing environment. For each issue that we set forth, we also outline some potential policy responses. These policy challenges and possible responses are presented in Table 5.1. While the set of challenges we present is not exhaustive, it does represent both some of the pressing ongoing concerns of governments as well as issues that are likely to intensify in importance over the coming decades. The fundamental assumption underlying the discussion of policy responses is that they require greater focus and flexibility and not that greater government involvement *per se* is required. Finally, while these policy challenges are not unique to North American nations, and while the discussion of potential policy responses may also be relevant for other industrialized countries, the discussion assumes a North American context.

The Persistence of the Plight of the Economically Disadvantaged
The previous discussion indicated that government policies that served an efficiency rationale (e.g. saved on costs elsewhere in the system) could survive under global competition with inter-jurisdictional competition for invest-

Table 5.1   *Key labour market policy issues and potential responses*

Policy challenge	Policy response
Persistence of the plight of the economically disadvantaged	Focus on the disadvantaged
Accounting for inter-generational concerns	Increasing inter-generational accountability in policy-making
Mismatch between macro-policies and individual requirements	Creating non-standard and flexible policy responses
Reducing the cost of labour–management conflict	Facilitating co-operative labour relations
Diversity in policy across jurisdictions	Enhancing co-ordination of policy across jurisdictions
Increased 'policy complexity'	Increased co-ordination across seemingly unrelated policy areas
Labour adjustment	Creation of active adjustment policies
Apparent conflict between policy and market forces	Accounting for market incentives and responses
Increased regionalism	Creating flexibility through regional policy approaches

ment and the associated jobs. Traditionally, the same cannot be said for policies that serve a pure equity-oriented or distributional function, such as assisting the more disadvantaged in society; they can conflict with efficiency, in which case a legitimate social trade-off between efficiency (a larger economic pie) and equity (a more equitably distributed pie) is involved.[19]

The labour policy dilemma is that, under globalization, it can become more difficult to finance the social programmes that assist the most disadvantaged; as indicated, costs cannot be shifted forwards to customers with increased global competition, nor can they be shifted backwards to capital given increased capital mobility, nor even to higher-paid labour given that their mobility allows them to escape the taxes. That leaves unskilled labour as the most immobile factor of production that cannot escape the taxes and, yet, this is the very group that is typically most in need of the assistance.

There are no easy answers to this policy dilemma. But, certainly, a legitimate response for governments is to *focus* policy initiatives on the disadvantaged rather than to have them dissipate to groups throughout the income distribution. This approach is made difficult by the fact that the disadvantaged are seldom represented at the political bargaining table when policies are established or changed; and policies that are initially established to assist the disadvantaged can often be accessed or 'captured' by the more advantaged groups.[20] Focusing on the disadvantaged is also made difficult by the fact that it can challenge notions of universality, and such notions often have broad political appeal (e.g. in Canada). Focusing on the disadvantaged can also mitigate against the effects of decentralization, at least for that aspect of public policy, because decentralization fosters the inter-jurisdictional competition that makes it difficult for any one jurisdiction to tax its residents for pure equity-oriented initiatives; and, in fact, it may serve as a magnet for drawing in the disadvantaged from other jurisdictions. A federal response (although not necessarily delivery) is more appropriate in such situations where mobile taxpayers can otherwise escape the burden, and mobile recipients can take advantage of different programmes.

Accounting for Inter-Generational Concerns

In political bargaining, not only are the disadvantaged seldom at the table, but also future generations are poorly represented. This creates a danger in that current generations may have incentives to foster policies that effectively pass the costs of such policies on to future generations of taxpayers. This can be the case, for example, with respect to pay-go schemes (such as the Canada Pension Plan or the Quebec Pension Plan) and workers' compensation, where substantial unfunded liabilities could be passed on to future generations.[21] Such inter-generational transfers can occur not only in pay-go systems, but also through such mechanisms as deferred compensation in the public sector, where lower current wages (that will benefit the current voters) are traded off for such components as pensions, job security and guaranteed promotions – the costs of which will be shifted somewhat to future generations of taxpayers.

Such schemes are balanced when there is stable population and economic growth, and the payouts are not questioned when there is a large taxpaying base of working age and a small population of recipients (as is currently the case). However, if that age triangle becomes inverted with the bulk of the population in the older age groups drawing benefits, and there is only a small taxpaying population of working age, then the system may not be sustainable. This could arise in Canada and the USA when the baby-boom population reaches the age of normal retirement (around the year 2010), drawing on pension benefits and incurring medical expenses, especially as life expectancy increases.[22]

Such inter-generational issues are therefore likely to be more important in the near future as the population ages and the baby boom reaches retirement age (e.g. see Foot and Stoffman, 1996) . Current policy initiatives must resist the temptation to shift the cost burden of policies to future generations. This can lead to several undesirable outcomes, including the imposition of an excessive burden on those generations that are not currently at the political bargaining table, and also to a withdrawal from such social contracts by future generations.[23]

Mismatch Between Macro-Policies and Individual Requirements

The share of total employment accounted for by non-standard forms of employment has generally increased throughout North America (see Commission for Labor Cooperation, 1997: Figure 29, p. 46). The rise of non-standard employment and the decline of traditional employment relationships create a potential mismatch between the requirements of individuals who no longer work at a traditional full-time, lifetime job in the same industry, or in a large, fixed work site, and existing policies that were designed when those traditional work characteristics were the norm. One alternative is to focus policies on individuals so that benefits and social plans are portable as workers move to any work site. In this way, non-standard employment may well require a non-standard policy response.[24] With respect to the delivery of programmes, it also highlights the need for customized assistance that is geared to the particular characteristics and needs of each individual. This can be facilitated by 'expert systems' computer programming that can more easily match the particular characteristics of individuals with the distinctive needs of employers.

Reducing the Cost of Labour–Management Conflict

The original labour relations policy frameworks of the Canadian and American industrial relations systems (i.e. the Wagner Act in the USA and PC1003 in Canada) have always recognized the importance of establishing the right of free collective association, free collective bargaining, and mitigating the costs associated with industrial and workplace conflict (Arthurs *et al.*, 1988; Kochan and Katz, 1988). Certainly, the legislation governing labour relations contains fairly elaborate and well-tuned provisions aimed at reducing the likelihood of work stoppages. More recently, however, both organized labour and management have placed increased emphasis on fostering labour–management co-operation (Verma and Cutcher-Gershenfeld, 1993; Kochan and Osterman, 1994; Walton *et al.*, 1994). This can range from new initiatives in collective bargaining to workplace participation, to voluntary employee buyouts and employee ownership (see Chaykowski and

Grant, 1995; Gunderson *et al.*, 1995).

Conflict during contract negotiations is also associated with the spill-over of adversarialism into the term of the collective agreement. Adversarialism and conflict in the workplace have potentially adverse effects on the efficiency of production and the quality of goods and services produced. Innovative approaches to collective bargaining that reduce conflict (e.g., mutual gains bargaining) could be supported through proactive government policies aimed at providing resources to the parties to pursue more co-operative bargaining techniques and to continue co-operative approaches into the term of the collective agreement (e.g. the provision of specialized training programmes and access to a bank of expert advisors) (Appelbaum and Batt, 1994; Chaykowski and Verma, 1994; Kochan and Osterman, 1994).

From the management viewpoint, the emphasis on employee commitment matches the objectives of fostering the new emphasis on quality and service. In other cases, employee involvement is itself a key element of a high-performance work system, while employee commitment is closely associated with the success of many of the other workplace innovations that are typically associated with high performance work systems. Management efforts to increase employee participation and involvement in the workplace appear to continue to extend to both unionized and non-unionized workplaces. While the emphasis on co-operative solutions has been heightened by competitive pressures, unions generally remain sceptical. The major concern of unions is that co-operation should not become either co-optation or a strategy to circumvent the role of the union (see Verma, 1995: p. 298).

Here the policy objective could be to create a two-way exchange whereby employee commitment to the organization can be fostered by organizational commitment to the employee. Information sharing and meaningful power-sharing can also foster true co-operative efforts. The current industrial relations systems in Canada and the USA can effectively allow for the development of joint union–management committees that support these two principles.[25] Labour relations policy could also readily focus on strengthening the development of joint workplace structures (e.g. committees).

Diversity in Policy Across Jurisdictions

The previous discussion highlighted the need for co-ordination across different levels of governments so as to prevent inter-jurisdictional competition that could dissipate equity-oriented social programmes.[26] Co-ordination across jurisdictions within a country may also be necessary to foster the internal mobility, trade and harmonization of standards that can enhance internal competitiveness as a pre-condition for external competitiveness.

This is the case, for example, with respect to requirements for occupational licensing, common skill certification, and training and education.

In Canada, one of the most conspicuous areas in which there is increasing diversity in policy across jurisdictions is in the sphere of labour relations. While the dissimilarities among existing labour relations legislation across Canadian jurisdictions is, arguably, less pronounced than Canada–US differences, there is an increasing tendency in some Canadian jurisdictions to benchmark policy objectives against American standards. In some jurisdictions, policy reforms are very reactive whereas in others policymakers are attempting to put forward a broad-based agenda. At present, there appears to be no co-ordination of strategies for reshaping labour relations policy (Chaykowski, 1995a).

Since product and capital markets are now global, international co-operation may also be necessary to ameliorate international competition on the basis of a dissipation of social programmes and labour standards. Promulgation of ILO (International Labour Organization) standards can help in this regard, as can social accords and labour side accords as part of trade agreements. The problem is that ILO standards are essentially voluntary (although the 'court of public opinion' can provide pressure) and it is notoriously difficult to enforce international agreements.[27] The complaint mechanisms in place under the North American Agreement in Labor Cooperation (NAALC) (the labour side-accord to the NAFTA) may provide a basis for more ambitious future 'upward harmonization' of labour standards in the region.[28]

Increased 'Policy Complexity'

The changing environment is requiring more co-ordination, not only across different governments, but also across different functional areas of government. Labour and human resource issues cannot be dealt with in isolation. They must be strategically co-ordinated with other government functions. For example, wage inequality within Canada has been mitigated considerably by the fact that the Canadian higher education system has extensively transformed potentially unskilled workers into skilled ones, reducing the supply of less skilled workers (thereby increasing their wages) and increasing the supply of skilled workers (thereby reducing their wages) (Freeman and Needels, 1993). In this case, the wage polarization is influenced by education policies. Similarly, labour issues are intricately linked to trade policies, as with labour accords being a potentially important aspect of trade policy (e.g. the NAALC and NAFTA). Issues such as payroll taxes have obvious implications for labour, not only because of the programmes that are financed by such policies, but also because of the potential for cost-shifting to labour (e.g. Abbott and Beach, 1997). Finally, child care policies can have an important effect on the labour force participation of women and on the type of work that is selected (Chaykowski and Powell, 1999).

The increased importance of co-ordinating across different functional areas of government is also highlighted by the fact that retrenchment in one area often leads to a substitution into other areas. For example, tightening up on disability benefits in workers' compensation can lead to a shift towards the use of disability benefits under the Canada Pension Plan/Quebec Pension Plan (CPP/QPP); tightening up on unemployment insurance can shift people to workers' compensation, and vice versa (Fortin and Lanoie, 1992).

Of even greater potential importance, there is growing realization that the health and well-being of individuals are influenced by the nature of their work, and especially by the control that lower-level workers can exercise over their own work. If the incidence of 'bad jobs' and unemployment can lead to bad health (see Grayson, 1989; and Jin *et al.*, 1995) and increased social costs, then increased unemployment and polarization into 'bad jobs' and 'no jobs' can have important implications beyond the labour market.[29]

Labour Adjustment

Competitiveness and equity can be fostered by active adjustment policies that facilitate the reallocation of labour from declining sectors and regions to expanding ones.[30] Such active adjustment policies include support for worker training, labour mobility and labour market information.[31] Encouraging marginal adjustment on a continuous basis is likely to be less disruptive than an approach whereby such adjustment pressures are allowed to build up and, inevitably, occur as inframarginal adjustments affecting whole communities and workers with little mobility. Also, reallocating labour from declining sectors towards expanding ones is likely to reduce wage inequality by reducing the supply of labour in the declining sectors and increasing it in the expanding ones. The active policy of the federal government in Canada to assist in the establishment of sectoral councils is a flexible and innovative response to the increased demand for support in the process of labour adjustment during the 1980s and 1990s.

Apparent Conflict Between Policy and Market Forces

The principle of the need to pay attention to market incentives involves a more general proposition that, in the design of policy initiatives, market responses (often subtle) have the potential to negate the effect of some policy initiatives, and can certainly lead to unintended adverse consequences.[32]

Employers can often shift the costs of labour market regulations even though they fall on employers in the first instance. This may be entirely appropriate, for example, when the costs of health and safety regulations are shifted forward to consumers so that the price they pay for the product reflects the true cost of producing it, including the health and safety costs that fall on workers. In other circumstances, however, the cost shifting is likely to be more subtle and an unintended by-product of the regulation. For example, the costs of private occupational pension plans can be shifted backwards to labour, and even the costs of reasonable accommodation requirements for injured workers are shifted back to those workers if they take a job with an employer other than the employer where their accident occurred (Gunderson *et al.*, 1992; Gunderson and Hyatt, 1996). As indicated previously, such cost shifting back to labour can be extremely difficult to absorb when real wages have already been stagnant since the mid 1970s, and when the cost shifting is likely to fall disproportionately on the immobile factor of production (i.e., less skilled labour) that is already being disadvantaged by the wage polarization that is leaving them behind.

These illustrations are not meant to imply that policies that regulate (e.g. terminations, overtime, pensions, or reasonable accommodation requirements) are negative; rather, the intention is to illustrate the subtle market adjustments that can occur, and that can lead to unintended outcomes. Rightly or wrongly, such adjustments are likely to become more prevalent where market forces are becoming more prominent. The design of policy initiatives must take into account these new realities, perhaps by harnessing the forces of the market when they can complement the policy initiatives.

Increased Regionalism

Policy initiatives could also try to harness the new sectoral and regional realities that are emerging (Chaykowski and Verma, 1992). As noted above, regional alliances are becoming stronger, reflecting the new trade patterns and common sources of comparative advantage. Increased policy attention is also being placed on the common management and labour problems and aspirations of specific industries. This is perhaps most evidenced by the emergence of sector councils in both Canada and the USA that deal with human resource issues such as adjustment, training and standards (Gunderson and Sharpe, 1998). These sectoral councils are much more developed in Canada, where they are actively supported by policy at the federal level.

One advantage of such sector councils is that they can harness the expertise and delivery mechanisms of specific industries at the same time as they serve as a viable mechanism to assist in the design and delivery of certain policy initiatives (e.g. the retraining of displaced workers). Most of the existing sectoral councils in Canada are essentially joint labour–management councils that operate at a much broader level than the establishment. Consequently, their ability to survive, in spite of an industrial relations system that is designed to have union–management relations function at the firm level, is an important development. Thus one policy opportunity challenge in Canada is to adjust the existing labour relations framework to facilitate union–management relations at the broader (sectoral) level, although to date there has been no strong lobby in favour of establishing industry-wide bargaining. In the USA, the policy objective would be a more modest attempt to foster the broad-based establishment of sectoral councils, although here, too, there appears to be little interest in such a government policy.

Since many of the labour market adjustments occur *across* industries, co-ordination at this level is also necessary, especially to facilitate the reallocation of labour from declining to expanding sectors. While policy related to training programmes or standards legislation may lend itself to greater cross-industry co-ordination than now exists, labour relations appears to be one area in which current policy does not.

The 'New Workplace', Labour Policy and the Diffusion of Workplace Innovation

The Emerging Workplace and 'Workplace Policy'

As the variants of the archetypal mass production model declined in importance across advanced industrialized economies following World War II, it was replaced by a variety of alternatives that were typically associated with specific nations. In Europe, several systems emerged including flexible specialization in Italy, diversified quality production in Germany and variants of socio-technical systems (e.g. in Sweden); and the lean production system evolved in Japan (Appelbaum and Batt, 1994). In many American and Canadian industries, firms that faced increasing competitive pressures eventually attempted to introduce some aspects of several of these production systems, giving rise to hybrids that, today, are often accompanied by new organizational structures, new forms of work organization, experimentation with a variety of human resource practices that are believed to increase productivity, and an increasing reliance on non-standard employment arrangements.

Dramatic changes have been occurring in the organizational structures of firms and in the characteristics of employment relationships (e.g. see Cappelli *et al.*, 1997; Kochan and Useem, 1992). Organizational flexibility has increased significantly relative to the more rigidly designed, hierarchial systems that emerged under scientific management: job classifications have become broader in scope as 'multi-tasking' and 'multi-skilling' have become more prominent; workplace teams and employee involvement have blurred traditional lines of demarcation across jobs. These changes in organizational structures have been facilitated by the reduction in the size of middle-management and the creation of flatter structures and more lateral (or horizontal) lines of authority relative to the traditional organizations that were characterized by more vertical, hierarchial structures. These types of changes have been reflected in workplace practices and human resource policies of firms. There is emerging evidence as well that, across many advanced industrialized countries (e.g. the United States, United Kingdom, Germany, Japan, Italy), in at least some industries, there are 'growing divergences in employment relations within countries . . . [but] convergence in employment systems across countries' (Katz and Darbishire, 2000, p. 263). Even so, it is also clear that the degree of uniformity of employment systems arising out of the mass production model is not likely to reappear in the near future.

Employment practices have also adapted to create more flexibility, primarily evidenced by the rise of non-standard employment in various forms (e.g. part-time, contract and self-employment contracts; and the use of temporary help agencies and subcontracting) (Krahn, 1995; Abraham, 1990). While some of the non-standard employment has been voluntary, especially among workers attempting to balance labour market and family responsibilities, much of it remains involuntary. Pay has become more flexible and geared to the performance of individual employees. In unionized firms, the ability of the organization to pay appears to have dominated contract settlements, as pattern bargaining has generally dissipated throughout Western industrialized countries (Katz, 1993). More-over, globalization has meant that multinationals have increased spatial discretion in the location of different aspects of their business: production and assembling in countries with low wages and labour standards; ware-housing and distribution facilities in countries with large markets; and research and development in home bases, although the concept of a home base is increasingly ephemeral. The ability of unions to 'take wages out of competition' has been severely restricted by this new corporate 'global leverage'.

Highly adaptive firms have typically undertaken changes in various dimensions of the workplace as well as human resource practices, including moves towards flexible work organization, team-based structures, increased employee involvement, investment in the enhancement of employee training and skills, and the use of variable pay systems (typically to complement base wages).[33] Together, workplaces with most of these characteristics have come to be referred to as 'high performance work systems' because they offer the prospect of delivering higher productivity (hence competitiveness). While many observers acknowledge that developing these characteristics is advantageous, there is a challenge: on the one hand, by the mid 1990s, adoption of these practices across Canadian and American organizations appeared to be very limited and even among those firms that had developed some of these characteristics, most had only adopted some of these elements; on the other hand, there is evidence that these practices will tend to deliver the desired outcomes when adopted together in 'bundles'.[34] Betcherman *et al.* (1994) and Ichniowski *et al.* (1997) present evidence on the impact of human resource practices. Thus there appears to be stickiness in the pace of adoption and a resulting 'adoption deficit'.

Consequently, some observers have suggested that there may be a 'facilitative' role for government in promoting and diffusing best practices. For example, Appelbaum and Batt (1994) and Kochan and Osterman (1994) suggest a range of supportive roles for government to perform to address such issues as the presence of market externalities, the rise of employment insecurity, and the persistence of informational and institutional barriers. The appropriate role of government in the 'workplace' area is different from the typical direct legislative route because these practices are internal to the firm and therefore involve the private decision-making of firms, just as in areas such as finance, marketing and production.[35] For others, this implies that governments should have no role outside the normal application of laws; that is, internal labour market decisions are best left up to the (private) parties with the internal expertise and responsibility for those decisions.

Challenges to Workplace Policy

The previous labour market policy discussion highlighted the implications of changes in the economic and political environment for the role of broader labour market policy in dealing mainly with adjustments that occur through external labour markets, in such forms as layoffs, job search and unemployment. However, growing emphasis in policy circles is being placed on the adjustments that are occurring within firms and in creating and sustaining 'good' jobs. The typical concerns are that, left to an imperfect market alone, the extent of innovation and pace of diffusion of innovations may be too slow to foster competitiveness, that firms may opt for a 'low road' of low wages and poor employment conditions as a path to competitiveness, or that the 'new workplace' may not generate a sufficient level of investment in human capital.

While the appropriate role of government policy with respect to workplace practices and human resource policies of firms will likely be subject to considerable debate into the future, a number of issues can be identified, and potential responses offered, to inform that debate. This is illustrated in the following discussion with respect to the potential rationale for government involvement with respect to certain internal workplace issues, and the appropriate form that involvement ought to take. See also Table 5.2.

Table 5.2 *Key workplace policy issues and potential responses*

Policy challenge	Policy response
Increasing the level and diffusion of successful innovation	Supporting the diffusion of workplace innovations in line with the public good nature of workplace innovations
Presence of negative 'training spillovers'	Sector councils; human capital loans
Adjustments that create dislocation and labour market and social costs	Supportive policies that cushion external adjustments
Spillovers from high-performance workplace strategies	Policies that support networks, employee involvement, teams, etc.
Presence of wage premia due to noncompetitive constraints	Encouraging the growth of 'good' jobs

Increasing the Level and Diffusion of Successful Innovation

Even if one takes the view that government policy is merited only when there are well-defined failures in the mechanisms of the private market or collective bargaining, this does not preclude a role for government policy with respect to the internal workplace practices and human resource policies of firms when workplace innovation has a public good aspect. It is well known that private markets will yield a less than socially optimal amount of innovation if the innovators cannot patent such innovations. In such circumstances, firms that innovate bear the full cost of the innovation but they are unable to appropriate the full benefits since successful innovations will be quickly adopted by competitors. The innovating firm would only have a slight lead in the market and the increasingly rapid diffusion of technological change only serves to exacerbate this problem. Innovation therefore has, in principle, the twin characteristics of public goods: the benefits are equally available to all; and the market does not exclude non-payers.

The same problem can prevail with respect to innovative workplace practice (see Gunderson, 1986, p. 127). Individual firms may therefore not have sufficient incentive to engage in such innovations, since they would bear the full cost of failures and yet competitors could share the benefits of successful ones.[36] Unlike in product markets where the appropriate incentives can be established by systems of patents, such patents are not possible with respect to innovative workplace and human resource practices. In such circumstances, it is possible that organizations could collectively become trapped in a 'low-innovation' equilibrium game, even though it could be in their collective best interest to co-operate and experiment with more innovative practices.

Certainly, workplace innovations do occur in spite of these problems. Innovations can give firms a temporary advantage in production, and organizations may benefit from a reputation as a progressive, innovative firm and this may, for example, in turn assist in their recruitment and retention of employees.[37] Whole production systems also can be 'shocked' into adopting new workplace and labour relations practices as occurred, for example, in the North American auto industry in response to Japanese approaches to enhance quality and commitment (Katz, 1985; Kochan et al., 1986). Over the past several decades, various elements of alternative production systems have been adopted by some Canadian and American firms, including aspects of Japanese lean production, Italian flexible production, and the Swedish socio-technical systems approach. While workplace innovation clearly does occur over time, the amount of such innovation may still be inhibited by the fact that private market forces provide insufficient (albeit not zero) incentives for innovative workplace practices.

Unfortunately, governments in Canada and the USA have relatively little experience in supporting the development and diffusion of workplace innovations. In this regard, policy makers may observe useful lessons from policies designed to support innovation in scientific research and development. One obstacle that policy in the area of workplace innovation may have more difficulty in overcoming in Canada and the United States, relative to Europe for example, is managerial resistance to the idea of a proactive policy.

Presence of Negative Training Spillovers

In advanced economies with a sizeable 'knowledge-based' industrial component, substantial investment in human capital is seen to be one of the key factors underpinning productivity growth and hence national competitiveness (for example see Thurow, 1992). Training, particularly that which is provided 'on-the-job', is an important component of a nation's overall investment in human capital. General training is precisely the type of training that is increasingly desirable (especially from an employee standpoint) given the increased likelihood that workers will be employed in different organizations over their lifetime.

Firms can be reluctant to provide such training, since they run the risk that their newly trained workers will simply be 'poached' by other firms that hire them away by paying higher wages. Individual workers should have an incentive to pay for general training since they will reap the benefits in the form of higher wages and greater employment opportunities. However, they may find it difficult to finance such training, and they may not be able to borrow because they cannot use their 'human capital' as collateral for a loan (unlike their ability to use physical assets to finance loans). National under-investment in training has long been of concern, so government programmes aimed at supporting investment in general (re)training would likely assist in easing worker job transitions as well as support overall labour productivity. To the extent that some sector councils in Canada have concentrated on providing advanced skills to workers, government support for joint labour–management councils is an example of this kind of policy (Gunderson and Sharpe, 1998).

Adjustments that Create Dislocation and Labour Market and Social Costs

Governments may also have a role to play with respect to the internal workplace and human resource practices of firms if they wish to avoid the prospect of fallout from difficult internal labour market adjustments (e.g. mass layoffs, unemployment). If so, then they may find it to be an expeditious 'second-best' policy to attempt to influence those internal adjustments *ex ante*, in order to reduce the negative consequences that ultimately fall on governments *ex post* in their role of dealing with the consequences of these internal adjustments in the external labour market and through other social programmes.

For example, governments may find it in their interest to encourage internal worksharing and voluntary early retirement to reduce short-term unemployment. Or, if job stress and lack of job control are important contributors to ill-health, then governments may find it expeditious to deal with such issues at the workplace level rather than through the residual fallouts on the workers' compensation or health-care systems. This suggests a role for government for supporting firm-level human resource practices and firm programmes that promote desirable outcomes.

Spillovers From High-Performance Workplace Strategies

In the endogenous growth literature,[38] both theory and empirical evidence suggest that there may be significant spillovers generated by the growth process itself – that is, 'growth begets growth'. This can occur through the forward and backward linkages and agglomeration externalities that are generated by the clustering of investments in physical and human capital. Diminishing returns to such investments does not occur because of the potential for infinite combinations of ingredients of inputs.

When applied to workplace practices and human resource policies, for example, this perspective would suggest that significant spillover benefits and positive interaction effects can prevail to clusters of firms that follow a 'high-road' human resource strategy and invest in a high-performance workplace and workforce;[39] in this case, the 'high road begets the high road'. Network externalities can generate significant information and new ideas in informal fashions. Such information flows can be fostered externally through organizational clusters and institutional mechanisms such as sector councils. They can also be fostered internally by employee involvement programmes and by workplace teams that share ideas. One of the recent concerns of downsizing, for example, has been the loss of experienced people who had inside information and networks (i.e. corporate memory) – intangibles that are not usually written out in every job description but which, nonetheless, constitute valuable productivity-enhancing skills and knowledge. This suggests a potential role for government in providing support for networks, employee involvement, etc.

Presence of Wage Premia Due to Non-competitive Constraints

As part of their internal workplace practices, firms may voluntarily pay efficiency wage premiums above the competitive norm. Such premiums can 'pay for themselves' by eliciting positive work behaviour and reducing costly turnover.[40] Jobs that pay such premia may have a range of characteristics associated with 'good jobs'. Jobs that pay efficiency wage premia are obviously preferred by employees because the premium is paid in return for positive work behaviour and commitment that does not generate disutility to workers. Jobs that pay efficiency wage premiums are also preferred by society since they have the potential to make both employers and employees better off.

Governments therefore may have a role in encouraging the formation of such 'good jobs'.

The problem is in identifying such jobs and distinguishing them from jobs that simply pay wage premia because of non-competitive constraints such as occupational licensing, unions, public sector employment, regulations, or monopoly profits. Also, jobs that pay efficiency wages are already likely to be higher-wage jobs, in which case the benefits would be going to the already advantaged rather than the disadvantaged.

Concluding Observations on Policy

While there has been some debate over whether or not the contemporary trend towards the increased globalization of financial and commodity markets is truly 'unprecedented', the general view is certainly that, regardless of how we may place the current globalization in historical context, it is having a profound effect on the social, political and economic fabric of nations.[41] Bordo et al. (1999, p. 57) also conclude that perhaps one of the most important factors that accounts for the relative economic stability enjoyed during the current trend towards globalization is the success of the institutional arrangements put in place at the national (e.g. social safety net) and international (World Trade Organization or the International Monetary Fund) levels. Ironically, in many countries, people fear that economic globalization will weaken the ability of nation states to exercise traditional policy levers in order to craft independent social policies, while others fear that international economic organizations will ultimately serve to weaken nation states' political and economic sovereignty. Whatever the final outcome, it would appear that by the close of the twentieth century the potentially diverse and far-reaching implications of globalization for governance continued to be a source of debate – as has the controversy over the role of government and the appropriate nature of labour policy.[42]

The discussion in this chapter has highlighted how the changing environment is giving rise to strategic responses on the part of both labour and management. Not surprisingly, governments must also restructure their policy initiatives if they are to remain relevant in the 'new economy and workplace'. With respect to the external labour market – the conventional purview of government policy – implications for a wide range of policy directions were outlined, including: focusing on the disadvantaged; increasing attention to inter-generational issues; focusing on the individual; emphasizing co-operation; developing co-ordination across different levels of government, including international initiatives; enhancing accord across related policy areas; developing active adjustment assistance to facilitate reallocation of labour from declining to expanding sectors; considering market incentives and responses in policy design; and supporting regional and sectoral initiatives. With respect to internal labour market issues involving workplace and human resource practices, new approaches and principles have to be developed because this is not a conventional area for government policy. We argued that the potential rationale for government involvement was linked to a variety of considerations: the public good nature of workplace innovation; the presence of training spillovers; a reduction of pressure on external labour market adjustments; potential for spillovers from high-performance workplaces; and the presence of efficiency wages. In most cases, the rationale for government policy intervention is related to spillover benefits to third parties that emanate from workplace practices, especially innovative practices. In such circumstances, the private parties themselves may not move with either sufficient intensity or rapidity in the development of such practices. Consequently, there may be a potential role for governments to foster such practices.

While there may be a *potential* role for governments, the appropriate *actual* role depends upon whether governments will be able to improve on what may be an otherwise imperfect solution that emerges from either private sector (management) decision-making or collective bargaining at the workplace. Given the difficulties in identifying the potential spillovers that are not internalized by the private parties, and the likelihood that a great deal of the benefits of government activity will be captured by special interest groups (who are not the disadvantaged) and by rent-seeking activity, there is good reason to question whether a potential rationale for government intervention should be taken as an actual basis for such intervention.

With that caveat in mind, a more limited role for governments in this area could encompass the dissemination of information on best practices. Awards for workplace innovations that have broader social implications would be merited, as would more extensive subsidies, although the best mechanism for such support is not obvious. Support for collective mechanisms for co-operation and for the exchange of such information (e.g. through sector councils) could also be merited. Governments could also engage in such innovative workplace practices internally, with the successful innovations providing a model that could be emulated in the private sector. In Canada, Crown corporations provide a potential vehicle for such experimentation, since they often run the spectrum from ones that essentially approximate government departments to ones that are very similar to private sector organizations.

Clearly, the role of government policy is changing in response to new pressures in both external labour markets and at the workplace level of firms. A fundamental rethinking of that changing role is necessary – especially with respect to the workplace practices of firms and the interaction between external and internal labour market adjustments. The absence of an active strategic policy response to the new environment invites a piecemeal, reactive approach that will simply lend itself to the deconstruction of the policies and institutions that have been built up, while the rapidly evolving forces that are giving rise to the challenges and opportunities that nations confront shape the future.

Notes

1. During the period of the late 1980s through the 1990s, there was a burgeoning literature on all aspects of globalization. Some examples of relevance to North American economic development include Thurow (1992; 1999), Ohmae (1995), Courchene (1997; 1999). In particular, Thurow has taken a broad view of American economic development and updated his views on the future path of development of the US economy.
2. Also, for Canada see the 1997 federal paper *Report of the Advisory Committee on the Changing Workplace,* and for the USA, refer to the 1994 document *Fact Finding Report: Commission on the Future of Worker–Management Relations.*
3. In Canada, under the constitution, in labour matters the federal government only has legislative powers within its own jurisdiction (which has tended to include roughly 10 per cent of the workforce employed in such industries as rail, shipping and air transportation, communications, and the federal public service), while each of Canada's provincial governments retains authority within its own territory.
4. See, for example, Appelbaum and Batt (1994), Kochan *et al.* (1986) and Cappelli *et al.* (1997) for the United States; for Canada, see Chaykowski and Verma (1992; 1994), Betcherman *et al.* (1994), and Gunderson and Riddell (1995; 1996), Verma and Chaykowski (1999).
5. The importance of the Auto Pact to the Canadian and US industries and the implications for industrial relations are described in Kumar and Meltz (1992), while the 'Open Skies' negotiations are discussed in Fisher and Kondra (1992). Other industry-level negotiations have occurred in industries in which trade is important, such as forestry and fishing.
6. Earnings losses in the neighbourhood of 10–30 per cent are typical for such displaced workers. See Jacobson *et al.* (1993) for a review.

7. Gottschalk and Smeeding (1997) provide a comprehensive comparative review of the trends in earnings and income inequality among OECD countries up to the early 1990s, while Karoly (1993) and Levy and Murnane (1992) provide thorough reviews of trends in inequality in the USA over earlier periods.

8. Canadian evidence is provided in Beach and Slotsve (1996), Morissette *et al.* (1995) and Picot (1996). The evidence also indicates that in Canada, relative to the USA, the polarization in hours worked is an important factor contributing to the polarization of earnings.

9. Most of the increase in economic inequality is attributable to a set of supply-side and demand-side factors that have shifted over time (e.g. see Levy and Murnane, 1992; Gottschalk and Smeeding, 1997; Johnson, 1997).

10. In Canada, the federal government has reduced transfer payments to the provinces and, in turn, in some provinces (e.g., Ontario or Alberta) responsibilities have been devolved to the local (i.e. municipal) level and funding for education and health care (both provincial responsibilities) either cut or frozen.

11. In Canada, both the federal and various provincial governments privatized major firms were that were once Crown corporations that symbolized government presence in key Canadian industries (e.g., at the federal level, the national airline (Air Canada) and one of two national rail lines (Canadian National) were privatized; and, as recently as 1999–2000 at the provincial level, the major provincial power utility, Ontario Hydro, was being broken up and undergoing some privatization) (see Thompson, 1995).

12. Particularly disappointing to the US labour movement was the failure of the Dunlop Commission, appointed during the first Clinton administration, to result in any reforms (USDL/USDC, 1994). There appears to be no prospect for further attempts at reforming labour legislation during the term of the first post-2000 presidency.

13. This was clearly a factor that weakened unions in the US (see Kochan *et al.*, 1986).

14. Theoretical issues pertaining to inter-jurisdictional competition and the harmonization of labour regulations, and the literature on that topic, are discussed in Gunderson (1997).

15. As other examples, termination and advance notice legislation can reduce employee resistance to efficient changes, and it can encourage early job search that can benefit both employees and employers. Employer contributions to public health care costs can save on private

health care insurance.

16. The empirical evidence on such cost shifting suggests that almost all of the costs of payroll taxes are shifted back to workers in the long run (Dahlby, 1993; Di Matteo and Shannon, 1995).

17. Otherwise, all that would be necessary is to inform employers that these policies are in their interests, and no resources would have to be devoted to enforcement. This is not to suggest that many employers do not fully account for the benefits that may accrue to them as a result of various government 'safety net' programmes. However, the costs/benefits may be unequally distributed across employers, and, on net, the benefits may accrue to employees.

18. This helps to explain the campaigns in Canada and the USA in the 1990s to boycott clothing manufactured overseas under conditions that do not meet basic international labour standards. In this case, the boycotts rely heavily upon moral suasion.

19. Such policies need not always conflict with efficiency if, for example, they 'buy' social stability or save on social services elsewhere in the system, or reduce resistance to otherwise efficient changes. Nevertheless, it is entirely legitimate for society to choose equity-oriented policies to assist the most disadvantaged, even if they conflict with efficiency objectives on a narrow cost-benefit evaluation.

20. It should not then be surprising that the more advantaged groups in society that rise to the top in the economic market place would not also be skilled in using the political marketplace.

21. For this situation to be stable across generations, the current generation essentially pays for the benefits of previous generations, in return for which future generations are expected to pay for the subsequent benefits that current generations can expect in the future.

22. This assumes, of course, that there is no dramatic change in the immigration policies in place.

23. This withdrawal need not be explicit. It can come in subtle forms, such as slow reductions in health care expenditures, de-indexing of pensions, clawing back of pension benefits, and more stringency in benefit payouts under workers' compensation.

24. In the training area, for example, this approach implies the need for generally usable training that can be used in a variety of work environments. It also highlights the need for modular training that can be built upon and repackaged in a process of lifelong (re)learning. In the collective bargaining arena it may require that policymakers develop means of representation that are more closely related to the

individual rather than linked to the workplace (see Betcherman and Chaykowski, 1996, p. 11).

25. Chaykowski (1997; 1999) examines a case that illustrates the broad development of joint committees in a very traditional labour relations context.

26. Such competition among different governments could, however, be desirable if it led to a dissipation of government policies that did not provide a public infrastructure in a cost-effective fashion or that simply protected the 'economic rents' of already privileged groups. Nevertheless, it can also inhibit governments from establishing purely equity-oriented policies that do not 'pay' on narrow efficiency criteria.

27. When they are incorporated as part of trade agreements, they run the risk of being simply thinly disguised forms of protectionism, especially when the high-wage developed countries try to have *their* more expensive labour standards imposed on the lower-wage countries.

28. The NAALC provides a mechanism by which a country may essentially lodge a complaint about the failure of another to enforce their own (national) standards.

29. It also highlights the difficulty of attributing cause and effect in workers' compensation systems when compensation is forthcoming only when the accident and disease can be attributed to events at the workplace. Even if workplace stress and lack of job control can be important contributors to disease and health problems, it is not likely that the separate and independent effect of workplace issues can be disentangled so as to provide workers' compensation for such cases. Clearly, labour policy issues are intricately related to broader policy issues, in this case to issues of general health and well-being.

30. Even so, income maintenance programmes obviously will likely still have a role to play, especially for those persons for whom labour market work is not a viable alternative.

31. These approaches are in contrast to the more passive income maintenance programmes that can discourage labour from leaving the declining sectors.

32. Regulations that make it more difficult or costly to lay off or terminate employees, for example, could become anticipated at the hiring stage, discouraging the hiring of employees who may subsequently have to be laid off. In essence, the expected termination costs become quasi-fixed costs at the hiring stage. This could discourage the hiring of new workers and encourage firms to employ their existing workforce overtime hours so as to amortize the quasi-fixed hiring costs. It could also encourage the

use of non-standard workforces (e.g. use of subcontracting, temporary help agencies or contract work) to avoid the quasi-fixed costs of hiring new workers.

33. Betcherman and Chaykowski (1996) provide a discussion of these dimensions of a high performance work system and the high-road versus low-road paths to competitiveness.

34. Betcherman *et al.* (1994) and Osterman (1994) provide survey evidence on the extent of usage of these characteristics of high performance work systems in Canada and the USA, respectively.

35. Such decisions are, of course, subject to constraints imposed by legislation and collective agreements, where applicable.

36. Nor do firms have a sufficient incentive to diffuse innovative workplace practices 'deeper' within the organization (since that would make them more transparent to competitors) or 'broader' to other organizations, since they cannot 'sell' the innovation.

37. Consulting firms obviously market their innovative practices across different organizations and, in fact, the increase in such firms may well be the market's response to this gap. Nevertheless, even here, it is difficult to prevent competitors from simply 'free riding' and copying the successful innovations, although consulting firms will try to inhibit such practices by 'customizing' their product to match as uniquely as possible the corporate culture of each organization.

38. A discussion of this literature, along with an application to labour market and human resource issues, is given in Gunderson (1996).

39. This is over and above the positive benefits to individual firms; Canadian evidence is discussed in Betcherman *et al.* (1994), Chaykowski and Grant (1995), Wagar (1995), Betcherman and Chaykowski (1996).

40. Note that these premia can include any form of compensation. Efficiency wage theories are analysed in Akerlof and Yellen (1986).

41. For example, Bordo *et al.* (1999) discuss the debate on the historical context of the current wave of globalization and argue that the extent of the current (economic) globalization process clearly exceeds that which occurred at the economic height of the British Empire during the late nineteenth century.

42. The scope of this debate over the implications of globalization is reflected in diversity of views across such work as that by Ohmae (1990), Rosencrance (1996), Ostry (1997) and Zacher (1997) .

REFERENCES

Abbott, M. and Beach, C. (1997) 'The Impact of Employer Payroll Taxes on Employment and Wages: Evidence for Canada, 1970–1993', in M. Abbott, C. Beach and R. Chaykowski (eds), *Transition and Structural Change in the North American Labour Market.* Kingston. ON: IRC Press, pp. 154–234.

Abraham, K. (1990) 'Restructuring the Employment Relationship: The Growth of Market-Mediated Work Arrangements', in K. Abraham and R. B. McKersie (eds), *New Developments in the Labor Market: Toward a New Institutional Paradigm.* Cambridge: The MIT Press, pp. 85–119.

ACIRRT (Australian Centre for Industrial Relations Research and Training) (1999) *Australia at Work: Just Managing?* Sydney: Prentice Hall.

Ackers, P., Smith, C. and Smith, P. (eds) (1996) *The New Workplace and Trade Unionism.* London: Routledge.

Adams, E. E. (1991) 'Quality Circle Performance', *Journal of Management,* 17, 25–39.

Advisory Committee on the Changing Workplace (1996) *Report of the Advisory Committee on the Changing Workplace.* Ottawa: Ministry of Public Works and Government Services Canada.

Aglietta, M. (1979) *A Theory of Capitalist Regulation.* London: Verso.

Akerlof, G. and Yellen, J. (eds) (1986) *Efficiency Wage Models of the Labor Market.* New York: Cambridge University Press.

Aktouf, O. (1991) 'Adhésion et pouvoir partagé. Le cas Cascades', *Annales des mines: gérer et comprendre,* 23, June, 44–57.

Albert, M. (1991) *Capitalism Contra Capitalisme.* Paris: Seuil.

Angle, H. L. and Perry, J. L. (1986) 'Dual Commitment and Labor-Management Relationship Climates', *Academy of Management Journal,* 29, 31–50.

Aoki, M. (1988) *Information, Incentives, and Bargaining in the Japanese Economy.* Cambridge: Cambridge University Press.

Appelbaum, E., Bailey, T., Berg, P. and Kalleberg, A. L. (1994) *Cross Industry Employee/ Employer Survey: Pilot Project Report to the Alfred P. Sloan Foundation.* Washington, DC: Economic Policy Institute, Unpublished Manuscript.

Appelbaum, E., Bailey, T., Berg, P. and Kalleberg, A. L. (2000) *Manufacturing Advantage: Why High-Performance Work Systems Pay Off.* Ithaca: Cornell University Press.

Appelbaum, E. and Batt, R. (1994) *The New American Workplace: Transforming Work Systems in the United States.* Ithaca: ILR Press.

Appelbaum, E. and Berg, P. (1996) 'Financial Market Constraints and Business Strategy in the USA', in J. Michie and J. G. Smith (eds), *Creating Industrial Capacity:*

Towards Full Employment. Oxford: Oxford University Press, pp. 192–221.

Appelbaum, E. and Berg, P. (1997) 'Work Reorganization and Flexibility in Job Design', in D. Lewin, D. J. B. Mitchell and M. A. Zaidi (eds), *The Human Resource Management Handbook.* Greenwich: JAI Press, pp. 45–62.

Armstrong, P. (1988) 'Labour and Monopoly Capital', in R. Hyman and W. Streeck (eds), *New Technology and Industrial Relations.* Oxford: Blackwell, pp. 143–59.

Arthur, J. B. (1992) 'The Link Between Business Strategy and Industrial Relations Systems in American Steel Minimills', *Industrial and Labor Relations Review,* 45 (3), 488–505.

Arthurs, H., Carter, D., Fudge, J. and Glasbeek, H. (1988) *Labour Law and Industrial Relations In Canada.* 3rd edn. Deventer: Kluwer; Toronto, ON: Butterworths.

Atkinson, J. (ed.) (1985) *Manpower Policy and Practice.* Aldershot: Gower.

Babson, S. (1996) 'A New Model Ford?', *Asia Pacific Business Review,* 2 (4), 82–98.

Baethge, M. and Wolfe, H. (1995) 'Continuity and Change in the '"German Model" of Industrial Relations', in R. Locke, T. A. Kochan and M. Piore (eds), *Employment Relations in a Changing World Economy.* Cambridge: The MIT Press, pp. 231–62.

Bailey, T. and Merritt, D. (1992) *Discretionary Effort and the Organization of Work: Employee Participation and Work Reform Since Hawthorne,* Working Paper, Teachers College and Conservation of Human Resources. New York: Columbia University.

Barker, J. R. (1993) 'Tightening the Iron Cage: Concertive Control in Self-Managing Teams', *Administrative Science Quarterly,* 38, 408–37.

Barley, S. and Kunda, G. (1992) 'Design and Devotion: Surges of Rational and Normative Ideologies of Control in Managerial Discourse', *Administrative Science Quarterly,* 37, 363–99.

Batstone, E. (1986) 'Labour and Productivity', *Oxford Review of Economic Policy,* 2 (3), 32–42.

Batstone, E., Boraston, I. and Frenkel, S. (1977) *Shop Stewards in Action.* Oxford: Blackwell.

Batt, R. (1995) *Performance and Welfare Effects of Work Restructuring: Evidence from Telecommunications Services.* Sloan School of Management,. Cambridge: The MIT Press.

Batt, R. and Appelbaum, E. (1995) 'Worker Participation in Diverse Settings: Does the Form Affect the Outcome, and If So, Who Benefits?', *British Journal of Industrial Relations,* 33 (3), 331–78.

Batt, R. and Strausser, M. (1997) *Labor Market Outcomes of Deregulation in Telecommunications Services.* Manuscript, Ithaca: Cornell University Press.

Beach, C. and Slotsve, G. (1996) *Are We Becoming Two Societies?: Income Polarization and the Myth of the Declining Middle Class in Canada.* The Social Policy Challenge 12, Toronto, ON: C.D. Howe Institute.

Beauvais, L. L., Scholl, R. W. and Cooper, E. A. (1991) 'Dual Commitment among Unionized Faculty: A Longitudinal Investigation', *Human Relations,* 44, 175–92.

Becker, B. and Gerhart, B. (1996) 'The Impact of Human Resource Management on Organizational Performance: Progress and Prospects', *The Academy of Management*

Journal, 39 (4), 779–801.

Becker, B. E. and Huselid, M. A. (1998a) *Human Resources Strategies, Complementarities, and Firm Performance.* Manuscript, Buffalo: School of Management, SUNY-Buffalo.

Becker, B. E. and Huselid, M. A. (1998b) 'High Performance Work Systems and Firm Performance: A Synthesis of Research and Managerial Implications', *Research in Personnel and Human Resources Management,* 16, 53–101.

Bélanger, J. (1989) 'Job Control and Productivity: New Evidence from Canada', *British Journal of Industrial Relations,* 27 (3), 347–64.

Bélanger, J., Berggren, C., Björkman, T. and Köhler, C. (eds) (1999) *Being Local Worldwide: ABB and the Challenge of Global Management.* Ithaca: Cornell University Press.

Bélanger, J. and Dumas, M. (1998) 'Teamwork and Internal Labour Markets: a Study of a Canadian Aluminium Smelter', *Economic and Industrial Democracy,* 19 (3), 417–42.

Bélanger, P. R. (1995) 'Mondialisation, productivité, réorganisation des pouvoirs', in R. Blouin, R. Boulard, P-A. Lapointe, A. Larocque, J. Mercier and S. Montreuil (eds), *La réorganisation du travail. Efficacité et implication.* Sainte-Foy: Les Presses de l'Université Laval, pp. 165–73.

Bélanger, P. R., Grant, M. and Lévesque, B. (eds) (1994) *La modernisation sociale des entreprises.* Montreal: PUM.

Bélanger, P. R. and Lévesque, B. (1994a) 'Modernisation sociale des entreprises: diversité des configurations et modèle québécois', in P. R. Bélanger, M. Grant and B. Lévesque (eds), *La modernisation sociale des entreprises.* Montreal: PUM, pp. 18–52.

Bélanger, P. R. and Lévesque, B. (1994b) 'Out of Fordism in North America: Regional Trends in Labour-Management Relations and Work Organisations', in W. Ehlert, R. Russell, G. Széll (eds), *Return of Work, Production and Administration to Capitalism.* Frankfurt am Main: Peter Lang, pp. 68–78.

Bell, D. (1999) 'The Axial Age of Technology, Foreword: 1999', *The Coming of Post-Industrial Society.* New York: Basic Books, ix–lxxxv (first published in 1973).

Bendix, R. (1956) *Work and Authority in Industry: Ideologies and Management in the Course of Industrialization.* Berkeley: University of California Press.

Benkhoff, B. and Peccei, R. (1997) 'Beware of Management Respondents', paper to British Universities Industrial Relations Association annual conference, University of Bath, July.

Berg, P. (1999) 'The Effects of High Performance Work Practices on Job Satisfaction in the United States Steel Industry', *Relations Industrielles/ Industrial Relations,* 54 (1), 111–35.

Berg, P., Appelbaum, E., Bailey, T. and Kalleberg, A. L. (1996) 'The Performance Effect of Modular Production in the Apparel Industry', *Industrial Relations,* 35 (3), 356–73.

Bergeron, J.-G. and Bourque, R. (1996) *Workplace Change in Québec. Public Policy and the Union Response.* Kingston: IRC Press, Queen's University.

Berggren, C. (1993a) 'Lean Production: The End of History?', *Work, Employment and*

Society, 7, 163–88.

Berggren, C. (1993b) *Alternatives to Lean Production*. Ithaca: ILR Press.

Berggren, C. and Nomura, M. (1997) *The Resilience of Corporate Japan: New Strategies and Personnel Practices*. London: P. Chapman.

Betcherman, G. (1995) 'Workplace Transformation in Canada: Policies and Practices', in B. Downie and M. L. Coates (eds), *Managing Human Resources in the 1990's and Beyond*. Kingston: IRC Press, Queen's University, pp. 102–19.

Betcherman, G. and Chaykowski, R. (1996) *The Changing Workplace: Challenges for Public Policy*, Research Paper no. R-96-13E, Applied Research Branch, Strategic Policy, Human Resources Development Canada. Ottawa: HRDC.

Betcherman, G., McMullen, K., Leckie, N. and Caron, C. (1994) *The Canadian Workplace in Transition*. Kingston: IRC Press.

Björkman, T. (1999) 'Lean Management in Practice: The Headquarters Perspective', in J. Bélanger, C. Berggren, T. Björkman and C. Köhler (eds), *Being Local Worldwide: ABB and the Challenge of Global Management*. Ithaca: Cornell University Press, pp. 36–60.

Blank, R. (1997) *It Takes A Nation: A New Agenda For Fighting Poverty*. Princeton, NJ: Princeton University Press.

Bluestone, B. and Bluestone, I. (1992) *Negotiating the Future: A Labor Perspective on American Business*. New York: Basic Books.

Boltanski, L. and Chiapello, È. (1999) *Le nouvel esprit du capitalisme*. Paris: Gallimard.

Bordo, M., Eichengreen, B. and Irwin, D. (1999) 'Is Globalization Today Really Different Than Globalization A Hundred Years Ago?', *National Bureau of Economic Research Working Paper* 7195 (June). Cambridge MA: NBER.

Bourque, G. L. (2000) *Le modèle québécois de développement. De l'émergence au renouvellement*, Québec, Presses de l'Université du Québec.

Bourque, G. L. and Lévesque, B. (1999) *Le modèle québécois en question*. Cahiers du CRISES, no. 9910.

Bourque, R. (1999) 'Coopération patronale-syndicale et réorganisation du travail', *Relations industrielles/Industrial Relations*, 54 (1), 136–67.

Bourque, R. and Rioux, C. (1994) 'Tendances récentes de la négociation collective dans l'industrie du papier au Québec', *Relations industrielles/ Industrial Relations*, 49 (4), 730–49.

Bourque, R. and Rioux, C. (1997) 'Industrial Restructuring and Union Response: The Experience of the Fédération des Travailleurs du Papier et de la Fôret in Québec', *Labor Studies Journal*, 22 (2), 3–20.

Boyer, R. (ed.) (1986) *La flexibilité du travail en Europe*. Paris: La Découverte.

Boyer, R. (ed.) (1988) *The Search for Labour Market Flexibility*. Oxford: Clarendon Press.

Boyer, R. (1993) 'Comment émerge un nouveau système productif', in J. P. Durand (ed.) *Vers un nouveau modèle productif?* Paris: Syros, pp. 31–92.

Boyer, R. (2000) 'Les mots et les réalités', in S. Cordellier (ed.) *La mondialisation au-delà des mythes*. Paris, La Découverte/Poche, pp. 13–56.

Boyer, R. and Hollingsworth, J. R. (1997) 'How and Why Do Social Systems of

Production Change?', in J. R. Hollingsworth and R. Boyer (eds), *Contemporary Capitalism: The Embeddedness of Institutions*. Cambridge: Cambridge University Press, pp. 189–96.

Boyer, R. and Orléan, A. (1994) 'Persistance et changement des conventions', in A. Orléan (ed.) *Analyse économique des conventions*. Paris: PUF, pp. 219–47.

Boyer, R. and Saillard, Y. (eds) (1995) *Théorie de la régulation: L'état des savoirs*. Paris: La Découverte.

Brody, D. (1980) *Workers in Industrial Democracy*. New York: Oxford University Press.

Bronfenbrenner, K., Friedman, S., Hurd, R. W., Oswald, R. A. and Seeber, R. L. (eds) (1998) *Organizing to Win: New Research on Union Strategies*. Ithaca, NY: ILR Press.

Brown, W. (1973) *Piecework Bargaining*. London: Heinemann.

Brown, W. (2000) 'Putting Partnership into Practice in Britain', *British Journal of Industrial Relations*, 38 (2), 299–316.

Burawoy, M. (1979) *Manufacturing Consent: Changes in the Labor Process Under Monopoly Capitalism*. Chicago: University of Chicago Press.

Buchanan, D. and Preston, D. (1992) 'Life in the Cell: Supervision and Team Work in a Manufacturing Systems Engineering Environment', *Human Resource Management Journal*, 2 (4), 55–76.

Callus, R., Morehead, A., Cully, M. and Buchanan, J. (1991) *Industrial Relations at Work: The Australian Workplace Industrial Relations Survey*. Canberra: Australian Government Publishing Service.

Cappelli, P. (1985) 'Competitive Conditions and Labor Relations in the Airline Industry', *Industrial Relations*, 22 (3), 316–38.

Cappelli, P. (1999) *The New Deal at Work: Managing the Market-Driven Workforce*. Cambridge: Harvard Business School Press.

Cappelli, P., Bassi, L., Katz, H. C., Knoke, D., Osterman, P. and Useem, M. (1997) *Change at Work*. Oxford: Oxford University Press.

Cappelli, P. and Rogovsky, N. (1994) *What Drives Commitment, 'Citizenship', and Performance: Employee Involvement or Task-Level Job Design?* Unpublished manuscript, Philadelphia, Wharton School, University of Pennsylvania.

Castaingts-Teillery, J. (2001) 'L'échange asymétrique: le cas des pays émergents', in D. Mercure (ed.) *Une société monde?* Sainte-Foy: Les Presses de l'Université Laval, 215–30.

Castells, M. (1996) *The Rise of Network Society*, vol. 1. Oxford: Blackwell.

Chandler, A. (1977) *The Visible Hand: The Managerial Revolution in American Business*. Cambridge: Harvard University Press.

Charest, J. (1999) 'Articulation institutionnelle et orientations du système de formation professionnelle au Québec', *Relations industrielles/Industrial Relations*, 54 (3), 439–68.

Chaykowski, R. (1995a) 'Industrial Relations Policy: Active or Reactive?', *Policy Options*, October, pp. 24–7.

Chaykowski, R. (1995b) 'Union Influences on Labour Market Outcomes and Earnings Inequality', in K. Banting and C. Beach (eds), *Labour Market Polarization and Social*

Policy Reform. Kingston: Queen's University School of Policy Studies, pp. 95–118.

Chaykowski, R. (1997) 'Joint Labour-Management Committees at Inco Limited: Innovation Within the Traditional Industrial Relations System', *Collective Bargaining Review,* September.

Chaykowski, R. (1999) 'Adaptation within the Traditional Industrial Relations System: The Development of Labour Relations at Inco Limited', in A. Verma and R. Chaykowski (eds), *Contract and Commitment: Employment Relations in the New Economy.* Kingston, ON: Queen's University, IRC Press, pp. 41–81.

Chaykowski, R. and Grant, M. (1995) 'From Traditional to Mutual Gains Bargaining: The Canadian Experience', *Collective Bargaining Review,* May, 79–88.

Chaykowski, R. and Powell, L. (1999) 'Women and the Labour Market: Recent Trends and Policy Issues', *Canadian Public Policy,* 25, Supplement.

Chaykowski, R. and Slotsve, G. (1996) 'A Distributional Analysis of Changes in Earnings Inequality Among Unionized and Nonunionized Male Workers in the United States, 1982–1990', *Canadian Journal of Economics,* 29, Special Issue, S109–13.

Chaykowski, R. and Thomason, T. (1995) 'Canadian Workers' Compensation: Institutions and Economics', in T. Thomason and R. Chaykowski (eds), *Research in Canadian Workers' Compensation.* Kingston, ON: Queen's University, IRC Press, pp. 1–42.

Chaykowski, R. and Verma, A. (1992) *Industrial Relations in Canadian Industry.* Toronto: Holt, Rinehart and Winston.

Chaykowski, R. and Verma, A. (eds) (1994) 'Innovation in Industrial Relations: Challenges to Organizations and Public Policy', in T. J. Courchene (ed.) *Stabilization, Growth and Distribution: Linkages in the Knowledge Era.* Bell Canada Papers on Economic and Public Policy, 2; Kingston, ON: John Deutsch Institute, Queen's University, pp. 367–401.

Clark, J. (1995) *Managing Innovation and Change.* London: Sage.

Clarke, S. (1992) 'What in the F–'s Name is Fordism', in N. Gilbert, R. Burrows and A. Pollert (eds), *Fordism and Flexibility: Divisions and Change.* London: Macmillan, pp. 13–30.

Cohen, S. and Bailey, D. (1997) 'What Makes Teams Work: Group Effectiveness Research from the Shop Floor to the Executive Suite', *Journal of Management,* 23 (3), 239–90.

Cohen, S. and Ledford, G. (1994) 'The Effectiveness of Self-Managing Teams: A Quasi-Experiment', *Human Relations,* 47 (1), 13–43.

Cohen, S., Ledford, G. and Spreitzer, G. (1996) 'A Predictive Model of Self-Managing Work Team Effectiveness', *Human Relations,* 49 (5), 643–76.

Collard, R. and Dale, B. (1989) 'Quality Circles', in K. Sisson (ed.) *Personnel Management in Britain.* Oxford: Blackwell, pp. 356–77.

Collinson, M., Edwards, P. K. and Rees, C. (1997) *Involving Employees in Total Quality Management.* London: Department of Trade and Industry.

Collinson, M., Rees, C., Edwards, P. K. and Innes, L. (1996) *Involving Employees in Total*

Quality Management: Employee Attitudes and Organizational Context in Unionized Environments. Warwick: IRRU, Warwick Business School, University of Warwick.

Comeau, Y. and Lévesque, B. (1993) 'Workers' Financial Participation in the Property of Enterprises in Québec', *Economic and Industrial Democracy,* 14 (2), 233–50.

Commission for Labor Cooperation (1997) *North American Labor Markets: A Comparative Profile.* Dallas: Commission for Labor Cooperation/Lanham, MD: Bernan Press.

Conlon, E. J. and Gallagher, D. G. (1987) 'Commitment to Employer and Union: Effects of Membership Status', *Academy of Management Journal,* 30, 151–62.

Conseil consultatif du travail et de la main-d'œuvre (CCTM) (1994) *Document d'orientation,* Québec, Gouvernement du Québec.

Conseil consultatif du travail et de la main-d'oeuvre (1997) *Document de réflexion sur une nouvelle organisation du travail.*

Cordery, J. L., Mueller, W. S. and Smith, L. M. (1991) 'Attitudinal and Behavioral Effects of Autonomous Group Working: A Longitudinal Field Study', *Academy of Management Journal,* 34, 464–76.

Coriat, B. (1990) *L'atelier et le robot.* Paris: Christian Bourgeois.

Coriat, B. (1991) *Penser à l'envers. Travail et organisation dans l'entreprise japonaise.* Paris: Christian Bourgeois.

Coriat, B. (1997) 'Globalization, Variety, and Mass Production: The Metamorphosis of Mass Production in the New Competitive Age', in R. J. Hollingsworth and R. Boyer (eds), *Contemporary Capitalism. The Embeddeness of Institutions.* Cambridge: Cambridge University Press, pp. 240–64.

Coriat, B. and Weinstein, O. (1995) *Les nouvelles théories de l'entreprise.* Paris: Librairie générale française.

Coté, D. and Luc, D. (1994) *Le profil des Coopératives de travailleurs actionnaires du Québec.* Montréal: Centre de gestion des coopératives, École des HEC.

Cotton, J. L., Vollrath, D. A., Froggatt, K. L., Lengnick-Hall, M. C. and Jennings, K. R. (1988) 'Employee Participation: Diverse Forms and Different Outcomes', *Academy of Management Review,* 13 (1), 8–22.

Courchene, T. (1997) *The Nation State in a Global/Information Era: Policy Challenges.* Bell Canada Papers on Economic and Public Policy, 5; Kingston, ON: John Deutsch Institute, Queen's University.

Courchene, T. (1998) *From Heartland to North American Region State,* Centre for Public Management Monograph Series on Public Policy and Public Administration, No. 6. Toronto: University of Toronto, Faculty of Management.

Courchene, T. (1999) *Room To Manoeuvre: Globalization and Policy Convergence.* Bell Canada Papers on Economic and Public Policy, 6; Kingston, ON: John Deutsch Institute, Queen's University.

Coutrot, T. and Parraire, J. L. (1994) 'Le développement récent des politiques de motivation de salaires', *Premières synthèses DARES,* Ministry of Labour, Employment and Vocational Training, Paris, no. 47.

Cressey, P. and MacInnes, J. (1980) 'Voting for Ford', *Capital and Class,* 11, 5–33.

Cully, M. and Marginson, P. (1995) *The Workplace Industrial Relations Surveys*. Coventry: Industrial Relations Research Unit, Warwick Papers in Industrial Relations (55).

Cully, M., O'Reilly, A, Millward, N., Forth, J., Woodland, S., Dix, G. and Bryson, A. (1998) *The 1998 Workplace Employee Relations Survey: First Findings*. London: Department of Trade and Industry (available at www.dti.gov.uk/emar).

Cusumano, M. A. (1985) *The Japanese Automobile Industry: Technology and Management at Nissan and Toyota*, Cambridge: Harvard University Press.

Cutcher-Gershenfeld, J. (1991) 'The Impact on Economic Performance of a Transformation in Workplace Relations', *Industrial and Labor Relations Review*, 44 (2), January, 241–60.

Cutcher-Gershenfeld, J., Nitta, M., Barrett, B., Belhedi, N., Bullard, J., Coutchie, C., Inaba, T., Ishino, I., Lee, S., Lin, W.-J., Mothersell, W. M., Ramanand, S., Strolle, M. E. and Wheaton, A. C. (1994) 'Japanese Team-Based Work Systems in North America: Explaining the Diversity', *California Management Review*, 37 (1), 42–64.

Cutcher-Gershenfeld, J. Nitta, M., Barrett, B., Belhedi, N., Sai-Chung Chow, S., Ishino, T., Lee, S., Lin, W.-J., Moore, M. L., Mothersell, W. M., Palthe, J., Ramanand, S., Strolle, M. E. and Wheaton, A. C. (1998) *Knowledge-driven Work: Unexpected Lessons from Japanese and United States Work Practices*. New York: Oxford University Press.

Dahlby, B. (1993) 'Payroll Taxes', in A. Maslove (ed.), *Business Taxation in Ontario*. Toronto: University of Toronto Press, pp. 80–170.

Dahrendorf, R. (1959) *Class and Class Conflict in Industrial Society*. Stanford: Stanford University Press.

Dawson, P. and Webb, J. (1989) 'New Production Arrangements: The Totally Flexible Cage?', *Work, Employment and Society*, 3 (2), 221–38.

Deery, S. J., Iverson, R. D. and Erwin, P. J. (1994) 'Predicting Organizational and Union Commitment: The Effect of Industrial Relations Climate', *British Journal of Industrial Relations*, 32 (4), 581–97.

Delery, J. E., Gupta, N. and Shaw, J. D. (1997) *Human Resource Management and Firm Performance: A Systems Perspective*. Paper presented at the 1997 Southern Management Association Meetings, Fayetteville: Department of Management, University of Arkansas.

Deutschmann, C. (1992) 'Works Councils and Enterprise-Level Industrial Relations in German Transplants of Japanese Firms', in S. Tokunga, N. Altmann and H. Demes (eds), *New Impacts on Industrial Relations: Internationalisation and Changing Production Strategies*. Munich: Iudicum, pp. 133–47.

Di Maggio, P. J. and Powell, W. W. (1983) 'The Iron Cage Revisited', *American Sociological Review*, 48 (1), 147–60.

Di Matteo, L. and Shannon, M. (1995) 'Payroll Taxation in Canada: An Overview', *Canadian Business Economics*, 3 (4), 5–22.

Dohse, K., Jürgens, U. and Malsch, T. (1985) 'From "Fordism" to "Toyotism"? The Social Organisation of the Labour Process in the Japanese Automobile Industry', *Politics and Society*, 14 (2), 115–46.

Doty, D. H. and Delery, J. E. (1997) *The Importance of Holism, Interdependence, and*

REFERENCES

Equifinality Assumptions in High Performance Work Systems: Toward Theories of the High Performance Work Force. Unpublished Manuscript, Fayetteville: Department of Management, University of Arkansas.

Drago, R. (1986) 'Participatory Management in Captialist Firms: An Analysis of "Quality Circles"', *Economic Analysis and Workers' Management*, 20 (3), 233–49.

Drucker, P. F. (1999) 'Knowledge-Worker Productivity: The Biggest Challenge', *California Management Review*, 41 (2), 79–94.

Duncan, G., Smeeding, T. and Rogers, W. (1993) 'W(h)ither the Middle Class? A Dynamic View', in D. Papadimitriou and E. Wolff (eds), *Poverty and Prosperity in the USA in the Late Twentieth Century*. New York: St Martin's Press, pp. 240–71.

Dunlop, J. (1958) *Industrial Relations Systems*. New York: Henry Holt.

Durand, C. (1978) *Le travail enchaîné: Organisation du travail et domination sociale.* Paris: Seuil.

Eaton, A. E. (1995) 'New Production Techniques, Employee Involvement and Unions', *Labor Studies Journal*, 20 (3), 19–42.

Eaton, A. E., Gordon, M. and Keefe, J. (1992) 'The Impact of Quality of Work Life Programs and Grievance System Effectiveness on Union Commitment', *Industrial and Labor Relations Review*, 45, 591–604.

Edling, C. and Sandberg, A. (1993) 'Ar Taylor dod och pyramidernna rivna? Nya former for foretagsledning och arbetsorganisation', *NUTEK: Att organisera for produkktivitet? En jamforelse av elektronikproduktion I Sverige och Tyskland.* B5, pp. 139–73.

Edwards, P. K. (1986) *Conflict at Work: A Materialist Analysis of Workplace Relations.* Oxford: Basil Blackwell.

Edwards, P. K. (1988) 'Patterns of Conflict and Accommodation', in D. Gallie (ed.), *Employment in Britain*. Oxford: Basil Blackwell, pp. 187–217.

Edwards, P. K. (1992) 'La recherche comparative en relations industrielles', *Relations Industrielles/ Industrial Relations*, 47 (3), 411–36.

Edwards, P. K., Collinson, M. and Rees, C. (1998) 'The Determinants of Employee Responses to Total Quality Management', *Organisation Studies*, 19 (3), 449–75.

Edwards, P. K. and Whitston, C. (1993) *Attending to Work*. Oxford: Basil Blackwell.

Edwards, R. (1979) *Contested Terrain*. London: Heinemann.

Elger, T. (1990) 'Technical Innovation and Work Reorganization in British Manufacturing in the 1980s: Continuity, Intensification or Transformation?', *Work, Employment and Society*, Special Issue, May, 67–101.

Elger, T. and Smith, C. (eds) (1994) *Global Japanization: The Transnational Transformation of the Labour Process*. London, New York: Routledge.

Emery, F. and Trist, E. (1960) 'Socio-Technical Systems', in C. W. Churchman and M. Verhulst (eds), *Management Sciences, Models and Techniques*. New York: Pergamon Press, pp. 83–97.

EPOC Research Group (1997) *New Forms of Work Organisation: Can Europe Realise its Potential?* Luxembourg: Office for the Official Publications of the European Communities.

EQW (1995) *The Educational Quality of the Workforce National Survey.* Philadelphia: National Centre on the Educational Quality of the Workforce.

Fairbrother, P. (1996) 'Workplace Trade Unionism in the State Sector', in P. Ackers, C. Smith and P. Smith (eds), *The New Workplace and Trade Unionism: Critical Perspectives on Work and Organization.* London: Routledge, pp. 110–48.

Fairbrother, P. and Yates, C. (eds) (2002) *Trade Union Renewal and Organizing: A Comparative Study of Trade Union Movements in Five Countries.* London: Continuum, forthcoming.

Fisher, E. and Kondra, A. (1992) 'Canada's Airlines: Recent Turbulence and Changing Flight Plans', in R. Chaykowski and A. Verma (eds), *Industrial Relations in Canadian Industry.* Toronto, ON: Holt, Rinehart and Winston, pp. 358–404.

Fletcher, B. and Hurd, R. W. (1999) 'Political Will, Local Union Transformation and the Organizing Imperative', in B. Nissen (ed.), *Which Direction for Organized Labor?* Detroit: Wayne State University Press, pp. 191–216.

Foot, D. K. and Stoffman, D. (1996) *Boom, Bust and Echo: How to Profit from the Coming Demographic Shift.* Toronto: MacFarlane, Walter & Ross.

Fortin, N. M. and Lemieux, T. (1997) 'Institutional Changes and Rising Wage Inequality: Is There a Linkage?', *Journal of Economic Perspectives,* 11 (2), Spring, 75–96.

Fortin, B. and Lanoie, P. (1992) 'Substitution Between Unemployment Insurance and Workers' Compensation', *Journal of Public Economics.* 49.

Fournier, L. (1991) *Solidarité Inc, Un syndicalisme créateur d'emplois.* Montréal, Québec/Amérique.

Freeman, R. B. (1996) 'Labor Market Institutions and Earnings Inequality', *New England Economic Review,* May–June, 157–68.

Freeman, R. B. and Dube, A. (2000) 'Shared Compensation Systems and Decision-Making in the US Job Market', Paper presented to the Annual North American Seminar on Incomes and Productivity, Mexico City, February, 46pp.

Freeman, R. B., Kleiner, M. M. and Ostroff, C. (1997) *The Anatomy and Effects of Employee Involvement.* Cambridge, MA: Department of Economics, Harvard University.

Freeman, R. and Needels, K. (1993) 'Skill Differentials in Canada in an Era of Rising Labor Market Inequality', in D. Card and R. Freeman (eds), *Small Differences that Matter: Labor Markets and Income Maintenance in Canada and the United States.* Chicago: University of Chicago Press, pp. 45–68.

Freeman, R. B. and Rogers, J. (1993) 'Who Speaks for Us? Employee Representation in a Nonunion Labor Market', in B. E. Kaufman and M. M. Kleiner (eds), *Employee Representation: Alternatives and Future Directions.* Madison: Industrial Relations Research Association, pp. 13–80.

Freeman, R. B. and Rogers, J. (1995) 'Worker Representation and Participation Survey: First Report of Findings', *Proceedings of the Forty-Seventh Meeting of the IRRA.*

Freeman, R. B. and Rogers, J. (1999) *What Workers Want.* Ithaca: Cornell University Press.

REFERENCES

Friedman, A. L. (1977) *Industry and Labour.* London: Macmillan.

Friedman, A. L. (1997) 'Managerial Strategies of Labour Control', Paper to annual conference of British Sociological Association, University of York, March.

Fröhlich, D. and Pekruhl, U. (1996) *Direct Participation and Organisational Change, Fashionable but Misunderstood?* Luxembourg: Office for the Official Publications of the European Communities.

Frost, A. (2000) 'Explaining Variation in Workplace Restructuring: The Role of Local Union Capabilities', *Industrial and Labor Relations Review*, 53 (4), 559–78.

FTQ (Fédération des travailleuses et travailleurs du Québec) (1999) *Pour rétablir un rapport de forces: les alliances locales* (Regaining the Balance of Power: Community Alliances). Montreal: Fédération des travailleurs et travailleuses du Québec.

Gallie, D. (1996) 'Skill, Gender and the Quality of Employment', in R. Crompton, D. Gallie and K. Purcell (eds), *Changing Forms of Employment*. New York: Routledge, pp. 133–59.

Gallie, D. and White, M. (1993) *Employee Commitment and the Skills Revolution.* London: PSI Publishing.

Gallie, D., White, M., Cheng, Y. and Tomlinson, M. (1998) *Restructuring the Employment Relationship.* Oxford: Clarendon Press.

Geary, J. F. (1993) 'New Forms of Work Organisation and Employee Involvement in Two Case Study Sites', *Economic and Industrial Democracy*, 14 (4), 511–34.

Geary, J. F. (1994) 'Task Participation: Employees' Participation Enabled or Constrained?', in K. Sisson (ed.), *Personnel Management: A Comprehensive Guide to Theory and Practice in Britain*. Oxford: Blackwell, pp. 634–61.

Geary, J. F. (1995) 'Work Practices: the Structure of Work', in P. K. Edwards (ed.), *Industrial Relations*. Oxford: Blackwell, pp. 368–96.

Geary, J. F. (1999) 'The New Workplace: Change at Work in Ireland', *International Journal of Human Resource Management*, 10 (5), 870–90.

Geary, J. and Roche, W. (2001) 'Multinationals and Human Resource Practices in Ireland: A Rejection of the ''New Conformance Thesis'' ', *The International Journal of Human Resource Management*, 12 (1), 1–19.

Geary, J. F. and Sisson, K. (1994) *Conceptualising Direct Participation in Organisational Change*. Luxembourg: Office for the Official Publications of the European Communities.

Giles, A., Lapointe, P.-A., Murray, G. and Bélanger, J. (1999) 'Industrial Relations in the New Workplace: Research, Policy and Practice, *Relations Industrielles/Industrial Relations*, 54 (1), 15–25.

Giles, A. and Murray, G. (1996) 'Trajectoires et paradigmes dans l'étude des relations industrielles en Amérique du Nord', in G. Murray, M.-L. Morin and I. da Costa (eds), *L'état des relations professionnelles*. Sainte-Foy: Les Presses de l'Université Laval/Octares Éditions, pp. 64–92.

Gilly, J.-P. and Pecqueur, B. (1995) 'La dimension locale de la régulation', in R. Boyer and Y. Saillard (eds), *Théorie de la régulation: L'état des savoirs*. Paris: La Découverte, pp. 304–12.

Gittleman, M., Horrigan, M. and Joyce, M. (1998) '"Flexible" Workplace Practices: Evidence from a Nationally Representative Survey', *Industrial and Labor Relations Review*, 52, 99–115.

Glover, L. and Fitzgerald Moore, D. (1998) 'TQM: Shopfloor Perspectives', in C. Mabey, D. Skinner and T. Clark (eds), *Experiencing Human Resource Management*. London: Sage, pp. 54–72.

Godard, J. and Delaney, J. T. (2000) 'Reflections on the "High Performance" Paradigm's Implications for Industrial Relations as a Field', *Industrial and Labor Relations Review*, 53, 482–502.

Goetschy, J. and Rozenblatt, P. (1992) 'France: The Industrial Relations System at a Turning Point?', in A. Ferner and R. Hyman (eds), *Industrial Relations in the New Europe*. Oxford: Blackwell, pp. 404–44.

Goodrich, C. L. (1920/75) *The Frontier of Control*. London: Pluto.

Gottschalk, P. (1997) 'Inequality, Income Growth, and Mobility: The Basic Facts', *Journal of Economic Perspectives*, 11 (2), Spring, 21–40.

Gottschalk, P. and Smeeding, T. (1997) 'Cross-National Comparisons of Earnings and Income Inequality', *Journal of Economic Literature*, 35, June, 633–87.

Graham, L. (1995) *On the Line at Subaru-Isuzu: The Japanese Model and the American Worker*. Ithaca: Cornell University Press.

Gramsci, A. (1971) *Selections from the Prison Notebooks of Antonio Gramsci*, edited and translated by Quintin Hoare and Geoffrey Nowell Smith. New York: International Publishers.

Grant, M., Bélanger, P. and Lévesque, B. (1997) *Nouvelles formes d'organisation du travail*. Paris and Montréal: L'Harmattan.

Grant, M. and Lévesque, B. (1997) 'Aperçu des principales transformations des rapports du travail dans les entreprises: le cas québécois', in M. Grant, P. R. Bélanger and B. Lévesque (eds), *Nouvelles formes d'organisation du travail Études de cas et analyses comparatives*, Paris and Montréal, L'Harmattan, 221–77.

Grayson, J. P. (1989) 'Reported Illness from the CGE Closure', *Canadian Journal of Public Health*, 80 (1), Jan/Feb, 16–19.

Green, W. C. (1996) 'The Transformation of the NLRA Paradigm: Labor-Management Relations in Post-Fordist Auto Plants', in W. C. Green and E. J. Yanarella (eds), *North American Auto Unions in Crisis. Lean Production as Contested Terrain*. Albany: State University of New York Press, pp. 161–90.

Griffin, R. (1988) 'Consequences of Quality Circles in an Industrial Setting: A Longitudinal Assessment', *Academy of Management Journal*, 31, 338–58.

Griffin, R. (1991) 'The Effects of Work Redesign on Employee Perceptions, Attitude and Behaviors: A Long-Term Investigation', *Academy of Management Journal*, 34, 425–35.

Grint, K. (1995) *Management: a Sociological Introduction*. Cambridge: Polity.

Guérin, G. and Wils, T. (1992) *Gestion des ressources humaines: du modèle traditionnel au modèle renouvelé*. Montréal: Les Presses de l'Université de Montréal.

Guest, D. (1990) 'Human Resource Management and the American Dream', *Journal of*

REFERENCES

Management Studies, 27, 377–97.

Guest, D. E. and Dewe, P. (1991) 'Company or Trade Union: Which Wins Workers' Allegiance? A Study of Commitment in the UK Electronic Industry', *British Journal of Industrial Relations*, 29, 75–96.

Gunderson, M. (1986) 'Alternative Mechanisms for Dealing with Permanent Layoffs, Dismissals and Plant Closings', in C. Riddell (ed.), *Adapting to Change: Labour Market Adjustment in Canada*. Toronto: University of Toronto Press, pp. 111–62.

Gunderson, M. (1996) 'Regional Productivity and Income Convergence in Canada Under Increasing Economic Integration', *Canadian Journal of Regional Science*, 19, Spring, 1–23.

Gunderson, M. and Hyatt, D. (1996) 'Do Injured Pay for Reasonable Accommodation?', *Industrial and Labor Relations Review*, 50, October, 92–104.

Gunderson, M. (1997) 'Harmonization of Labour Policies Under Free Trade', University of Toronto Centre for Industrial Relations, mimeo.

Gunderson, M., Hyatt, D. and Pesando, J. (1992) 'Wage-Pension Trade-Offs in Collective Agreements', *Industrial and Labor Relations Review*, 46, October, pp. 146–60.

Gunderson, M. and Riddell, C. (1995) 'Jobs, Labour Standards and Promoting Competitive Advantage: Canada's Policy Challenge', *Labour*, S125–48.

Gunderson, M. and Riddell, C. (1996) 'The Changing Nature of Work: Implications for Public Policy'. Ottawa: Institute for Research on Public Policy.

Gunderson, M., Sack, J., McCartney, J., Wakely, D. and Eaton, J. (1995) 'Employee Buyouts in Canada', *British Journal of Industrial Relations*, 33, September, 417–42.

Gunderson, M. and Sharpe, A. (1998) *Forging Business-Labour Partnerships: the Emergence of Sectoral Councils in Canada*. Toronto: University of Toronto Press.

Hackman, J. R. (1987) 'Conclusion: Creating More Effective Work Groups in Organizations', in J. R. Hackman (ed.), *Groups That Work (And Those That Don't): Creating Conditions for Effective Teamwork*. San Francisco: Jossey-Bass, pp. 479–504.

Hackman, J. R. and Lawler, E. (1971) 'Employee Reactions to Job Characteristics', *Journal of Applied Psychology*, 55, 259–86.

Hackman, J. R. and Oldham, G. R. (1975) 'Development of the Job Diagnostic Survey', *Journal of Applied Psychology*, 60, 159–70.

Hackman, J. R. and Oldham, G. R. (1976) 'Motivation Through the Design of Work: Test of a Theory', *Organizational Behavior and Human Performance*, 16, 250–79.

Hackman, J. R. and Oldham, G. R. (1980) *Work Redesign*. Reading: Addison-Wesley.

Hackman, J. R. and Wageman, R. (1995) 'Total Quality Management: Empirical, Conceptual and Practical Issues', *Administrative Science Quarterly*, 40, June, 309–42.

Hammer, M. and Champy, J. (1993) *Reengineering the Corporations: A Manifesto for Business Revolution*. New York: Harper Business.

Harley, B. (1999) 'The Myth of Empowerment: Work Organisation, Hierarchy and Employee Autonomy in Contemporary Australian Workplaces', *Work, Employment and Society*, 13 (1), March, 41–66.

Harley, B., Ramsay, H. and Scholarios, D. (1999) *High Tide and Green Grass: Employee*

Experience in High Commitment Work Systems. Paper presented at the Academy of Management Meetings, Chicago.

Harrison, B. (1994) *Lean and Mean: The Changing Landscape of Corporate Power in the Age of Flexibility*. New York: Basic Books.

Harrisson, D. and Laplante, N. (1994) 'Confiance, coopération et partenariat. Un processus de transformation de l'entreprise québécoise', *Relations industrielles/ Industrial Relations*, 49 (4), 696–729.

Harrisson, D. and Laplante, N. (1996) 'Trade Union and Cooperation: Case Studies in Quebec Manufacturing Plants', *Economic and Industrial Democracy*, 17 (1), 99–129.

Head, T. C., Molleston, J. L., Sorenson, P. F. and Gargano, J. (1986) 'The Impact of Quality Circles on Employee Task Perceptions', *Group and Organization Studies*, 11 (4), 360–73.

Hebdon, R. and Warrian, P. (1999) 'Coercive Bargaining: Public Sector Restructuring Under the Ontario Social Contract: 1993–1996', *Industrial and Labor Relations Review*, 52 (2), 196–212.

Heller, F., Pusic, E., Strauss, G. and Wilpert, B. (1998) *Organizational Participation Myth and Reality*. Oxford: Oxford Press.

Hendry, C. (1993) 'Personnel Leadership in Technical and Human Resource Change', in J. Clark (ed.), *Human Resource Management and Technical Change*. London: Sage, pp. 78–100.

Herzberg, F. (1962) *Work and the Nature of Man*. New York: Thomas Y. Crowell.

Herzenberg, S. A., Alic, J. A. and Wial, H. (1998) *New Rules for a New Economy: Employment and Opportunity in Postindustrial America*. Ithaca: Cornell University Press.

Hill, S. (1991) 'Why Quality Circles Failed But Total Quality Management Might Succeed', *British Journal of Industrial Relations*, 29 (3), 541–68.

Hirst, P. and Zeitlin, J. (1997) 'Flexible Specialization: Theory and Evidence in the Analysis of Industrial Change', in J. R. Hollingsworth and R. Boyer (eds), *Contemporary Capitalism: The Embeddedness of Institutions*. Cambridge: Cambridge University Press, pp. 220–39.

Hodson, R. (1996) 'Dignity in the Workplace Under Participative Management: Alienation and Freedom Revisited', *American Sociological Review*, 61, 719–38.

Hodson, R., Creighton, S., Jamison, C. S., Rieble, C. and Welsh, C. (1993) 'Is Worker Solidarity Undermined by Autonomy and Participation? Patterns from the Ethnographic Literature', *American Sociological Review*, 58, 398–416.

Hodson, R., Creighton, S., Jamison, C. S., Rieble, C. and Welsh, C. (1994) 'Loyalty to Whom? Workplace Participation and the Development of Consent', *Human Relations*, 47, 895–913.

Hollingsworth, J. R. and Boyer, R. (eds), (1997) *Contemporary Capitalism: The Embeddedness of Institutions*. Cambridge: Cambridge University Press.

Holmstrom, B. and Milgrom, P. (1994) 'The Firm as an Incentive System', *American Economic Review*, 84 (4), 972–91.

Huselid, M. A. (1995) 'The Impact of Human Resource Management Practices on

REFERENCES

Turnover, Productivity, and Corporate Financial Performance', *Academy of Management Journal*, 38, 635–70.

Hyman, R. (1997) 'La géométrie du syndicalisme. Une analyse comparative des identités et des idéologies', *Relations industrielles/ Industrial Relations*, 52 (1), 7–37.

Ichniowski, C. (1992) 'Human Resource Practices and Productive Labor-Management Relations', in D. Lewin, O. S. Mitchell and P. D. Sherer (eds), *Research Frontiers in Industrial Relations and Human Resources*. Madison: Industrial Relations Research Association, pp. 239–71.

Ichniowski, C., Kochan, T. A., Levine, D., Olson, C. and Strauss, G. (1996) 'What Works at Work: Overview and Assessment', *Industrial Relations*, 35 (3), 299–333.

Ichniowski, C., Shaw, K. and Prennushi, G. (1997) 'The Effects of Human Resource Management Practices on Productivity: A Study of Steel Finishing Lines', *The American Economic Review*, 87 (3), June, 291–313.

ILO (International Labour Organization) (1997) *World Labour Report: Industrial Relations, Democracy and Stability*. Geneva, Switzerland: International Labour Organization.

Jacobson, L., Lalonde, R. and Sullivan, D. (1993) *The Cost of Worker Dislocation*. Kalamazoo: Upjohn Institute for Employment Research.

Jin, R., Shah, C. and Svoboda, T. (1995) 'The Impact of Unemployment on Health: A Review of the Evidence', *Canadian Medical Association Journal*, 153, September, 529–40.

Johnson, G. E. (1997) 'Changes in Earnings Inequality: The Role of Demand Shifts', *Journal of Economic Perspectives*, 11 (2), Spring, 41–54.

Kamata, S. (1983) *Japan in the Passing Lane*. London: Allen and Unwin.

Kandel, E. and Lazear, E. P. (1992) 'Peer Pressure and Partnerships', *Journal of Political Economy*, 100 (4), 801–17.

Karoly, L. (1993) 'The Trend in Inequality Among Families, Individuals, and Workers in the United States: A Twenty-Five Year Perspective', in S. Danziger and P. Gottschalk (eds), *Uneven Tides: Rising Inequality in America*. Russell Sage Foundation, pp. 19–97.

Katz, H. C. (1985) *Shifting Gears: Changing Labor relations in the US Automobile Industry*. Cambridge: The MIT Press.

Katz, H. C. (1993) 'The Decentralization of Collective Bargaining: A Literature Review and Comparative Analysis', *Industrial and Labor Relations Review*, 47 (1), 3–22.

Katz, H. C. and Darbishire, O. (2000) *Converging Divergences: Worldwide Changes in Employment Systems*. Ithaca: ILR Press.

Katz, H. C., Kochan, T. A. and Weber, M. R. (1985) 'Assessing the Effects of Industrial Relations Systems and Efforts to Improve the Quality of Working Life on Organizational Effectiveness', *Academy of Management Journal*, 28, 509–26.

Katz, H. C. and Sabel, C. (1985) 'Industrial Relations and Industrial Adjustment in the Car Industry', *Industrial Relations*, 24 (3), 295–315.

Kelly, J. E. (1982) *Scientific Management, Job Design and Work Performance*. London: Academic.

Kemp, N., Wall, T., Clegg, C. and Cordery, J. (1983) 'Autonomous Work Groups in a Greenfield Site: A Cooperative Study', *Journal of Occupational Psychology*, 56, 271–88.

Kern, H. and Schumann, M. (1989) *La fin de la division du travail?* Paris: Maison des sciences de l'homme.

Kjellberg, A. (1992) 'Sweden: Can the Model Survive?', in A. Ferner and R. Hyman (eds), *Industrial Relations in the New Europe*. Oxford: Blackwell, pp. 88–142.

Klein, J. A. (1991) 'A Reexamination of Autonomy in Light of New Manufacturing Practices', *Human Relations*, 44, 21–38.

Kleinschmidt, M. and Pekruhl, U. (1994) 'Kooperation, Partizipation und Autonomie: Gruppenarbeit in deutschen Betrieben', *Arbeit – Zeitschrift fur Arbeitsforschung*, 2, 150–72.

Knights, D. and McCabe, D. (1998a) 'Dreams and Designs on Strategy: A Critical Analysis of TQM and Management Control', *Work, Employment and Society*, 12 (3), September, 433–56.

Knights, D. and McCabe, D. (1998b) 'What Happens When the Phone Goes Wild. BPR, Stress and the Worker', *Journal of Management Studies*, 35 (3), 163–94.

Kochan, T. A. (2000) 'Building a New Social Contract at Work: A Call to Action', Draft text of Presidential Address to the 52nd Annual Meeting of the Industrial Relations Research Association, mimeo.

Kochan, T. A., Cutcher-Gershenfeld, J. and MacDuffie, J.-P. (1989) 'Employee Participation, Work Redesign and New Technology: Implications for Public Policy in the 1990s. Commission on Workforce Quality and Labor Market Efficiency', in *Investing in People*. Washington, DC: Department of Labor. II, pp. 1831–92.

Kochan, T. A. and Katz, H. C. (1988) *Collective Bargaining and Industrial Relations: From Theory to Practice*. 2nd edn, Homewood: Richard D. Irwin, Inc.

Kochan, T. A., Katz, H. C. and McKersie, R. B. (1986) *The Transformation of American Industrial Relations*. New York: Basic Books.

Kochan, T. A., Katz, H. C. and McKersie, R. B. (1991) 'Strategic Choice and Industrial Relations Theory: An Elaboration', in H. C. Katz (ed.), *The Future of Industrial Relations: Proceedings of the Second Bargaining Group Conference*. Ithaca: Cornell University Press, Institute of Collective Bargaining, pp. 104–15.

Kochan, T. A., Katz, H. C. and Mower, N. (1984) *Worker Participation and American Unions: Threat or Opportunity?* Kalamazoo: W. E. Upjohn.

Kochan, T. A., Lansbury, R. D. and MacDuffie, J. P. (1997) 'Conclusion', in T. A. Kochan, R. D. Lansbury and J. P. MacDuffie (eds), *After Lean Production*. Ithaca: Cornell University Press, pp. 303–24.

Kochan, T. A. and Osterman, P. (1994) *The Mutual Gains Enterprise*. Cambridge: Harvard Business School Press.

Kochan, T. A. and Useem, M. (eds) (1992) *Transforming Organizations*. New York: Oxford University Press.

Krahn, H. (1995) 'Non-standard Work on the Rise', *Perspectives on Labour and Income*, 7, Winter, 35–42.

Kumar, P. (1995) *Unions and Workplace Change in Canada*. Kingston, ON: IRC Press.

REFERENCES

Kumar, P. (2000) 'Rethinking High Performance Work Systems', in *Incomes and Productivity in North America: Papers of the 2000 Seminar*. Washington: Commission for Labor Cooperation, North America Agreement on Labor Cooperation.

Kumar, P. and Meltz, N. M. (1992) 'Industrial Relations in the Canadian Automobile Industry', in R. Chaykowski and A. Verma (eds), *Industrial Relations in Canadian Industry*. Toronto: Holt, Rinehart and Winston, pp. 39–86.

Kumar, P. and Murray, G. (2001) 'Canadian Union Strategies in the Context of Change', *Labor Studies Journal* (forthcoming).

Kumar, P. and Murray, G. (2002) 'Strategic Dilemma: The State of Union Renewal in Canada', in P. Fairbrother and C. Yates (eds), *Trade Union Renewal and Organizing: A Comparative Study of Trade Union Movements in Five Countries*. London: Continuum, forthcoming.

Lane C. (1995) *Industry and Society in Europe: Stability and Change in Britain, Germany and France*. Aldershot: Edward Elgar.

Lapointe, P.-A. (1995) 'La réorganisation du travail: continuité, rupture et diversité', in R. Blouin, R. Boulard, P.-A. Lapointe, A. Larocque, J. Mercier and S. Montreuil (eds), *La réorganisation du travail, efficacité et implication*. Sainte-Foy: Les Presses de l'Université Laval, pp. 3–43.

Lapointe, P.-A. (1997) 'Succès et durabilité de la réorganisation, recette miracle ou construits sociaux spécifiques?', *Psychologie du travail et des organisations*, 3 (1/2), 91–117.

Lapointe, P.-A. (1998) 'Identités ouvrières et syndicales, fusion, distanciation et recomposition', *Sociologie et sociétés*, 30 (2), 189–212.

Lapointe, P.-A. (2000) *Participation and Democracy at Work*. Paper to the 12th World Congress, IIRA, Tokyo, June.

Lapointe, P.-A. and Bélanger, P. R. (1996) 'La participation syndicale à la modernisation sociale des entreprises', in G. Murray, M. L. Morin and I. da Costa (eds), *L'état des relations professionnelles. Traditions et perspectives de recherche*. Sainte-Foy and Toulouse: Les Presses de l'Université Laval/Octarès, pp. 284–310.

Lapointe, P.-A., Lévesque, C. and Murray, G. (2000) Les innovations en milieu de travail dans l'industrie des équipements de transport terrestre au Québec: Rapport synthèse. Étude soumise au comité sur l'organisation du travail de la table de concertation de l'industrie, Québec and Montréal, Université Laval and HEC.

Lawler III, E. E. (1995) 'Strategic Human Resource Management: An Idea Whose Time Has Come', in B. Downie and M. L. Coates (eds), *Managing Human Resources in the 1990s and Beyond : Is the Workplace Being Transformed?* Kingston, ON: IRC Press, pp. 46–70.

Lawler III, E. E., Mohrman, S. and Ledford, G. (1992) *Employee Involvement and Total Quality Management: Practices and Results in Fortune 1000 Companies*. San Francisco: Jossey–Bass.

Lawler III, E. E., Mohrman, S. A. and Ledford, G. (1995) *Creating High Performance Organizations*. San Francisco: Jossey-Bass.

Lazes, P. and Savage, J. (1996) 'A Union Strategy for Saving Jobs and Enhancing

Workplace Democracy', *Labor Studies Journal*, 21 (2), 96–121.

Lazonick, W. (1983) 'Technological Change and the Control of Work: The Development of Capital-Labor Relations in US Manufacturing', in H. F. Gospel and C. R. Littler (eds), *Managerial Strategies and Industrial Relations: An Historical and Comparative Study*. London: Heinemann, pp. 111–36.

Leborgne, D. and Lipietz, A. (1988) 'L'après-fordisme et son espace', *Les Temps modernes*, 501, April.

Ledford, G., Lawler III, E. E. and Mohrman, S. (1988) 'The Quality Circle and Its Variations,' in R. Campbell and J. Campbell (eds), *Productivity in Organizations: New Perspectives from Industrial and Organizational Psychology*. San Francisco: Jossey-Bass, pp. 255–94.

Leion A. (1992) *Den nyttiga kompetensen*.Ystad: AB Timbro, Ystads Centraltryckeri.

Lemieux, T. (1993) 'Unions and Wage Inequality in Canada and the United States', in D. Card and R. Freeman (eds), *Small Differences that Matter: Labor Markets and Income Maintenance in Canada and the United States*. Chicago: University of Chicago Press, pp. 69–108.

Lemieux, T. (1997) 'Institutional Changes and Rising Wage Inequality: Is There a Linkage?', *Journal of Economic Perspectives*, 11 (2), Spring, 75–96.

Lévesque, B. (1994) 'Une forme originale d'association capital-travail: les coopératives de travailleurs actionnaires au Québec', *Revue des études coopératives, mutualistes et associatives*, 251, 49–60.

Lévesque, B., Bélanger, P. R. and Mager, L. (1999) 'La réingénierie des services financiers: un secteur exemplaire de l'économie des services. Le cas des Caisses populaires et d'écocomie Desjardins', *Lien social et Politiques – RIAC*, 40, 89–103.

Lévesque, C. and Murray, G. (1998) 'La régulation paritaire à l'épreuve de la mondialisation', *Relations industrielles/Industrial Relations*, 53 (1), 90–122.

Lévesque, C. and Murray, G. (2002) 'Local Versus Global: Rethinking and Reactivating Local Union Power in the Global Economy', *Labor Studies Journal*, 16 (4).

Lévesque, C., Murray, G., Le Queux, S. and Roby, N. (1997) 'Workplace Restructuring and Worker Representation: the Impact of Work Reorganization on the Local Union', in R. Chaykowski, P. A. Lapointe, G. Vallée and A. Verma (eds), *Worker Representation in the Era of Trade and Deregulation*. Quebec: ACRI/CIRA, pp. 115–30.

Levine, D. I. and Tyson, L. D. (1990) 'Participation, Productivity and the Firm's Environment', in A. S. Binder (ed.), *Paying for Productivity. A Look at the Evidence*. Washington: The Brookings Institution, pp. 183–243.

Levy, F. and Murnane, R. (1992) 'US Earnings Levels and Earnings Inequality: A Review of Recent Trends and Proposed Explanations', *Journal of Economic Literature*, 30, September, 1333–81.

Lewchuk, W. and Robertson, D. (1996) 'Working Conditions under Lean Production: A Worker-Based Benchmarking Study', *Asia Pacific Business Review*, 2, 60–81.

Lincoln, J. R. and Kalleberg, A. L. (1990) *Culture, Control, and Commitment: A Study of Work Organization and Attitudes in the United States and Japan*. Cambridge: Cambridge University Press.

REFERENCES

Lipietz, A. (1989) *Choisir l'audace. Une alternative pour le XXIe siècle.* Paris: La Découverte.

Lipietz, A. (1994) 'Fordism and Post-Fordism', in W. Outhwaite and T. Bottomore (eds), *The Blackwell Dictionary of Twentieth-Century Social Thought.* Oxford: Blackwell, 230–1.

Lipsig-Mummé, C. (1995) 'Labour Strategies in the New Social Order: A Political Economy Perspective', in M. Gunderson and A. Ponak (eds), *Union-Management Relations in Canada.* Toronto: Addison-Wesley, pp.195–225.

Locke, R. (1995) 'The Transformation of Industrial Relations? A Cross-National Review', in K. S. Wever and L. Turner (eds), *The Comparative Political Economy of Industrial Relations.* Madison: Industrial Relations Research Association, pp. 9–31.

Locke, R., Kochan, T. A. and Piore, M. (eds) (1995) *Employment Relations in a Changing World Economy.* Cambridge: The MIT Press.

Locke, R. and Thelen, K. (1995) 'Apples and Oranges Revisited: Contextualised Comparisons and the Study of Comparative Labor Politics', *Politics and Society*, 23 (3), 337–67.

MacDuffie, J. P. (1995a) 'International Trends in Work Organisation in the Auto Industry: National-Level vs. Company-Level Perspectives', in K. S. Wever and L. Turner (eds), *The Comparative Political Economy of Industrial Relations.* Madison: Industrial Relations Research Association Series, pp. 71–114.

MacDuffie, J. P. (1995b) 'Human Resource Bundles and Manufacturing Performance: Organizational Logic and Flexible Production Systems in the World Auto Industry', *Industrial and Labor Relations Review*, 48, 197–221.

MacDuffie, J. P. (1995c) 'Workers' Roles in Lean Production: The Implications for Worker Representation', in S. Babson (ed.), *Lean Work: Empowerment and Exploitation in the Global Auto Industry.* Detroit: Wayne State University Press, pp. 54–69.

MacDuffie, J. P. and Krafcik, J. F. (1992) 'Integrating Technology and Human Resources for High Performance Manufacturing: Evidence from the International Auto Industry', in T. A. Kochan and M. Useen (eds), *Transforming Organizations.* New York, Oxford: Oxford University Press, pp. 209–26.

Magenau, J. M., Martin, J. E. and Peterson, M. M. (1988) 'Dual and Unilateral Commitment among Stewards and Rank-and-File Union Members', *Academy of Management Journal*, 31, 359–76.

Marchington, M., Wilkinson, A., Ackers, P. and Goodman, J. (1993) 'The Influence of Managerial Relations on Waves of Employee Involvement', *British Journal of Industrial Relations*, 31 (4), 553–76.

Marchington, M., Wilkinson, A., Ackers, P. and Goodman, J. (1994) 'Understanding the Meaning of Participation', *Human Relations*, 47 (4), 867–94.

Marginson, P., Armstrong, R., Edwards, P. K., Purcell, J. and Hubbard, N. (1993) *The Control of Industrial Relations in Large Companies: An Initial Analysis of the Second Company Level Industrial Relations Survey.* Coventry: Industrial Relations Research Unit, Warwick Papers in Industrial Relations (45).

Marginson, P. and Sisson, K. (1994) 'The Structure of Transnational Capital in Europe: The Emerging Euro-Company and its Implications for Industrial Relations', in R. Hyman and A. Ferner (eds), *New Frontiers in European Industrial Relations*, Oxford: Blackwell, pp. 15–51.

Marks, M., Mirvis, P., Hackett, E. and Grady, J. (1986) 'Employee Participation in a Quality Circle Program: Impact on Quality of Work Life, Productivity, and Absenteeism', *Journal of Applied Psychology*, 71, 61–9.

Mars, G. (1982) *Cheats at Work*. London: Counterpoint.

Marshall, R. (1992) 'The Future Role of Government in Industrial Relations', in M. F. Bognanno and M. M. Kleiner (eds), *Labor Market Institutions and the Future Role of Unions*. Oxford: Blackwell, pp. 31–49.

Maschino, D. (1992) 'Les changements de l'organisation du travail dans le contexte de la mondialisation économique', *Le marché du travail*, 13 (7), 6–8 and 73–90; (8), 6–10 and 73.

Maurice, M, Sellier, F. and Silvestre, J.-J. (1982) *Politique d'éducation et organisation industrielle en France et en Allemagne: essai d'analyse sociétale*. Paris: PUF.

McArdle, L., Rowlinson, M., Procter, S., Hassard, J. and Forrester, P. (1995) 'Total Quality Management and Participation: Employee Empowerment or the Enhancement of Exploitation?', in A. Wilkinson and H. Willmott (eds), *Making Quality Critical; New Perspective on Organizational Change*. London: Routledge, 156–72.

Meltz, N. and Verma, A. (1995) 'Developments in Industrial Relations and Human Resource Practices in Canada: An Update from the 1980s', in R. Locke, T. A. Kochan and M. Piore (eds), *Employment Relations in a Changing World Economy*. Cambridge: MIT Press, pp. 91–130.

Micklethwait, J. and Wooldridge, A. (1996) *The Witch Doctors*. New York: Random House.

Milgrom, P. and Roberts, J. (1995) 'Complementarities and Fit: Strategy, Structure, and Organizational Change in Manufacturing', *Journal of Accounting & Economics*, 19, 179–208.

Millward, N. (1994) *The New Industrial Relations?* London: Policy Studies Institute.

Millward, N., Stevens, M., Smart, D. and Hawes, W. R. (1992) *Workplace Industrial Relations in Transition*. The ED/ESRC/PSI/ACAS Surveys, Aldershot: Dartmouth.

Mintzberg, H. (1979) *The Structuring of Organizations*. Englewood Cliffs: Prentice Hall.

Mohrman, S. and Novelli, L. (1985) 'Beyond Testimonials: Learning from a Quality Circles Programme', *Journal of Occupational Behaviour*, 6, 93–110.

Moody, K. (1997) *Workers in a Lean World*. London/New York: Verso.

Morehead, A., Steele, M., Alexander, M., Stephen, K. and Duffin, L. (1997) *Changes at Work: The 1995 Australian Workplace Industrial Relations Survey*. Melbourne: Addison Wesley Longman.

Morissette, R., Myles, J. and Picot, G. (1995) 'Earnings Polarization in Canada, 1969–1991', in K. Banting and C. Beach (eds), *Labour Market Polarization and Social Policy Reform*. Kingston: Queen's University School of Policy Studies, pp. 23–50.

Murakami, T. (1995a) 'Introducing Team Work', *Industrial Relations Journal*, 26 (4), 293–305.

REFERENCES

Murakami, T. (1995b) 'Team Work and the Structure of Representation at Vauxhall and Adam Opel', PhD thesis, University of Warwick.

Murray, G. (2001) 'La reconstruction des institutions du travail dans les sociétés mondialisées', in D. Mercure (ed.), *Une société monde?* Sainte-Foy: Les Presses de l'Université Laval, 239–252.

Murray, G., Lévesque, C., Roby, N. and Le Queux, S. (1999) 'Isolation or Integration? The Relationship between Local and National Union in the Context of Globalization', in J. Waddington (ed.), *Globalization and Patterns of Labour Resistance.* London: Mansell, pp. 160–91.

Murray, G., Lévesque, C. and Vallée, G. (2000) 'The Re-regulation of Labour in a Global Context: Conceptual Vignettes from Canada', *The Journal of Industrial Relations,* 42 (2), 234–57.

Murray, G. and Verge, P. (1999) *La représentation syndicale.* Sainte-Foy: Les Presses de l'Université Laval.

Nakamura, K. and Nitta, M. (1995) 'Developments in Industrial Relations and Human Resource Practices in Japan', in R. Locke, T. Kochan and M. Piore (eds), *Employment Relations in a Changing World Economy.* Cambridge, MA: MIT Press, pp. 325–58

Nichols, T. and Beynon, H. (1977) *Living with Capitalism.* London: Routledge.

Nissen, B. (ed.) (1997) *Unions and Workplace Reorganization.* Detroit: Wayne State University Press.

Nissen, B. (ed.) (1999) *Which Direction for Organized Labor? Essays on Organizing, Outreach and Internal Transformations.* Detroit: Wayne State University Press.

NUTEK (Swedish National Board for Industrial and Technical Development) (1996) *Towards Flexible Organisations.* Stockholm: NUTEK.

OECD (1989) *Labour Market Flexibility and Trends in Enterprises.* Paris: OECD.

Ohmae, K. (1990) *The Borderless World.* London: Collins.

Ohmae, K. (1995) 'Putting Global Logic First', *Harvard Business Review,* January/February, 119–25.

Offe, C. (1985) 'New Social Movements', *Social Research,* 52 (4), 817–68.

Oliver, N. (1997) 'High Performance Manufacturing: Management Practices vs. Institutional Context', Seminar paper, Graduate School of Business, University College, Dublin, 25 April.

Oliver, N. and Wilkinson, B. (1989) 'Japanese Manufacturing Techniques and Personnel and Industrial Relations Practice in Britain: Evidence and Implications', *British Journal of Industrial Relations,* 27 (1), 73–91.

Ondrack, D. A. and Evans, M. G. (1987) 'Job Enrichment and Job Satisfaction in Greenfield and Redesign QWL Sites', *Group and Organization Studies,* 12, 5–22.

Ortiz, L. (1998) 'Union Response to Team Work: the Case of Opel Spain', *Industrial Relations Journal,* 29 (1), 42–57.

Osberg, L. and Xu, K. (1999) 'Poverty Intensity: How Do Canadian Provinces Compare?', *Canadian Public Policy,* 25 (2), 179–97.

Osterman, P. (1988) *Employment Futures: Reorganization, Dislocation, and Public Policy.*

New York: Oxford University Press.

Osterman, P. (1994) 'How Common is Workplace Transformation and Who Adopts It?', *Industrial and Labor Relations Review*, 47, 173–88.

Osterman, P. (1998) 'Changing Work Organisation in America: What Has Happened and Who Has Benefitted', *Transfer*, 4 (2), 246–63.

Osterman, P. (1999) *Securing Prosperity: The American Labor Market: How it has Changed and What to Do about it.* Princeton: Princeton University Press.

Osterman, P. (2000) 'Work Reorganization in an Era of Restructuring: Trends in Diffusion and Effects on Employee Welfare', *Industrial and Labor Relations Review*, 53, 179–96.

Ostry, S. (1997) 'Globalization and the Nation State', in T. Courchene (ed.), The Nation State in a Global/Information Era: Policy Challenges. Bell Canada Papers on Economic and Public Policy, Vol. 5. Kingston, Ontario: John Deutsch Institute, Queen's University, pp. 57–65.

Ouchi, W. (1981) *Theory Z: How American Business can meet the Japanese Challenge.* Reading: Addison-Wesley.

Parker, M. and Slaughter, J. (1988) *Choosing Sides: Unions and the Team Concept.* Boston: South End Press.

Parker, M. and Slaughter, J. (1993) 'Should the Labor Movement Buy TQM?', *Journal of Organizational Change Management*, 6 (4), 43–56.

Parker, M. and Slaughter, J. (1994) *Working Smart: A Union Guide to Participation Programs and Reengineering.* Detroit: A Labor Notes Book.

Pearson, C. A. L. (1992) 'Autonomous Workgroups: An Evaluation at an Industrial Site', *Human Relations*, 35, 423–55.

Peters, T. J. and Waterman, R. J. (1982) *In Search of Excellence: Lessons from America's Best-Run Companies.* New York: Harper and Row.

Petrella, R. (1994) 'Pour un contrat social mondial', *Le monde diplomatique*, July.

Picot, G. (1996) 'Working Time, Wages and Earnings Inequality in Canada', Conference on Working Time in Canada and the United States, Ottawa: Statistics Canada.

Pil, F. K. and MacDuffie, J. P. (1996) 'The Adoption of High–Involvement Work Practices', *Industrial Relations*, 35 (3), July, 423–55.

Pil, F. K. and MacDuffie, J. P. (2000) 'The Adoption of High-Involvement Work Practices', in C. Ichinowski, D. I. Levine, C. Olson and G. Strauss (eds), *The American Workplace: Skills, Compensation and Employee Involvement.* Cambridge: Cambridge University Press, pp. 137–71.

Piore, M. (1991) 'The Future of Unions', in G. Strauss, D. G. Gallagher and J. Fiorito (eds), *The State of the Unions.* Madison: Industrial Relations Research Association, pp. 387–410.

Piore, M. (1995) *Beyond Individualism: How Social Demands of the New Identity Groups Challenge American and Political Life.* Cambridge: Harvard University Press.

Piore, M. and Sabel, C. (1984) *The Second Industrial Divide: Possibilities and Prosperity.* New York: Basic Books.

Pollert, A. (1996) 'Team Work on the Assembly Line: Contradiction and the Dynamics of Union Resilience', in P. Ackers, C. Smith and P. Smith (eds), *The New Workplace and Trade Unionism*. Routledge: London, pp. 178–209.

Pontusson, J. (1992) 'Unions, New Technology and Job Redesign at Volvo and British Leyland', in M. Golden and J. Pontusson (eds), *Bargaining for Change*. Ithaca: Cornell University Press, pp. 277–306.

Ramsay, H. (1977) 'Cycles of Control', *Sociology*, 11 (3), 481–506.

Ramsay, H. (1996) 'Managing Sceptically: A Critique of Organizational Fashion', in S. Clegg and G. Palmer (eds), *The Politics of Management Knowledge*. London: Sage Publications, 155–72.

Rankin, T. (1990) *New Forms of Work Organization: The Challenge for North American Unions*. Toronto: University of Toronto Press.

Rees, C. (1995) 'Quality Management and HRM in the Service Industry', *Employee Relations*, 17 (3), 99–109.

Rees, C. (1998) 'Empowerment Through Quality Management', in C. Mabey, D. Skinner and T. Clark (eds), *Experiencing Human Resource Management*. London: Sage, pp. 33–53.

Regalia, I. (1995) *Humanise Work and Increase Profitability? Direct Participation in Organisational Change Viewed by the Social Partners in Europe*. EF/95/21/EN. Luxembourg: Office for the Official Publications of the European Communities.

Regalia, I. and Regini, M. (1995) 'Between Voluntarism and Institutionalisation: Industrial Relations and Human Resource Practices in Italy', in R. Locke, T.A. Kochan and M. Piore (eds), *Employment Relations in a Changing World Economy*. Cambridge: The MIT Press, pp. 131–64.

Regalia, I. and Ronchi, R. (1991) *Le Relazioni Industriali nelle Imprese Lombarde. Annual Survey*. Milan: IRES Lombardia.

Regini, M. (1995) *Uncertain Boundaries: The Social and Political Construction of European Economies*, Cambridge: Cambridge University Press.

Rifkin, J. (1996) *The End of Work: The Decline of the Global Labor Force and the Dawn of the Post-Market Era*. New York: Tarcher/Putnam.

Rinehart, J., Huxley, C. and Robertson, D. (1997) *Just Another Car Factory: Lean Production and its Discontents*. Ithaca: Cornell University Press.

Rodrik, D. (1997) *Has Globalization Gone Too Far?* Washington, DC: Institute for International Economics.

Rogers, J. K. (2000) *Temps: The Many Faces of the Changing Workplace*. Ithaca: Cornell University Press.

Rogers, J. and Streeck, W. (1995) 'The Study of Works Councils: Concepts and Problems', in J. Rogers and W. Streeck (eds), *Works Councils: Consultation, Representation, and Cooperation in Industrial Relations*. Chicago: The University of Chicago Press, pp. 3–26.

Rosencrance, R. (1996) 'The Rise of the Virtual State', *Foreign Affairs*, 75 (4), July/August, 45–61.

Rosenthal, P., Hill, S. and Peccei, R. (1997) 'Checking Out Service: Evaluating

Excellence, HRM and TQM in Retailing', *Work, Employment and Society*, 11 (3), 481–503.

Rouillard, J. (1989) *Histoire du syndicalisme québécois*. Montreal: Boréal.

Rubinstein, S., Bennett, M. and Kochan, T. A. (1993) 'The Saturn Parnership: Co-Management and the Reinvention of the Local Union', in B. E. Kaufman and M. M. Kleiner (eds), *Employee Representation Alternatives and Future Directions*. Madison: IRRA, pp. 339–70.

Sabel, C. F. (1995) 'Bootstrapping Reform: Rebuilding Firms, the Welfare State, and Unions', *Politics & Society*, 23 (1), 5–48.

Sabel, C. and Zeitlin, J. (1985) 'Historical Alternatives to Mass Production: Politics, Markets and Technology in Nineteenth Century Industrialization', *Past and Present*, 108, 133–76.

Sauerwein, R. G. (1993) 'Gruppenarbeit im westdeutschen Maschinenbau: Diffusion und Merkmale – Ergebnisse des NIFA-Pannels 1991 und 1992', Sonderforschungs-bereich 187 der Ruhr-Universitat Bochum, Arbeitpapier Z2-1/93, Bochum.

Sayles, L. R. (1958) *Behavior of Industrial Work Groups*. New York: Wiley.

Scarborough, H. and Terry, M. (1997) 'United Kingdom: the Reorganisation of Production', in T. A. Kochan, R. D. Lansbury and J.-P. MacDuffie (eds), *After Lean Production*. Ithaca: Cornell University Press, pp. 137–54.

Schenk, C. (2002) 'Social Movement Unionism: Beyond the Organizing Model', in P. Fairbrother and C. Yates (eds), *Trade Union Renewal and Organizing: A Comparative Study of Trade Union Movements in Five Countries*. London: Continuum, forthcoming.

Scott, A. (1994) *Willing Slaves? British Workers Under Human Resources Management*. Cambridge: Cambridge University Press.

Scott, J. (1991) 'Networks of Corporate Power: a Comparative Assessment', *Annual Review of Sociology*, 17, 181–203.

Seers, A., Petty, M. M. and Cushman, J. F. (1995) 'Team-Member Exchange under Team and Traditional Management: a Naturally Occurring Quasi-Experiment', *Group and Organizational Management*, 20 (1), 18–38.

Sennett, R. (1998) *The Corrosion of Character: The Personal Consequences of Work in the New Capitalism*. New York/London: W. W. Norton & Company.

Sewell, G. (1998) 'The Discipline of Teams: The Control of Team-based Industrial Work through Electronic and Peer Surveillance', *Administrative Science Quarterly*, 43 (2), June, 397–428.

Sewell, G. and Wilkinson, B. (1992) 'Someone to Watch Over Me: Surveillance, Discipline and the JIT Labour Process', *Sociology*, 26 (2), 271–89.

Shaiken, H., Lopez, S. and Mankita, I. (1997) 'Two Routes to Team Production: Saturn and Chrysler Compared', *Industrial Relations*, 36 (1), 17–45.

Sisson, K. (1995) 'Change and Continuity in British Industrial Relations: Strategic Choice or Muddling Through?', in R. Locke, T. A. Kochan and M. Piore (eds), *Employment Relations in a Changing World Economy*. Cambridge: The MIT Press, pp. 33–58.

Smith, A. (1993) 'Canadian Industrial Relations in Transition', *Relations industrielles/*

Industrial Relations, 48, 641–60.

Smith, C. and Thompson, P. (1998) 'Re-Evaluating the Labour Process Debate', *Economic and Industrial Democracy*, 19 (4), 551–77.

Sommet sur l'économie et l'emploi (1996) *Les faits saillants*. Québec: Secrétariat du Sommet, November.

Springer, R. (1999) 'The End of New Production Concepts?', *Economic and Industrial Democracy*, 20 (1), 117–46.

Standing, G. (1997) 'Globalization, Labour Flexibility and Insecurity: The Era of Market Regulation', *European Journal of Industrial Relations*, 3, 7–37.

Statistics Canada (1998) *The Evolving Workplace: Findings from the Pilot Workplace and Employee Survey*. Ottawa: Statistics Canada.

Steel, R. P., Jennings, K. R. and Lindsey, J. T. (1990) 'Communications Forum Interventions: a Longitudinal Case Study', *Leadership and Organization Development Journal*, 9 (5), 3–9.

Steel, R. P. and Shane, G. S. (1986) 'Evaluation Research on Quality Circles: Technical and Analytical Implications', *Human Relations*, 39, 449–68.

Storey, J. (1992) *Developments in the Management of Human Resources*. Oxford: Blackwell.

Storey, J. and Harrison, A. (1999) 'Coping with World Class Manufacturing', *Work, Employment and Society*, 13, 643–4.

Streeck, W. (1981) 'Qualitative Demands and the Neo-Corporatist Manageability of Industrial Relations: Trade Unions and Industrial Relations in West Germany at the Beginning of the Eighties', *British Journal of Industrial Relations*, 14 (2), 146–69.

Streeck, W. (1991) 'On the Institutional Conditions of Diversified Quality Production', in E. Matzner and W. Streeck (eds), *Beyond Keynesianism. The Socio-Economics of Production and Full Employment*. Brookfield: Elgar, pp. 21–61.

Streeck, W. (1992) *Social Institutions and Economic Performance*. London: Sage Publications.

Streeck, W. (1995) 'Works Councils in Western Europe: from Consultation to Participation', in J. Rogers and W. Streeck (eds.), *Works Councils: Consultation, Representation and Co-operation in Industrial Relations*. Chicago: University of Chicago Press, 313–48.

Supiot, A. (2000) 'Les nouveaux visages de la subordination', *Droit social*, 2 February, 131–44.

Task Force on Review of the Canada Labour Code (1997) *Seeking a Balance: Review of Part I of the Canada Labour Code*. Report, Ottawa.

Taylor, F. W. (1911) *The Principles of Scientific Management*. New York: Harper.

Taylor, S. (1997) '"Empowerment" or "Degradation'? Total Quality Management in the Service Sector', in R. K. Brown (ed.), *The Changing Shape of Work*. Basingstoke: Macmillan, pp. 171–202.

Thacker, J. W. and Fields, M. W. (1987) 'Union Involvement in Quality of Worklife Efforts: A Longitudinal Investigation', *Personnel Psychology*, 40, 97–111.

Thacker, J. W. and Rosen, H. (1986) 'Dynamics of Employee Reactance to Company and Union: Dual Allegiance Revisited and Expanded', *Relations Industrielles/*

Industrial Relations, 41, 128–44.

Thompson, E. P. (1968) *The Making of the English Working Class*. Harmondsworth, Middlesex: Penguin.

Thompson, M. (1995) 'The Industrial Relations Effects of Privatization: Evidence From Canada', in G. Swimmer and M. Thompson (eds), *Public Sector Collective Bargaining in Canada*. Kingston, ON: Queen's University IRC Press, pp. 164–79.

Thompson, M. and Ponak, A. (1992) 'Restraint, Privatization and Industrial Relations in the Public Sector in the 1980s', in R. Chaykowski and A. Verma (eds), *Industrial Relations in Canadian Industry*. Toronto, ON: Holt, Rinehart and Winston, pp. 284–322.

Thurow, L. (1992) *Head to Head*. New York: William Morrow.

Thurow, L. (1999) *Building Wealth: The New Rules for Individuals, Companies and Nations in a Knowledge-Based Economy*. New York: Harper Collins.

Tixier, P.-E. (1992) *Mutation ou déclin du syndicalisme? Le cas de la CFDT*. Paris: PUF.

Touraine, A. (1973) *Production de la société*. Paris: Seuil.

Towers, B. (1997) *The Representation Gap: Change and Reform in the British and American Workplace*. Oxford: Oxford University Press.

Trist, E. L. and Bamforth, K. W. (1951) 'Some Social and Psychological Consequences of the Longwall Method of Coal-Getting', *Human Relations*, 4, 1–38.

TUC (Trades Union Congress) (1999) *Partners for Progress: New Unionism in the Workplace*. London: Trades Union Congress.

Tuckman, A. (1995) 'Ideology, Quality and TQM', in A. Wilkinson and H. Willmott (eds), *Making Quality Critical: New Perspective on Organizational Change*. London: Routledge, pp. 54–81.

Turnbull, P. J. (1988) 'The Limits to Japanization: Just-in-Time, Labour Relations and the UK Automotive Industry', *New Technology, Work and Employment*, 4, 7–20.

Turner, L. (1991) *Democracy at Work: Changing World Markets and the Future of Labor Unions*. Ithaca: Cornell University Press.

US Department of Labor and US Department of Commerce (USDL/USDC) (1994) *Fact Finding Report: Commission on the Future of Worker-Management Relations*, May.

Vallas, S. P. (1999) 'Rethinking Post-Fordism: The Meaning of Workplace Flexibility', *Sociological Theory*, 17 (1), 68–101.

Vallas, S. P. and Beck, J. P. (1996) 'The Transformation of Work Revisited', *Social Problems*, 43 (3), 339–61.

Veltz, P. (2000) *Le nouveau monde industriel*. Paris: Gallimard.

Verma, A. (1987) 'Employee Involvement Programs: Do They Alter Worker Affinity Towards Unions?', *Proceedings of the Thirty-Ninth Annual Meetings of the Industrial Relations Research Association*, 39, 306–12.

Verma, A. (1995) 'Employee Involvement in the Workplace', in M. Gunderson and A. Ponak (eds), *Union-Management Relations in Canada*. Toronto: Addison–Wesley, pp. 281–308.

Verma, A. and Chaykowski, R. (eds) (1999) *Contract and Commitment: Employment Relations in the New Economy*. Kingston, ON: Queen's University, IRC Press.

REFERENCES

Verma, A. and Cutcher-Gershenfeld, J. (1993) 'Joint Governance in the Workplace: Beyond Union-Management Cooperation and Worker Participation', in B. E. Kaufman and M. M. Kleiner (eds), *Employee Representation: Alternatives and Futures Directions*. Madison: IRRA, pp. 197–234.

Voss, K. and Sherman, R. (1999) 'You Just Can't Do It Automatically: The Transition to Social Movement Unionism in the United States', Paper Presented to the Seminar on Trade Union Innovation, Adaptation and Renewal from Different Countries, Cardiff University, November.

Voos, P. B. (1994) 'An Economic Perspective on Contemporary Trends in Collective Bargaining', in P. B. Voos (ed.), *Contemporary Collective Bargaining in the Private Sector*. Madison: IRRA, pp. 1–23.

Wagar, T. (1995) *Human Resource Management Practices and Organizational Performance*. Kingston, ON: IRC Press.

Wall, T., Kemp, N., Jackson, P. and Clegg, C. (1986) 'Outcomes of Autonomous Workgroups: a Long-Term Field Experiment', *Academy of Management Journal*, 29 (2), June, 280–304.

Walton, R., Cutcher-Gershenfeld, J. and McKersie, R. (1994) *Strategic Negotiations: A Theory of Change in Labour-Management Relations*. Cambridge: Harvard Business School Press.

Walton, R. E. (1985) 'From Control to Commitment in the Workplace', *Harvard Business Review*, 63 (2), 77–84.

Weiler, P. C. (1983) 'Promises to Keep: Securing Workers' Rights to Self-Representation under the NLRA', *Harvard Law Review*, 96, 1769–1827.

Weiler, P. C. (1993) 'Governing the Workplace: Employee Representation in the Eyes of the Law', in B. E. Kaufman and M. M. Kleiner (eds), *Employee Representation: Alternatives and Future Directions*. Madison: Industrial Relations Research Association, pp. 81–104.

Weinstein, M. and Kochan, T. A. (1995) 'The Limits of Diffusion: Recent Developments in Industrial Relations and Human Resource Practices in the United States', in R. Locke, T. A. Kochan and M. Piore (eds), *Employment Relations*. Cambridge: The MIT Press, pp. 1–31.

Wells, D. M. (1993) 'Are Strong Unions Compatible with the New Model of Human Resource Management?', *Relations industrielles/Industrial Relations*, 48 (1), 56–85.

Wells, D. M. (1996) ''New Dimensions for Labor in a Post-Fordist World', in W. C. Green and E. J. Yanarella (eds), *North American Auto Unions in Crisis. Lean Production as Contested Terrain*. Albany: State University of New York Press, pp. 191–207.

Wever, K. S. (1995) *Negotiating Competitiveness. Employment Relations and Organizational Innovation in Germany and the United States*. Boston: Harvard Business School Press.

Whitfield, K. (2000) 'High-Performance Workplaces, Training, and the Distribution of Skills', *Industrial Relations*, 39 (1), 1–25.

Wilkinson, A., Godfrey, G. and Marchington, M. (1998) 'Bouquets Brickbats and Blinkers: Total Quality Management and Employee Involvement in Practice', *Organisation Studies*, 18 (5), 799–819.

Williams, K., Haslam, C., Williams, J., Cutler, T., Adcroft, A. and Johal, S. (1992) 'Against Lean Production', *Economy and Society*, 21 (3), 321–54.

Windolf, P. (1989) 'Productivity Coalitions and the Future of European Corporatism', *Industrial Relations*, 28 (1), 1–20.

Wite, J. F. (1980) *Democracy, Authority, and Alienation in Work*. Chicago: University of Chicago Press.

Womack, J. P., Jones, D. T. and Roos, D. (1990) *The Machine that Changed the World*. New York: Harper Perennial.

Wood, S. (1999) 'Getting the Measure of the Transformed High-Performance Organization', *British Journal of Industrial Relations*, 37 (3), 391–417.

Work in America (1993) *Report of a Special Task Force to the Secretary of Health, Education, and Welfare*. Cambridge: The MIT Press.

Wright, M. and P. K. Edwards (1998) 'Does Teamworking Work, and, if so, Why? A Case Study in the Aluminium Industry', *Economic and Industrial Democracy*, 19, 59–90.

Zacher, M. (1997) 'The Global Economy and the International Political Order: Some Diverse and Paradoxical Relationships', in T. Courchene (ed.), *The Nation State in a Global/Information Era: Policy Challenges*. Bell Canada Papers on Economic and Public Policy, Vol. 5. Kingston, Ontario, John Deutsch Institute, Queen's University, pp. 67–82.

Zuboff, S. (1988) *In the Age of the Smart Machine: The Future of Work and Power*. New York: Basic Books.

INDEX